COMIX

A History of Comic Books in America

COMIX

A History of Comic Books in America

THUD

MISS
UNDER
STOOD

BY **LES DANIELS**

GRAPHICS BY
MAD PECK (F)
STUDIOS

BONANZA BOOKS · NEW YORK

517110377

Copyright © MCMLXXI by Les Daniels and
Mad Peck Studios

Library of Congress Catalog Card Number:
75-169-104

This edition is published by Bonanza Books,
a division of Crown Publishers, Inc. by arrangement with Outerbridge & Lazard, Inc.
abcdefgh

Manufactured in the United States of America.

Acknowledgments

We wish to express our gratitude to the following individuals without whose cooperation this book would not have been possible.

For permission to reproduce comics:

Bernard Kashdan (National Periodical Publications), T. T. Scott (Real Adventures Publishing), George Sherman (Walt Disney Studios), William Gaines (E. C. Publications), Patricia Papangelis (Playboy), Harvey Kurtzman (Humbug Publishing), James Warren (Warren Publishing), Charles Goodman (Magazine Management Co.), Bill Beckman, Robert Crumb, Gilbert Shelton, Greg Irons, Jay Lynch, Skip Williamson, Spain Rodrigues, Justin Green, Kim Deitch, Trina Robbins.

For information and advice:

J. Michael Barrier, Don Thompson, Roy Thomas, Jerry De Fuccio.

For access to comics collections:

Robert Krywy, Kenny Weinstein, Kenny Kneitel, Joe Pilati, Rob Kincaid, Alec Chalmers, Norma Asbornsen, and Stephen Halpert.

And for production assistance:

Gloria Derderian and Maizy Day.

Contents

Introduction

Comic books have been with us now for almost four decades, and the newspaper comic strips from which they sprang have been part of our culture for twice as long. Yet the medium has received scant serious attention until very recently. Even the relatively frequent celebrations of newspaper comics have treated the comic book as a derivative and somewhat deplorable offspring of respectable ancestors.

This situation has changed considerably in the last couple of years. Somehow comic books have taken on new overtones of "relevance." There are even courses on the subject in a number of colleges and universities. Concrete proof of the seriousness with which the subject can be taken has been provided by the rapid growth of the market for comic book collectors, where some issues once priced at ten cents are bought and sold for hundreds of dollars. And the industry has institutionalized itself with the creation of the Academy of Comic Book Arts, designed to enlighten the uninitiated and award worthy workers in the field.

The reasons for this burgeoning interest are many. The passage of time has made these flamboyant publications familiar; they have been around too long now to be dismissed as a fly-by-night enterprise. Generations have grown up with them, and they have acquired the value produced by nostalgic memories. At the same time, their traditional role as the reading matter of the young has given them greater importance in this era when youth has become an arbiter of taste. The fashionable popularity of McLuhanesque methods of analyzing media has inspired a new outlook that judges works on their own terms, and such an approach compensates the comic book for its lack of legitimate tradition.

The fact is that millions and millions of comic books are sold every year; it would be futile to deny the idea that they have helped to shape the American scene. Whether their effect has been positive or negative is open to debate, at least among those who are sociologically inclined. There can be little doubt, however, that the comic book is a positive success as an art, at least in the most basic sense of attracting and holding an audience. And fluctuations in the style and content of these periodicals serve to mirror changes in the attitudes of both artists and audience.

It is because these variations seem to have some significance that an attempt has been made in this book to cover more topics than those usually included in considerations of the comic book. The general tendency has been to treat the whole medium in terms of its most obvious manifestation: the costumed superhero syndrome. Certainly this theme set the industry on its feet, and just as certainly it has remained the most consistently popular. But there is more in comic books than fantasies of fisticuffs. Other topics worthy of attention range from the innocent antics of anthropomorphic animals to the irreverent ideas of the latest underground comics, from snickering satires to sinister studies of the supernatural. If these variations have not always enjoyed the widest popularity, they are nevertheless important in expanding the potential of the art.

As confining as the emphasis on superheroes has been the promotion of the concept of the "Golden Age" of comic books, a term used to designate the period between 1938 (the year in which the germinal *Superman* feature first appeared) and 1945. This was, admittedly, the era in which many of the most famous characters and creators got their start; it was the time when comic books came into their own. But it was also a period which began with crude drawing and somewhat simple-minded scripting, a period sustained more by the excitement of novelty than by excellence of performance. The emotional attachment which commentators have for this era is demonstrated by the fact that the three books which have emerged to date as histories of comic books deal with the "Golden Age" exclusively, as though subsequent achievements were hardly worth mentioning. It would be unfair to deny the charm of some early efforts, or even to suggest that the "Golden Age" failed to produce some authentically first-rate work, but the most remarkable thing about this era, really, is the speed with which the level of performance was raised. There is in all likelihood no case in which the debut of an artist or a hero constituted his finest moment, yet the first appearance is invariably the most prized of collectors' items. In selecting the stories which are reproduced in this volume, an attempt has been made to choose pieces which either typify trends or offer unusual variations, rather than concentrating on historical "firsts" which in most cases are not really representative.

The "Golden Age" was also a time in which a great deal of derivative work was done; innumerable characters rose and fell who offered only the slightest variations on established themes, and most of them are probably best forgotten. In dealing with this period it seems wiser to concentrate on those achievements whose quality or durability made them outstanding. An exhaustive list of comic book heroes would be exhausting as well, and might become an exercise in trivia rather than an examination of significant trends.

The alternative approach is to consider the history of the comic book as a collection of selected topics. Admittedly this involves a certain kind of proportional imbalance, as in the case of the underground comics which here receive the same coverage as other types of much larger circulation. Yet it is only by contrasting the various schools of the comic book art that a real sense of its possibilities can be suggested. This book is intended to complement those which have treated a narrower view of the field with correspondingly greater detail.

Of course one of the most important features of this volume is the generous selection of complete comic book stories which it contains. Truly a picture is worth a thousand words, and never more so than in an examination of a form which is primarily pictorial. Yet spot illustrations or cover reproductions can only suggest the flavor of a series. Clearly, uncut episodes are desirable for demonstration purposes, and it is satisfying to have been able to include so many. Some potential selections proved to be impossible to obtain, but it seems safe to say that no book to date has contained such a wide range of comic book tales. Where else can one find in the same volume such divergent personalities as the Old Witch and Donald Duck, or Captain America and Those Fabulous Furry Freak Brothers?

The publishers, creators, collectors and advisors whose welcome cooperation made this book possible are listed on the acknowledgments page, but a word is in order here concerning those who contributed directly to the writing. Frank Muhly is responsible for a substantial portion of the third chapter, and the entire text of the seventh chapter was prepared by Mad Peck Studios, which also secured many of the most important copyright releases.

Les Daniels
Providence, Rhode Island
May 1971

MEANWHILE:

WELL FOLKS, LIKE THE MAN SAYS ABOVE, COMICS ARE SWELL! UNFORTUNATELY, THEY ARE MOSTLY PRINTED ON SLEAZY PAPER THAT FALLS APART IN FIFTEEN YEARS. SERIOUS COMIC BOOK COLLECTORS PROTECT THEIR COMICS IN PLASTIC BAGS BUT THEN NOBODY GETS TO READ 'EM. CONSEQUENTLY, WE WERE MOVED TO COMPILE THIS TOME SO THAT YOU CAN HAVE A BUNCH OF COMICS TO LOOK AT WHENEVER YOU WANT! NOT ONLY THAT BUT YOU GET ALL THEM SWELL WORDS BY MR. DANIELS TOO. BEFORE I FORGET, I WANNA THANK JEFF AND BILL DOWN AT STERLING PHOTO FOR SLAVING OVER THEIR 31 INCH ROBINSON PHOTO MECHANICAL CAMERA. BUT MOST OF ALL I WANNA THANK ME MOTHER WHO HAD ENOUGH SENSE TO NOT THROW OUT MY COMICS.

KIDS FOR EARTH

← THE MAD PECK

Chapter One: The Coming of Comics

Comics are the accidental art form. They stand with twentieth century innovations like cinema and broadcasting, but for various reasons they lack the credentials of these other forms because they were not apparently the technical achievement of a great inventor. No perspiring genius burst from his laboratory with "Eureka!" emblazoned on a thought-balloon emanating from his fevered brain. Comics were not created—they evolved. And any mode of the imagination that develops this way is always controversial. Arbiters of taste and judgment operate on a system that ascribes value only to that which has already been found worthy by posterity. So the history of ideas marches sullenly forward into an unimagined future, its eyes cast resolutely back over its shoulder at the useless but reassuring guideposts of the past.

Defenders of the comics medium have a tendency to rummage through recognized remnants of mankind's vast history to pluck forth sanctioned symbols which might create among the cognoscenti the desired shock of recognition. Prehistoric wall paintings, oriental ideographs, Egyptian hieroglyphics, Medieval tapestries, illuminated manuscripts, journalistic cartoons, religious and political pamphlets, even arcane or occult symbol-sets like the Tarot—all have been cited as forms of the comics to reassure serious thinkers that the bad boy of the arts was no orphan, and might even have royal blood in his veins. The kid has even been praised as a patriot: sons of the revolution like Benjamin Franklin and Paul Revere used the comics form, complete with speech balloons, and this was actually a common practice as the eighteenth century stabilized and standardized the periodical press. Indeed, this child of the times has some brilliant leaves on his family tree.

But he himself is more than the sum of his definable parts. A strange union of literature and art, a union which was also intended as a piece of merchandise and a public relations gimmick, the kid was

1

something unusual and certainly colorful.

The Kid to begin with was Yellow.

There was something more special in his flamboyant display of this primary color than might have been realized by even his most amazed admirers. It constituted a technical breakthrough, one so familiar and widespread today that we take it for granted—even more, we treat it condescendingly. Yet it was a monumental task to transfer this missing link of the spectrum into the grayish halftone world of newsprint. Red and blue seemed to fall naturally onto the white of the American newspaper, but yellow remained elusive, its hue so deformed by massive presses that the sickly shade seemed to connote cowardice more than solar cheer. In 1893, the New York *World* had presented newspaper readers with the first complete color page, although it was something less than brilliant. Real relief arrived some three years later on February 16, 1896, when the new color formula was applied to a humorous drawing. It had been perfected by Charles Saalburgh, the *World*'s engraving foreman; the art was the work of Richard Outcault. Yet Outcault created the first hero of the comics inadvertently, presenting him as not much more than a spear-carrier among the crowd of kid carousers at "The Great Dog Show in M'Googan Avenue," just around the corner from Hogan's Alley. The "Hogan's Alley" designation was as close as the *World* or its readers had come to naming this series of Outcault cartoons, but when the yellow ink hit his nightshirt, the anonymous child of the slums became the "Yellow Kid" by popular acclaim, and so gave the strip his own new name.

It was not even a strip as we know it today: it was one drawing, not a series, and it failed to display the white speech balloon, outlined in black, which we consider characteristic of the comics form. Yet because the talents of the printer and artist had combined to produce a character who could command the public's attention, this is the beginning of newspaper comic strips, and thus the first step toward comic books.

What the Kid had going for him was vulgarity. It radiated from his lurid garment and from his big-eared, bald, and beady-eyed countenance. He existed in a world that was crude, noisy, sordid and eccentric, and he commented disdainfully upon it, first with wry expressions of his idiot's face, later with phonetically rendered slang inscribed on his expansive nightshirt. There was nothing overtly attractive about him; his appeal seemed to be a function of his offensiveness. Such was the power of the medium he embodied that it made a delight out of what was apparently rude and tasteless. Of course, he had his critics as well as his fans. The critics presumably held the cartoon responsible for the ugliness it depicted, while enthusiasts viewed it as a commentary on what already existed but was rarely exposed.

It should be noted in connection with this comics art controversy that the proprietor of the *World*, and the original publisher of *The Yellow Kid*, was no less a personage than Joseph Pulitzer, whose name has endured to the present in connection with the most widely known and respected annual American awards for journalistic excellence, the Pulitzer prizes. In retrospect, the Pulitzer name trails clouds of glory. In the gay nineties, however, it signified a man totally committed to a cut-throat competition for the newspaper readers of New York City. It was hardly necessary for the *World* to launch an elaborate investigation of aesthetics once it had been determined that color comics increased the paper's circulation. The public had spoken; there would be no looking backward.

There would be more than a few turnabouts, though. Pulitzer's chief rival was William Randolph Hearst, who had recently acquired the New York *Journal*. The classic film by Orson Welles, *Citizen Kane*, in part a fictionalized account of Hearst's career, contains an amusing sequence in which Kane launches a newspaper and uses a large capital outlay to hire the staff of the most successful daily for his own operation. This had its parallel in history, as Hearst lured Outcault and the Kid into his camp with more cash. Pulitzer did his part for inflation by bringing them back to the *World* with still another increase, but the indefatigable Hearst raised the ante again, and finally won the game. He had Outcault, so Pulitzer hired another artist (who eventually was to become famous for his painting), George Luks, to render the Kid. Lack of legal precedent concerning copyright apparently made it possible for both competitors to feature the same character.

The publicity accompanying these fast maneuvers struck some observers as less than dignified. They smeared that little spot of printer's ink all over the rival publications and coined the epithet of "Yellow Press" to characterize the new style of journalism which offered its readers something more than hard news. It was quite a contrast to the "good gray" New York *Times*, which presented the public with "All the news that's fit to print," and which has remained unique among American newspapers by refusing to commit itself to something as common as comics. Yet the *Times* is isolated in its elitism, and the "Yellow" formula of information liberally laced with entertainment is now a national standard.

If the comics succeeded, though, it is because they paid a certain price. To flow freely into the mainstream of the culture, the savage intensity of the original impulse would have to be diluted. The Kid was an iconoclast, a graven image whose primary function was to counterbalance the prevalent surface image of a self-satisfied society. As such, his career was to be short-lived. He was too crude. The same jolting impact which made him a sensation demanded his early demise. Even as the success of Outcault's conception established the comics' tradition of mutual imitation, his career would typify its dramatic fluctuation between intensity and acceptability. Outcault's next major effort was the creation of a new type of child star, Buster Brown, who made his debut in the New York *Herald Tribune* and was ultimately acquired, once again, by the irresistible Hearst. Buster, as opposed to his predecessor, was blatantly bourgeois in both conception and execution.

In contrast to the Kid's scandalous state of undress, Buster wore an elaborate and almost effeminate outfit of short pants, middy blouse and a broad-brimmed hat. The Kid's "skinhead" hairdo was replaced by an elegant crop of shoulder-length blond curls, a style as repulsive to the boys of that day as it would be attractive to those of the present era, and one which firmly established Buster as establishment-orientated. True, he was mischievous, but the trouble he made was small-time domestic stuff like getting the floor wet or dirtying his clothes, and he could usually put a share of the blame on his pet bulldog, Tige. Worse yet, he developed the obnoxious habit of ending each of his Sunday adventures with a painfully moralistic summation of the lessons to be learned from his day's activities, emblazoned on a large, hand-painted sign entitled "Resolved," which had all the depth and sincerity of an essay written as a part of a schoolboy's punishment. A typical example (1905) read: "Resolved! That the loss of my clothes does not worry me— To lose one's self respect is the only serious loss. Clothes are nothing, character counts; 'tis *everything*—your happiness, your *success*, and your eternity. I didn't fool my Aunt Emeline. I fooled *myself*. That's what always happens. Don't try to *fool* people—try not to fool 'em—that's the way to win. It's neither honest nor kind, and where is the pinhead who doesn't know that honesty is the best policy." There is more, but this should be sufficient. Of course, the syndrome of sin and repentance would repeat itself in the next installment anyway.

Outcault's career is almost a capsule history of the comics, in both newspaper strip and comic book manifestations. The recurring theme is one of a devilish impulse creating a sensation, then gradually being watered down into a conformist norm, leaving a vacuum which would be filled again by some new challenge to the sanctity of society and the printed page. Time and again the snickering anarchy first embodied by the Yellow Kid would be blanketed by the smiling hypocrisy typical of Buster Brown, but it would never be muffled for long. There were rewards for playing it safe: Buster Brown became the trademark for a firm manufacturing children's shoes which

has survived considerably longer than its namesake; nobody would tie up his product with the Yellow Kid. But the impulse that brought forth the Kid was always present. The shoe line that took Buster as its symbol eventually was successful enough to spawn media spinoffs including giveaway comic books and radio and television broadcasts. Yet the hero of these was not Buster, who had become a mere commercial figurehead, but an iconoclastic amphibian named Froggy the Gremlin, whose principal activity was to disrupt the stolid formats with his grotesque antics. Of course, all his disturbances were programmed into the proceedings, but it is significant that the characters had come full circle as the sanctimonious Buster yielded the stage to a green demon who might almost have been the reincarnation of Outcault's original hero.

Substance aside, the shift from the Kid to Buster brought some progress in the technical development of the medium: Outcault's second major effort was presented in the now standard format of multiple panels to indicate the passage of time, with dialogue firmly established in speech balloons. Both devices had preceded comic strips, but by the turn of the century were combined and consolidated into a recognizable entity.

This was a period of innovations in a number of fields, some of which had a powerful if indirect effect on the progress of the comics. The rise of literacy through mass education created at least low-level reading ability on a wide scale. Comics, with the built-in visual aid of pictorial representation, provided an opportunity for the slightly skilled reader to exercise such talents as he possessed; it was a new kind of reading. Studies and surveys have also indicated from time to time that the new medium had and still has a positive effect in teaching the art of reading even to the totally untrained. This is apparently true despite the "common sense" idea promoted by various theorists that comics, less rigidly defined than blocks of print, might cripple literary aspirations. After all, reading primers have traditionally relied on illustrations to amplify the meaning of the printed word, and the most obvious distinction between them and the bad boy of the arts is that the comics are geared to create the greatest possible entertainment value, and, thus, reader interest. Textbooks, by contrast, have their basis in educational theories which are never tested in the marketplace, so style and content are defined by arbitrary idealizations rather than actual appeal.

If increasing literacy made the comics accessible, the development of photography made them inevitable. The new method of making pictures turned the whole world of the visual arts upside down. The role of the artist as the precise recorder of events was to be supplanted totally and permanently by the cam-

3

era. For the professional illustrator, this had some frightening implications. The career of the illustrator as reporter was coming to an end. Heretofore illustrations had complemented the words of news stories and had been created (on the scene or from reports) by staff artists. The camera changed the pen-wielders' range of opportunities; pedestrian accuracy of detail became less important than creative concepts and striking style. As the newspaper story closed down as a potential market, opportunities grew in the areas of advertising art and the comics. Indeed, as has already been suggested, comics were a form of advertising, inaugurated and instituted because they increased the circulation of the publications in which they were featured.

The appearance of the camera served to bring about fundamental changes in the orientation of the artist. In the field of the fine arts, the release from the restrictions of realism would provide the chance for dramatic new experiments. Painters reacted with impressionism and expressionism, the surreal and the abstract. Imagination rather than information became the new criterion by which works would be judged.

It was in such an atmosphere that comics came to the fore. There were no groundrules, no direct traditions on which to draw. Theoretically, any kind of approach might have evolved, with a range of content as wide or wider than any other existing means of expression. What actually happened was that progress was made, but much more slowly than might have been anticipated. Sometimes it seemed that, for every step forward, there would be two taken backwards. Each innovation which occurred or might occur was subject to the scrutiny of editors on individual newspapers, and, more significantly, to the control of the national syndicates, whose growth was largely an offshoot of the enormous popularity of the comic strips.

Artistic control fell into the hands of the syndicates when it became apparent that their method of widespread distribution would involve financial rewards far greater than could ever be garnered from a strip appearing on a strictly local basis—and enjoying the relative autonomy that went with it. Attempts to promote and insure wide appeal took an inevitable toll in standardization.

The nature of the change was foreshadowed by Bud Fisher's long-lasting *Mutt and Jeff*. The first important daily newspaper strip (as distinguished from those which appeared in the color Sunday supplements), it began in 1907, under the original title *A. Mutt*, in the San Francisco *Chronicle*. Mutt was first presented as a racetrack character with dubious morals, and the comedy grew out of the lifestyle of the shiftless gambler type. Early strips even went so far as to offer authentic tips on the races. However, as Mutt and his pint-sized pal Jeff moved eastward across the country through syndi-

cation, the racy was increasingly qualified by the respectable. Mutt acquired as if by osmosis a wife, a home, and a secure, if ill-defined career. His distinctiveness as a character was lost, as was the setting which made him unique, by the time he became a national institution. Such was to be the price of fame.

An exception of sorts is offered by the oldest of all currently continuing comic strips, *The Katzenjammer Kids*, begun in 1896 by Rudolph Dirks for Hearst's New York *Journal*. Following in the footsteps of Outcault, Dirks eventually left the paper, with his popular creation under his arm—although not as firmly as he might have thought. Things had become a bit more official since the days when the same strip could be running in two competing publications at the same time. There were copyrights to be reckoned with, and the law had to be called in. It rendered its decision in 1912. The result had overtones of the judgment of Solomon, as the court gave *both* Dirks and his former publisher the right to the *characters*, with the understanding that the artist would have to leave his title, *The Katzenjammer Kids*, behind him. H. Knerr was hired by the *Journal* to work under the old logo, while Dirks continued his format, unaltered, calling it *The Captain and the Kids*. While the comic was diluted in theory by this strange duality, both versions managed to maintain a good deal of punch in the adventures of Hans and Fritz, two rambunctious juveniles who display a violent contempt for pompous authority. Even though the trend, unfortunately, was away from such vigorous anarchy, the Kids have kept it up, probably because they are not depicted as part of the American scene, but as Teutonic castaways, existing in microcosmic society in a nameless jungle.

More and more the Kids were the exception. The comic strips were becoming the first of the mass media, creating and unifying a national sensibility. Somewhere, somehow, it was decided that what the people needed was reassurance—perhaps the people themselves decided it—that what should be going into millions of homes all over the United States was a comforting and conformist version of the lives that were lived in those homes. Time and again, strips were sterilized and homogenized to meet a national norm, which, until the coming the comics, had been nonexistent.

The first thirty-odd years of comic strips consisted of a gradual narrowing of focus in which comedy—the only genre to be explored by the medium—would become increasingly domesticated. If the strips seemed more civilized, it was by and large because they chose to ignore most of the problems of civilization, in order to concentrate on the veneer of the society. Increasingly smug and self-satisfied, comic strips reflected and re-affirmed the roles and goals of the middle class, and abandoned the art of puncturing balloons full of hot air in favor of the art of pumping them up. The result was something which could be considered more dignified only in the most debased sense of the term, something less urbane than, to coin a phrase, sub-urbane.

There were a few exceptions, excursions into the worlds of the surreal or symbolistic like Winsor McCay's *Little Nemo* or George Herriman's *Krazy Kat*, but, in the big game, the dye had been cast. The wholesome, harmless, inoffensive family strip was coming into its own, with the same pervasiveness by which the situation comedy format would conquer television in the second half of the century. It appeared that the fate of A. Mutt was to be the fate of all mankind, at least as far as newspaper comic strips were concerned.

The four titles that signaled the domestic takeover were (with the years of their debuts) George McManus's *Bringing Up Father* (1912), Harry Hershfield's *Abie the Agent* (1914), Sydney Smith's *The Gumps* (1917) and Frank King's *Gasoline Alley* (1919). The logical culmination of the trend was Chic Young's *Blondie*, which, beginning in 1930, rapidly became the most widely circulated strip in the country and in the world, a position which it apparently continues to hold to the present day.

Bringing Up Father, by virtue of its age, is the least bland of the group, including as it does both healthy doses of slapstick and some satirical overtones. Its principal characters are a nouveau riche Irish couple, Jiggs and Maggie, and the plot conflicts invariably revolve around the contrast between their attitudes toward their improved social status. Jiggs longs for the simple life of his former friends, as symbolized by corned beef and cabbage at Dinty Moore's, while Maggie is a snob with cultural pretensions which dissolve into the most vulgar sort of mayhem as she moves to block her husband's backsliding tendencies. The strip has come to be considered a sort of classic (it has been continued after the original artist's death) and owes much of its popularity to the clean, limber line of the McManus style, which made most of its predecessors look crude, cluttered or scratchy by comparison. It is unfortunate that the longstanding success of *Bringing Up Father*, combined with its aesthetic advance, should have obscured its message. For, although the author's intention is to defend the humanistic outlook represented by Jiggs, the cumulative effect of the hero's endless frustration is to make him a fool. The visual effect of Maggie's brutality overcomes the irony to make her appear triumphant. Thus a major move toward a materialistic matriarchy was made in the mass media and in some part of the mass mind.

The misery of Jiggs, whose fortune made him an object of contempt, was lost on his followers Abie the Agent and Andy Gump, who pursued the good life with earnest enthusiasm. Neither was ever successful enough to permit his family to turn on him, and, without personal conflict, the humor in these strips just about disappeared. Even the most devout defenders of comic strips have been hard pressed to find a good word to print about Andy Gump, the chinless wonder with the calculating mind. Yet he was a national institution for years, and the cornerstone of the incredibly successful New York *Daily News* syndicate. The cutback in its comedy was less apparent because the drawings continued to have a discernible relation to the form which had once evoked laughter. Yet the self-satisfied nature of its contents, which invited members of an upwardly mobile society to, quite literally, enjoy themselves, was inimical to the imaginative potential of the medium and to the critical attitude which creates the catharsis of authentic self-recognition.

A further development came with *Gasoline Alley*, which extended the implications of the "slice of life" school by introducing the element of time into the comic strip. Previous family-style strips existed in a vacuum of eternity where, once the basic problem had been established, the calendar would never lose a page, thus demonstrating to readers, at least on a subliminal level, that the stories bore a very slight relationship to reality. Frank King allowed his Gasoline Alley characters to age, so that the foundling infant Skeezix eventually became the head of his own family group. The result was that readers were able to participate even more fully in the life of the characters, absorbed in an existence which now presented a more complete parallel, however bizarre, to what the readers might imagine themselves to be.

A more or less simultaneous development was the appearance of a group of titles which promised something new in the form of a subdued sex interest. These were the strips like Cliff Sterrett's *Polly and Her Pals* (1912), Martin Branner's *Winnie Winkle* (1920), Westover's *Tillie the Toiler* (1921) and Martin's *Boots*. Each featured an attractive heroine and offered, at least in theory, the prospect of some glamour and romance. In point of fact, though, the girls were respectable in the extreme, and offered only the slightest variation on the domestic themes which were becoming the newspaper standard. Each was part of a family group, and it soon became evident that what was being offered was only a slight shift of focus toward the distaff side. This was what the standard strips were promoting anyhow, though never more obviously than in *Blondie*, which used the girl strip as a come-on for the introduction of the ultimate situation-comedy type.

How many of those millions who follow the endless harassments of the poor overworked, browbeaten, henpecked Dagwood Bumstead realize or remember that he began his public career as a millionaire playboy? Sad but true. The Blondie of the title was a foolish flapper who caught his roving eye and held it with a grip of iron. Rather than lose her as his life-long lover, Dagwood allowed himself to be disinherited by parents whose judgment regarding his prospective bride was probably sounder than his own. He was to become the classic example of the down-trodden male, bolstering his wounded ego with his notorious sky-high sandwiches, yet still helpless against the machinations of his implacable wife. An object of contempt to his spouse, his offspring, his employer, and even his dog Daisy, Dagwood remains incredibly cheerful, and somehow his family and their relationships have become something of a national ideal. The correspondence between his lifestyle and that of his actual counterparts among the bread-winners of the United States is difficult to define explicitly, but it seems unfortunate at best that the most popular representation of the person who is at once the backbone of the family and the economy should be as a helpless buffoon.

The success of the female protagonist was combined with the proven appeal of the kid strip in 1924 when Harold Gray produced *Little Orphan Annie*. A paragon of independence and enterprise, Annie represented traditional American values which were often outlined quite specifically in political pronouncements with a distinctly conservative tone. This viewpoint was emphasized by the presence of Annie's occasional guardian, Daddy Warbucks, a munitions manufacturer with a huge fortune and high-handed methods for preserving it. There have been objections to Gray's views, but there can be no doubt that he made an important contribution to the history of comics. *Little Orphan Annie* paved the way for strips with melodramatic themes, and was a pioneer in the concept of using strips as a forum for serious commentary.

It was inevitable that the increasingly feminized world of the comic strips would create its own reaction with something that carried with it the masculine love for high adventure, a theme which had received short shrift from a medium which was ideally designed for it. The standard, and certainly the most significant, date for marking the birth of the new concept is January 7, 1929. The two strips which bowed simultaneously on that day threw startled newspaper readers backwards into the passionate, primeval past of the jungle, and forward into the fantastic future of space travel and science-fiction. They were *Tarzan*, by Harold Foster, and *Buck Rogers*, written by Philip Nowlan and rendered by Dick Calkins.

Both titles were commissioned by the heads of their syndicates, who apparently sensed the need for a new style at the same time. The search for adventure had led the syndicates to the pulp magazines for source material: *Tarzan*, of course, was drawn from the Edgar Rice Burroughs stories which had first appeared in *All-Story* (later *Argosy*), and *Buck Rogers* was derived from Nowlan's own stories for the science-fiction pulps. Within a decade, the feedback from these pioneering action strips would put a number of pulp publishers into the comic book business.

Along with fantastic action and thrills, the strips offered artistic innovation by depicting human beings in a realistic manner, as caricature gave way to illustration. Yet there was quite a contrast in the amount of talent employed in the technique. Calkins' drawing for *Buck Rogers* was wooden, cluttered, and two-dimensional; Foster rapidly developed into the most impeccable draftsman ever to grace a newspaper page, offering accurate anatomy, dramatic composition, and crisp rendering.

The year 1929 was also the year of the great Depression. Although *Tarzan* and *Buck Rogers* were nine months ahead of the crash, they and their successors doubtlessly owed some of their popularity to a desire for escaping from the grim truth of the economic situation. Certainly it had been demonstrated that the standard comic strip version of the happy home in the suburbs had hardly scratched the surface of human experience.

Still, violent conflict was brought back from space and the jungle to the streets of the United States by Chester Gould's *Dick Tracy* in 1931. Here was a hero who moved from the civilian world to a metropolitan police force when gangsters murdered his fiance's father in their home. This brutal shooting was something new to comics, justified by the indignation Gould and his boss, Joseph Patterson of the Chicago *Tribune* syndicate, shared concerning crime and criminals. It was the first civilized murder to be committed in the funnies. Gould's style was representational without being truly realistic; he compared it to a blueprint, and his hero's profile became increasingly rigid and squared-off as the years went by. The artist's insistence on bloody brutality and grotesque villains (the most popular was Flattop, the weirdest was probably Flyface) has caused more than a few papers to drop some of the more lurid episodes, and his rigidly defined version of the struggle between good and evil prefigures the melodramatic theme which was to dominate the comic book.

The second of the science-fiction comic strips, *Brick Bradford*, drawn by Clarence Gray and written by William Ritt, bowed in 1933. Brick used a flying time-traveling device to good effect, but he was almost immediately overshadowed by the appearance, in 1934, of the ultimate space epic, Alex Raymond's *Flash Gordon*. Like Foster, Raymond abandoned speech balloons in favor of subsidiary blocks of text. Visually, the Raymond strip offered everything that the groundbreaking work of Calkins in *Buck Rogers* had lacked. Raymond's settings were lush, his perspective enthralling, and his figures heroic. Using the same trio of standard protagonists as *Buck Rogers* (a man, a girl, and their eccentric, scientific mentor), Raymond infused his tales with an incredible glamour which bypassed concern with scientific gimmickry to revel in the potential for fantasy found in an unexplored universe where anything was possible. He also came up with the most satisfying villain ever to sneer and leer his way across a Sunday page, Ming the Merciless, lord of the planet Mongo and interplanetary scourge. Raymond was responsible during the same period for two other strips, *Secret Agent X-9* (scripted for a time by Dashiell Hammett) and *Jungle Jim*, but it was on the worlds beyond our own that he created his masterpiece.

Two comparatively minor achievements of the banner year 1934 were Vince Hamlin's *Alley Oop*, whose protagonist was a prehistoric man who teamed up with a time-traveling professor, and Lee Falk's brainchild, *Mandrake the Magician*. These were overshadowed by Raymond on the one hand, and Milton Caniff on the other. Caniff's *Terry and the Pirates* dropped a boy into an incredible world of criminal intrigue, and never called time out. With his unofficial guardian, Pat Ryan, Terry Lee lived the melodramatic life that his fans could only dream about. Caniff's solid, deceptively simple illustration, with its vivid contrast between light and shadow, stood in comparison to the classicism of Foster's *Tarzan* and the romanticism of Raymond's *Flash Gordon*, making him the realist of comic strip artists. His salty dialogue and elaborate plots marked him as a skillful writer. *Terry* also produced a devastating female counterpart to Raymond's Ming: the lucious and lethal Eurasian opium dealer, the Dragon Lady, who was shot to death in her first sequence by a heartbroken admirer, but later revived to become a comic strip immortal. Caniff's world is populated with pulchritude, but there is only one Dragon Lady.

The first truly satirical strip in newspaper history also put in its first appearance in 1934; this was *Li'l Abner*, the creation of Al Capp, who had previously assisted Ham Fisher on his saccharine boxing strip,

Joe Palooka. Like just about every other cartoonist, it took Capp a while to hit his stride, but what eventually resulted would be the most discussed and dissected piece of work in the history of the medium. To put the achievement simply, Capp exaggerated the flaws of society by contrasting them with the mental purity of his naive hillbilly hero. His attacks on the ethics of big business earned him the love of the political leftists; perhaps his most powerful creation (despite his later disclaimers) was the Shmoo, a lovable beast capable of providing free all the necessities of life, and doomed to extinction to preserve the economic status quo. Equally remarkable was the concept of "Fearless Fosdick," a strip within the strip, read religiously by Abner, which parodies *Dick Tracy*. In fact, Abner's slavish imitation of his "ideel" drove him in 1952 to marriage with the patiently passionate Daisy Mae, an event which Capp himself proclaimed to be an act of submission to public pressure, as distinguished from artistic integrity. Since this capitulation, the strip has become increasingly critical of the left which once embraced it, although Capp insists that he occupies the same position, and that it is the world that is changing. A creature called the Bald Iggle, featured in the strip some years ago, had the power to evoke the truth from anyone it encountered. Under its pressure, a critic was forced to admit that the reason he attacked the young was because he was no longer one of them. Whether or not this is the case with Capp, there is no doubt that, all in all, he has served comics and the public well by evoking controversy and possibly even thought.

In 1936, Hal Foster left *Tarzan* to the vigorous pen of Burne Hogarth and created the most elaborate and finely wrought of comic strips, the Arthurian epic *Prince Valiant*. *Prince Valiant* was perhaps the culmination of the comic strip. In the same year arrived a figure whose character embodied the traits that unknowingly heralded the birth of comic books. Created by Lee Falk, the character of the Phantom, with his costume of black mask and purple tights and his secret identity, manifested two of the essential features which would make comic books a vigorous and independent industry within two years. And not a minute too soon.

Chapter Two: The Birth of the Comic Book

The spectacular event that signaled the success of the comic book as an independent entity was the debut of Superman in the first issue of *Action Comics* in June 1938. But this was the culmination of a spasmodic series of efforts which date back almost to the first successes of the comic strip in newspapers. There was even a *Yellow Kid* comic book published in New York by Howard Ainslee during the period when the Kid was employed by Hearst's *Journal*. The Chicago *American* issued a *Mutt and Jeff* book in 1911 which was given away for coupons as a circulation builder. There were numerous other examples of such one-of-a-kind comic books, some of which will probably never be recovered or recorded again.

A Philadelphia publisher produced a few square-shaped books featuring Walt Disney's Mickey Mouse after Mickey's success in motion pictures had produced a newspaper strip in the early thirties. An experiment which had a longer life was Whitman's Big Little Books, which adapted popular newspaper strips and some movies into an unusual format. The Big Little Books were in effect profusely illustrated novels, although by literary standards somewhat simple-minded. Each left-handed page contained text, and the opposite page an illustration. Brief descriptive slugs under each picture made it possible to follow a crude version of the narrative without reference to the more forbidding blocks of type. The pictures were actually a step back from comic strips, since they dropped the speech balloons in favor of printed captions, but they were at least telling a complete and self-sustained story in the incredibly thick, three-inch-square books with the colorful pasteboard covers. Among the characters to appear in the Big Little Books were Buck Rogers, Flash Gordon, Dick Tracy, Terry and the Pirates, the Phantom, and Tarzan (who split up his activities between his cartoon incarnations and books that relied on stills from his successful career as a hero in the movies). Adaptations of major films like *David Copperfield* and

Lost Patrol made the Big Little Books an important indicator of the relationship between the comics and the cinema, two visual methods of storytelling which developed simultaneously and had a profound effect on each other, not only by providing source material, but also by suggesting to each other new methods of composition and new techniques for visual progression.

James Steranko's *History of Comics* mentions an unsuccessful experiment by George Delacorte (who, over the years, was to become among the most successful of publishers). *The Funnies* was a full-color tabloid of original comics material produced in 1929 and was available on newsstands for a run of thirteen issues before it was dropped. The quality of the material may have had something to do with its failure, or possibly the time was not ripe. Even the ungainly size may have been a factor. Regardless, it would take only four years more before the birth of the comic book would be officially recorded.

The most significant factor in the creation of the comic book was the presence of a New York firm called the Eastern Color Printing Company. It was here that *The Funnies* had been printed, and more to the point, it was here that the Sunday color comics sections were printed for many of the major newspapers in the Northeast. Marshall McLuhan's dictum that "the medium is the message" finds a great deal of justification in the events which took place here. Even as progress in color printing had produced *The Yellow Kid*, the presence of the gigantic, technically advanced color press at Eastern would finally lead to the comic book.

The two individuals who transformed the potential of the press into the reality of the comic book were Harry I. Wildenberg and M. C. Gaines, both Eastern employees. Wildenberg was sales manager, and Gaines was a salesman. (Another person in the firm who would eventually have an important place in the industry created at Eastern Color Printing was Leverett S. Gleason, Wildenberg's advertising manager.)

Wildenberg eventually became a cigar jobber in Florida, and in later years, he viewed his comic book inspiration with distress. Interviewed by John Vosburgh (*The Commonweal*, May 20, 1949) at the height of an early, if ineffectual attack on the comic book, Wildenberg disowned his brainchild while describing the sequence of events which gave it birth. "I don't feel proud that I started the comic books," he declared. "If I had had an inkling of the harm they would do, I would never have gone through with the idea." This "harm," of course, was largely theoretical, one of the charges—never proved—that were brought upon the form because it was new and lacked "official" sanction. Wildenberg insisted that he never read comics, not even newspaper strips, so the source

of his dismay must have been second-hand information. "You must remember," he continued, "that in the beginning I gave little thought to the social aspects of the matter. In business a man seldom thinks beyond profits. The social aspect of an idea, an invention, is secondary, if he contemplates it all. It was my business to sell comics and it did not even occur to me to weigh the effects they would have." The millions of Americans who have enjoyed comic books for years can only be grateful for their inventor's blind spot, and may even find some enjoyment in the irony of his remarks.

Amazed by the seemingly endless sheets of newspaper comics pouring off the presses, and cognizant of their power to improve newspaper circulation (the strips were, in fact, the most frequently read part of every newspaper carrying them), Wildenberg hit upon the idea that comics might be used to sell something else. Gulf Oil Company was convinced, and had original material worked up to be printed in tabloid form at Eastern and used as a premium at service stations. Millions were circulated. It was a step forward, but in form it was still not a comic book.

The format which was to become the standard one was dictated by the presses. They were geared to print sheets of the standard newspaper size which, when folded in half, produced tabloids. Folding this once more in an idle moment, Wildenberg hit upon the ideal size for a comic magazine as if by accident. Here was something compact and convenient which could be printed on the same press that did the newspaper work. One newspaper sheet could be folded and trimmed to produce sixteen comic book pages, measuring slightly more than eight by eleven inches.

An arrangement was made with a syndicate for Wildenberg to reprint newspaper strips at ten dollars per page, and salesman M. C. Gaines got an order from soap manufacturers Proctor and Gamble for one million copies of the first standardized comic book, thirty-two pages of *Funnies on Parade*, available for coupons clipped from the packaging of Proctor and Gamble products. Other manufacturers were sold on the same idea and the comic book had been established, at least on a limited basis, in 1933.

But comic books were still being used to sell something other than their own contents, and each premium printing might be the last. Gaines proved a point by demonstrating that local newsstands could sell the premiums at a retail price of ten cents, then approached Delacorte, who took a chance for a second time, ordered a comparatively small printing and sold it out without convincing himself he was on to a good thing. He did not renew, pleading a lack of advertising contracts for the suspicious new type of magazine. Later, Delacorte's company, Dell Publishing, would become one of the leaders in the field, but the whole concept still looked questionable at the time.

What finally happened was that Eastern set out on its own, spurred by the possibility of a larger profit than it could offer any of its customers. The result was a sixty-four page *Famous Funnies* in July 1934 distributed by the American News Company. As with *Funnies on Parade*, the issue consisted of material previously published as comic strips. A second issue appeared in September, then the publication became a monthly. Circulation increased with each issue until it was near a million. After almost four decades, the comic book had proved that comics could stand on their own feet.

The scramble for sales began, with new titles appearing which would soon exhaust the source of newspaper strips. Gaines produced *Popular Comics* for Dell (February 1936), and Lev Gleason engineered *Tip Top Comics* (April 1936) for the United Features Syndicate. But it was the earliest tabloid efforts like the Gulf giveaway and Delacorte's first short-lived comic, *The Funnies*, which would set the pace for comic books, which would achieve major impact only when they started printing original material.

Probably the motivation for this move was financial (more publishers wanted to get into the lucrative new field than the syndicates could supply with material), but the results were to have artistic implications as well. The newspaper action strips which became the comic book norm were essentially advertisements for themselves. The idea behind them was less to offer the reader a total aesthetic experience than to keep him coming back for more in search of a resolution which was rarely offered. A story read in one-minute bursts over weeks or months is hardly a story at all. Even the reprint books like *Famous Funnies* fell into the same problem, since they did not have room to present an entire story sequence from beginning to end. The earliest of the independent and original comic books were certainly crude, but they were on the right track.

The most important contribution to the shift to original material came when pulp publisher Harry Donenfeld bought out a moribund independent comic book outfit along with its few titles to begin *Detective Comics* in March 1937. This title also served as a name for Donenfeld's firm which, although it later became National Periodicals, continued to emblazon D. C. in a circular slug on the covers of all its comic books. (A world of complex business arrangements is often submerged beneath the unchanging corporate name which permits the public to identify the product by its publisher. Some companies would not be producers, but simply distributors or, in the case of A. C. G.—American Comics Group—advertising contractors.)

Donenfeld's comic book company, hereafter called D. C., became the unquestioned leader in the field when his plans to inaugurate a new title, *Action Comics*, came to the attention of Gaines, who was now agent for a newspaper syndicate. On Gaines's desk was an action strip which seemed too *outre* for his employers, but might be just right for a comic book. So he passed it along to Donenfeld, who decided to give it a try. The strip was *Superman*. Strangely enough, its creators, writer Jerry Siegel and artist Joe Shuster, were already working for *Detective Comics*, where they produced a variety of fairly unimpressive characters including "Slam Bradley." Apparently they had never even submitted *Superman* to Donenfeld because they had seen it rejected for years everywhere they had taken it. It would soon prove to be the most successful and imitated idea in comic books. In fact, it guaranteed that comic books would survive.

Superman, a foundling rocketed to Earth by his parents from the doomed planet Krypton, was adopted by two earthlings, Mr. and Mrs. Kent. He grew up under protective coloration to take the secret identity of Clark Kent, mild-mannered reporter for the *Daily Planet*. Beneath his simple suit and spectacles was the Man of Steel, and a skin-tight blue costume with red trunks, boots, and a cape, with just a little yellow behind the red "S" on his chest. As an alien, he was invulnerable, with apparently unlimited strength. At first only a fantastic jumper, he gained the freedom of pure flight when animators commissioned to do a series of motion picture cartoons found his early means of propulsion to be somewhat ludicrous.

Superman, the ultimate expression of human aspirations to power and pure freedom, was an instant triumph, a concept so intense and so instantly identifiable that he became perhaps the most widely known figure ever created in American fiction. Almost immediately it became apparent that he was too super to ever lose his war against crime. Once it was known who he was, it was known what would happen to him—for all intents and purposes, nothing. Consequently, it might have been possible that his very invulnerability would have been the source of his defeat, in the public eye if not in his adventures. Some devices, like the introduction of Kryptonite, the alien element with a deleterious effect on the Man of Steel, were to prove reasonably useful in keeping up interest. What really made the series a success, however, was already built into the story.

The most fascinating feature of *Superman*, and the most elaborately analyzed by students of the medium, is the tension existing between Superman and his alter ego, Clark Kent, especially as it reflects itself in the problems both have with their "love interest," girl reporter Lois Lane. As has often been noted, Superman is unique among the vast number of heroes with secret identities in that it is not the heroic role which he adopts, but rather the average. Clark Kent, and not that fantastic flying figure, is the phony. Some practical reasons have been offered for this impersonation. It frees the hero from constant harassment and frees his friends from potential peril. It also has a certain value in increasing sales, since the frail half of the dual character makes an immediate reader identification with the hero more feasible. Yet this factor, operating as it does outside the framework of the tales, does not provide the internal logic which can be sensed lurking below the surface of Superman. Since Superman, loved by Lois, maintains the guise of Kent, whom Lois despises, commentators like James Steranko and Jules Feiffer have suggested that he may be somewhat masochistic. In fact, however, his amusement with this eternal triangle suggests that the element at work here is less a capacity for neurotic suffering than for entertaining himself. What makes the apparent contradictions work cohesively is Superman's sense of humor, which was to be emphasized more and more as his career progressed.

A story which goes a long way toward illuminating this puzzling relationship is "Lois Lane, Superwoman," reprinted here from *Action Comics* No. 60 (May 1943). Here the idea of righting wrongs has been clearly subordinated to the problems which were built into the series. The villain is much less of a menace than the threat to the status quo represented by Lois Lane's brief vision of glory. The reversal gives Superman a taste of his own medicine, and the girl reporter's accident also forces a unique confession from the hero (as he becomes his super self): "Without her, life wouldn't be worth living for me." Superman's headstrong proposal on the last page indicates that only a change like the one Lois has undergone could ever end her frustration, but the "all a dream" syndrome interrupts to prevent a resolution and assure readers that the life of the series would go on as before. Thus the story is a predecessor of the increasingly prevalent use of "imaginary" stories which made it possible to bend the format of *Superman* in any direction without actually breaking it. The cleverness of the plot reflects a trend away from the vigorous simplicity of its originators, Siegel and Shuster, who, having supplied the most powerful single conception in the history of comic books, actually produced only a comparative handful of the stories, although their names continued to appear on title pages like this one.

A similar status was enjoyed by Bob Kane, who received all the credit for *Batman*, a feature which was to become D. C.'s second giant, and to establish the company as the leader in the field. Working with writer Bill Finger (and soon to be joined by artist Jerry Robinson), Kane created the Caped Crusader

for *Detective Comics* No. 27 (May 1939). *Batman Comics* bowed in spring 1940, following *Superman Comics* (summer 1939). Here at last were two original characters good enough to carry their own comic book titles. Batman immediately distinguished himself from his alien predecessor and his host of imitators by being a mere mortal, with no fantastic powers at all. What he had instead was the powerful motivation supplied by a gun-toting thug who left him a wealthy orphan with a fantastic hatred for criminals. By day playboy Bruce Wayne, by night as Batman he wore the menacing mask and billowing cape designed to strike fear into the hearts of evildoers. In his role as an avenger, in his squarish anatomy, and in his tendency to encounter grotesque villains, Batman was the comic book descendant of Chester Gould's Dick Tracy.

The early adventures of Batman featured a macabre atmosphere which was never entirely dispelled, although it was to be toned down by a series of events which stabilized the qualities of the trend-setting D. C. line. Batman had carried a gun, and shot down a few of his opponents. Editors finally decreed ·that this was carrying the spirit of grim vengeance too far to make for an appealing hero, and eventually a code of ethics was drawn up which defined the limits of acceptable behavior (and was in many respects the basis for the Comics Code to be inaugurated in 1954). There was also an economic motive for the survival of the villains who might prove to be popular with the audience. A case in point was the Joker, originally slated to die in the same first issue of *Batman* in which he had been born. It was recognized that the character was something too striking to abandon, and the story was redone.

The Joker, a green-haired, white-faced clown with a morbid sense of humor, was not the only classic villain to emerge in the first issue of *Batman*. Also appearing was the Cat, a glamorous and feline female villainess who later become Catwoman. Somehow she seemed a natural counterpoint to Batman, complete as she was with a set of cat-paraphernalia which matched the hero's own growing storehouse of equipment. Yet she lacked the uncompromising quality of a dyed-in-the-wool menace, as it became increasingly evident that what motivated her life of crime was a lovelorn desire to attract Batman's attention. In this sense, she was less a Dragon Lady than a Lois Lane. The bad girl who really meant business would find her home in other companies where careful considerations of good taste were less of an issue than uninhibited displays of elemental conflict.

Batman's move away from his hard-line approach was signaled by the introduction of Robin, the Boy Wonder, in *Detective Comics* No. 38. Born Dick Grayson, orphan son of a pair of acrobats, he was adopted by Bruce Wayne to become half of a new team, the "Dynamic Duo." Robin was to relieve the gloom of isolation, demanding by his very presence that the bitter Batman become more sympathetic, more human. He also provided an opportunity for some needed dialogue, and gave younger readers a character with whom they could identify. The bright colors of his red, yellow and green costume lightened the dark tone of the entire series, and set a major precedent for later heroes, very few of which would spring up without a kid companion in tow.

A third member of the *Batman* hierarchy of villains who has impressed the critics is Two-Face. In his comparatively few appearances, he became the graphic embodiment of the split personality, a good man turned bad when half his face was disfigured by acid. His habit of flipping a coin to determine his plan always left virtue at least a theoretical possibility, but somehow the "good" side hardly ever came up. He is represented here in his final bow, "Two-Face Strikes Again," from *Batman* No. 81. This tale, which was published in February 1954, is a fond look backward at a character who would have no place under the restrictions of the Comics Code which was to come into force just a few months later. Two-Face, resurrected to permanent hideousness after an earlier cure through plastic surgery, asserted the dark side of humanity with his final flip of a gigantic coin that was undeniably loaded. The hairbreadth escapes and huge props in this piece vividly represent the extravagant style of *Batman*, which was to slip briefly into a mockery of itself under the influence of a deliberately humorous television program in the mid-sixties. The artwork represents the definitive *Batman* style, elaborated (as with virtually all comic books) from a relatively crude beginning, yet still not slipping into the later slick illustrative technique which somehow diminished the tone.

Holding the rights to the two most impressive characters in comics, D. C. and Donenfeld expanded by taking on M. C. Gaines, who had supplied *Superman*, to produce a new, affiliated line of comics, All-American, which, sparked by writer Gardner Fox, unleashed a torrent of super characters including the Flash, Hawkman, and Green Lantern. *All-Star Comics*, inaugurated in 1940, put them all together in the same comic with the formation of the Justice Society of America. Soon they were all appearing in the same fragmented, but book-length story.

The line's most impressive achievement, however, was the debut of Wonder Woman, who first showed up in *All-Star Comics* No. 8, became the lead character in *Sensation Comics*, inaugurated in January 1942, and took off with *Wonder Woman*, her own title, in 1942. She was originated and scripted by psychologist William Moulton Marston to answer a specific call for a series to appeal to potential female readers. Not content to be just a woman who could perform as incredibly as her male counterparts, her stories contained incidents and attitudes which suggested, and perhaps even embodied, militant feminism on a scale unprecedented in any mass medium. Masculine critics have viewed her with a mixture of contempt and alarm, but she lasted longer than almost any of the male characters created concurrently, a fact which suggests that she and Marston knew just what they were doing. In the hands of artist Harry Peter she was perhaps the least visually attractive of comic book heroines, but, again, this seems to have been just what the doctor ordered.

Naturally, D. C. could not remain alone in the field that their efforts had made so rewarding. Numerous competitors sprang up overnight; some fell just as quickly, but a few of them were able to attract a sizable share of the public's dimes. The hottest contest developed when a character named Captain Marvel appeared in *Whiz Comics* No. 2 (despite the numbering, this was the first issue) in February 1940. *Captain Marvel Adventures* followed in 1941. Created by writer Bill Parker and artist C. C. Beck (Otto Binder was an important later author), *Captain Marvel* was to become the best seller in the field, and Superman's most impressive rival. A product of Fawcett Publications, which also produced magazines like *Mechanix Illustrated*, Captain Marvel was to have the strangest fate of any comic book hero: he was put out of business by a lawsuit. This was launched by D. C., who viewed the Captain as an infringement on the *Superman* copyright. Litigation went on for years, and a judgment was never reached, but an exhausted Fawcett Publications finally agreed to settle out of court and kill off their hero permanently. This was in 1953, when the type of comic book under dispute was in a temporary decline anyway.

Perhaps it is because of the legal guarantee that Captain Marvel will never fly again that such a mystique has grown up around him. Yet the popularity he enjoyed during his thirteen years of existence suggests that he was something more than a simple imitation of the Man of Steel. After all, an earlier defendant in a similar case, *Wonder Man*, had died without a whimper in 1941. At the same time, it seems safe to assert that, if there had been no *Superman* in 1938, there would have been no *Captain Marvel* two years later. If he fell, as opposed to a host of others working the same vein, it must have been because he was such a big target.

He was, in fact, "the big red cheese," to borrow a snide epithet from his arch rival, the bald, bespectacled mad scientist Dr. Sivana, whose crazy laugh ("Heh! Heh! Heh!") and crazier inventions made him the most lovable villain in an overcrowded field. Sivana's sneering remark set the tone for the stories which relied increasingly for their success on elements of self-satire and comedy. Again and again, Captain Marvel, for all his might, ended up in situations where even in triumph he came out looking just a little foolish. The most famous example of this was the uncovering of the brains behind an incredible array of villains which called itself the Monster Society of Evil. It took the Captain many issues of his comic to unmask the leader of this deadly conglomeration, who turned out to be Mr. Mind, a miniscule worm. Such irony was typical of the series, and no doubt it was Captain Marvel's ability to take a joke which made him such a favorite. He rarely punched his way out of a predicament before it had been milked for laughs. (In the sixties two companies would use the name for new heroes but, lacking the flavor of the original, they had short careers.)

Captain Marvel also gained some of his popularity through the way in which he acquired his powers. In real life, he was Billy Batson, boy broadcaster for radio station WHIZ. An ancient wizard whom he discovered dwelling for no apparent reason in an abandoned subway tunnel gave him the power to transform himself into the red-clad giant by speaking the old man's name, "Shazam!" Youthful readers were doubtless entranced by the possibility of receiving magical abilities just by shooting off their mouths, and the device of combining the hero and his boy companion into one (they apparently shared the same consciousness) was certainly a master stroke.

Captain Marvel gave birth to the comic books' first important spinoff character when he took Freddy Freeman, a boy injured by the fiendish Captain Nazi, to the subway. Here he became Captain Marvel Junior, who could transform himself by chanting "Captain Marvel!" All this took place in *Whiz* No. 25, which left Captain Nazi unpunished and which shamelessly advised readers to go out and buy another title. Captain Marvel told his namesake, "I'm going to send you into *Master Comics* to take care of Captain Nazi." And so it came to pass. Later Mary Marvel would join the ranks, featured in *Wow Comics*.

Other Fawcett heroes included Spy Smasher and Bulletman, but the best was Ibis the Invincible, also featured in *Whiz*. The fact that he appeared to be quietly cohabiting with his beautiful Princess Taia gave an added fillip to the adventures of this ancient Egyptian wizard in modern times. The company also produced eight issues of *Nickel Comics* in 1940, one of several short-lived experiments with a "half-priced" comic book.

The year 1941 set loose a remarkable number of new characters. It was, of course, the year when the United States entered the Second World War, but few comic book heroes found it necessary to wait for Pearl Harbor before they chose sides. The most obvious triumph was Captain America, who inspired a whole new crew of red, white and blue imitators. He and his cohorts in the Timely-Atlas-Marvel line will be considered in a later chapter.

A company with more than a few important contributions and an outstanding flair for off-beat melodramatics was the Quality Comics Group (officially Comic Magazines). Its most impressive title was *Police Comics*, which began in August 1941. Bowing in the first issue were the voluptuous Phantom Lady and the incredible Plastic Man. The eleventh issue offered the origin of one of the most powerful and highly praised of comic book heroes, Will Eisner's Spirit.

Will Eisner occupies a unique place among comic book men as an innovator of unparalleled ingenuity. Equally skilled as a writer and an artist, he brought a dramatic flair to everything he touched, and left an indelible mark on every series he created, even though he often remained with a series only long enough to get the thing launched. The comparatively few number of pages on which he worked is completely overshadowed by the effect they had on the rest of the industry. A master at conveying moods through weird angle shots and imaginative composition, he was equally effective at the creation of colorful, unexpected plots and vigorous vernacular dialogue. His comic book characters included the Ray, the Hawk, Doll Man, the Black Condor, and Uncle Sam. The creation with the most durability was the belligerent Blackhawk, but the character for which Eisner has received the most recognition is undoubtedly the Spirit.

Denny Colt was the secret identity of this character, who stood out from the mass of comic book heroes because of his nondescript appearance and lack of bizarre powers. He was officially dead, and used Wildwood Cemetery as a base of operations, but there was nothing supernatural about this man who wore ordinary street clothes and employed only the smallest of masks to disguise the fact that Colt was still among the living. What made the Spirit so impressive was his no-nonsense approach to the problem of crimefighting. In a medium where flamboyance was to become commonplace, his sardonic underplaying was a welcome change of pace, and one which put the emphasis back where it belonged, on the story. Ingenious detection alternated with bizarre flights of fancy to produce a wide variety of plots.

While the three top characters at D. C., Superman, Batman and Wonder Woman, enjoyed the distinction of being published in serial versions as newspaper strips, the Spirit began in 1939 as a strange sort of newspaper supplement which was actually a short comic book, and included a complete color story each Sunday. After moving into the more recognizable *Police Comics* format, he got his own Quality comic book in 1944. Eisner entered the armed services during the war, but his character was to be continued by others, notably Lou Fine.

Eisner himself may not have gone to war until 1942, but he put seven fierce fighters on the Allied side with the Blackhawk series which began with the first issue of the Quality title *Military Comics* in August 1941. This would become *Modern Comics* with the end of the war. *Blackhawk* bowed as a title in 1944, taking over with issue No. 9 from the moribund *Uncle Sam*. There were actually six Blackhawks, organized by the leader (who answered to no other name) as an independently wealthy guerrilla force without official government ties. Blackhawk's international followers were Andre, Chuck, Olaf, Stanislaus and Hendrickson. The seventh member, Chop Chop, a diminutive Chinese, was added in *Military Comics* No. 3. He was to be the source of some controversy, since it was possible to view his comic appearance as a racial slur. Yet the intention was obviously quite the opposite, since Chop Chop was clearly distinguished from the fiendish Japanese who were unquestionably caricatured in this and every other comic book (and every other mass medium) during the war. Readers who actually followed his adventures soon realized that Chop Chop was an integral part of the team, and one whose activities often determined the success of a mission. He was certainly preferable to stereotyped black characters like *Captain Marvel's* Steamboat Willie (was he named for the first talking Mickey Mouse movie?) and the Spirit's Ebony, although it can be said that the condescending treatment afforded to Negroes was a national characteristic during this period, and not an exclusive comic book manifestation. Attempts in the declining years of *Blackhawk* to alter Chop Chop's appearance only succeeded in destroying his individuality, turning him into a quasi-Caucasian who seemed less interesting and was probably even more insulting.

The importance of *Blackhawk* as a powerful concept has been largely overlooked. Beginning as a reaction to the Axis menace, and employed in the fifties to battle the threat of communism, the series achieved what may have been its finest moments during the lull between American commitments, when it became quite clear what this fighting team represented. The theme of the series is specifically political, and the possibility that a small group of armed, determined men from beyond a nation's borders might topple or sustain its government has parallels in modern reality. Working with mythical countries and symbolic situations, *Blackhawk* emphasized the transformation of the world from states of independence to states of interdependence.

The story represented here, "Karlovna Had a True Underworld," first appeared in *Blackhawk* No. 14, published for spring 1947. The extravagant air of menace and the presence of a glamorous villainess demonstrate some of the typical features of the Quality product. The visual influence of Eisner is everywhere, although the artwork is probably that of Lou Fine. The alluring, ambiguous figure of the queen of the Dragon People dominates the action. Banker Rambin, who turns out to have provided the material motive for the Dragon rebellion is, within the context of the story, just a formalized figurehead, fulfilling the role which the queen is ostensibly playing. Her behavior under pressure (at the end of the story, where she appears in her real identity as Wilna) reveals that she has an emotional involvement in her role as a revolutionary which transcends simple profiteering. As a representative of the unattractive but oppressed Dragon People, she moves toward an embodiment of pure anarchy, the negative side of rebellion which arises from practical or philosophical desperation. Wilna polarizes Blackhawk's pattern of violence, suggesting that his heroic stance in favor of a certain kind of freedom is simultaneously a sort of repressiveness. This problem is posed beneath the surface despite the obvious Blackhawk position as a free "third world" force, beyond political manipulation. Ultimately the hero, by virtue of his virtue, is a reactor rather than an actor. Without a villain, he would be out of work, and his true task is not creation, but the selective destruction which produces a creative atmosphere.

In the final analysis, the Blackhawks and the Dragon People are almost allies, as they discover a common enemy in banker Rambin, who simultaneously represents the government and seeks to undermine it. This might seem a mere device to close the action with a plot reversal, yet it relates directly to the issues which the story raises, as outsiders and undergrounders realize simultaneously that an established authority may represent no interests but those of its own power brokers. So, although the rebellion is countered, it also achieves a legitimate end by exposing the corruption which gave it birth. For all its fantastic elements, this piece functions powerfully as it probes the problems of political power.

Another outstanding Quality creation, Plastic Man, is one of the most imaginative characters in the history of comics. He began as a gangster, the Eel, who was abandoned by his comrades when wounded during a robbery. Nursed back to health by a sympathetic monk, the Eel discovered that a chemical which had entered the wound gave him the ability to distort his body in any shape. This unlikely result, combined with his brief taste of monastery life, reformed the Eel, who returned as Plastic Man to subdue his old gang. His alter ego soon abandoned, he kept his red stretch tights on all the time and became, strangely enough, an agent for the Federal Bureau of Investigation, which usually prefers more conservative employees. His own comic book, *Plastic Man*, began in 1944.

Eisner has claimed some of the credit for the concept of this character, but the man who made him come alive was Jack Cole, who drew the first story and soon evolved a fluid, cartoon-oriented style which set the series apart from anything else ever published. The comparative flatness of work by his successors made it clear how much had been lost when Cole abandoned the series. In his heyday, Plastic Man was the most surreal of comic book heroes, utilizing his extraordinary gift not only for battles, rescues and disguises, but also is a spirit of free play which was a constant visual delight. Cole's ability to distort and contort the basic figure was incredible, and he made the most ordinary of transition scenes into hilarious sight gags. To question a witness in a penthouse apartment, Plastic Man once stretched his neck the entire height of the building, dropped his head into the man's drink and poked it up through the tiny opening in the soda straw. The effect was staggering, and Plastic Man was distinguished as the hero who was most obviously enjoying himself while ostensibly fighting crime. The humorous element was intensified by the presence of the rotund Woozy Winks. The genial, emotional, simpleminded glutton who became Plastic Man's constant companion, first appeared in *Police Comics* No. 13. Woozy was perhaps the ideal sidekick, providing comedy relief in a series that was already loaded with comedy, and avoiding the sense of improbability which battling boy companions often left in their wake. Woozy was refreshingly useless, and somewhat accident prone; his only value lay in his ability to get himself into trouble, bringing his incredible friend into a new and bizarre adventure.

Certainly one of Plastic Man's most colorful encounters was with "Amorpho," a creature from outer space who shared the hero's talents and eventually impersonated him. The few panels at the end of the story of their incredibly convoluted fist fight atop the girders of an unfinished building were a riot of entwined plastic limbs. But Amorpho was perhaps carrying a good thing too far, and no opponent provided a more dramatic contrast with the softest man in comic books than the hardest woman in comic books, Sheila Sorrell, the Granite Lady, whose story from *Police Comics* No. 51 (February 1946) is featured here. The absurdity of minor characters like the members of the Myers mob exemplifies Cole's humorous approach, but it is even more evident in the twisted logic which extends the "heart of stone" metaphor into a physical fact. The masterful rendering of Sheila makes her simultaneously seductive and ridiculous, and her transformation into a woman of stone reveals something about the unpredictable pretensions of science, and more about the problems of frustrated women who feel that they have no real

opportunities except the opportunity to be ogled. Here the misguided act of an admirer who ought to know better gives the comparatively helpless singer a chance to express her seething indignation, complete with the convenient out of temporary amnesia. The fact that she commits apparent murders which later turn out to be harmless represents the extent to which her brief career of crime is an expression of fantasy fulfillment. She remains a sympathetic figure even in her most fearsome moments, not only because of the light tone of the entire story, but because her resentment seems justified, even if her behavior, and her singing, are not.

Quality published numerous other characters, though none as great as Spirit, Blackhawk or Plastic Man. One who deserves recognition for his unique presence and amusing irreverence is Kid Eternity, who originated in *Hit Comics* No. 25, and got his own comic book in 1946. A ghost with a fat, bald spiritual adviser named Mr. Keeper, the Kid had the power to summon any character from history with the word "eternity." The frivolous use to which he put some of these people made for some amusing twists.

If D. C. (with Superman, Batman and Wonder Woman), Timely (whose Captain America and others will be discussed later), Fawcett (with Captain Marvel) and Quality (with the Spirit, Blackhawk and Plastic Man) were the leaders in the production of comic book heroes, a few other companies also deserve mention. Chief of these is Fiction House (Real Adventures Publishing Company). Originally a publisher of pulp fiction magazines, this company simply transformed its major titles into comic books. These included *Planet Comics, Jungle Comics, Fight Comics, Wings Comics, Ranger Comics* and *Ghost Comics*. First and foremost was *Jumbo Comics*, which began as a black and white oversized comic book at the early date of September 1938. *Jumbo*, which was soon transformed into the more usual format, featured from its inception one of the most important, durable and attractive of comic book heroines, Sheena, Queen of the Jungle, by "W Morgan Thomas" (S. R. Powell). A sort of female·Tarzan, clad in an elaborate but brief leopard skin outfit, Sheena, striding through the jungle, was never equalled as a vivid expression of primitive female freedom. With a male companion, Bob, in tow (the text referred to him as "her mate"), she was the gigantic blond mistress of a savage kingdom. While some of her adventures concerned themselves with battling warlike native tribes, her primary opponents were white exploiters who moved into the jungle to rob it and its inhabitants of products and purity. She was a defender of the natural order whose justice was swift and often remorseless. *Sheena*, a comic book devoted entirely to her exploits, appeared in spring 1942. What distinguished her was neither the plotting, which was painfully simplistic, nor the dialogue, which became ludicrously stilted in its attempts to achieve a lofty tone. The appeal was primarily visual, embodied in the alluring figure of the jungle queen herself. On the comparatively innocent level of the pin-up art of the forties, she had sex appeal. Although never producing a character of equal stature or longevity, the entire Fiction House line seems to have been based on the promise that a good story was one that featured a well-proportioned, scantily clad young woman. This attractive formula made one of the company's titles much like another, but they undeniably presented an entertaining surface, if not much depth. A typical Sheena adventure (equally typical of all Fiction House productions) is reproduced here from *Jumbo Comics* No. 112 (June 1948).

Much in the same vein was the Fox Publications line, which critics like Don Thompson have accused of going too far in their enthusiasm for exaggerated female anatomy. Certainly Fox's girls were rendered with loving care, but they still never appeared in anything less than a two-piece bathing suit. In light of the current fashion in various media for total exposure of the human body, it seems reasonably clear that comic books dealt with the presentation of glamour as distinguished from raw sex. Fox's biggest character was Blue Beetle, featured in his own magazine from winter 1939. *Phantom Lady*, moving from the pages of Quality's *Police Comics*, began in August 1947. Other titles included *Dagar, Desert Hawk* and *Jo-Jo, Congo King*.

There were a number of western-flavored titles published during the early years of comic books. Most of these were relatively undistinguished, achieving their popularity by arranging to feature the names of prominent cowboy stars from the motion pictures. The most consistent producers of such material were Dell and Fawcett. Magazine Enterprises came up with the most colorful variation in Ghost Rider, a character who appeared in several titles besides his own, usually drawn by Dick Ayers. The hero's fearsome phosphorescent disguise and some weird plots made him a fascinating hybrid of the traditional cowboy and comic book modes.

Another character who deserves mention is the Black Cat, a heroine who bowed in the experimental *Pocket Comics* (August 1941) from Harvey Publications. She later moved into *Speed Comics*, and kicked off *Black Cat* comics in June 1946. The red-haired, motorcycle-riding judo expert was the after-hours role of Hollywood movie star Linda Turner.

She exhibited a certain playful quality which distinguished her from the more forbidding comic book heroines.

Costumed heroes and heroines in comic books existed in vast numbers; it would be virtually impossible to compile an exhaustive list of all of them, and only a few of the most interesting have been mentioned here, though hopefully enough to capture the flavor of the syndrome that defined the comic book and made it a permanent fixture on the American scene. If these characters dominated the medium, there were a few other variations besides the western. One was the kid gangs, sparked by Joe Simon and Jack Kirby's Boy Commandos, who bowed in *Detective Comics* No. 64, and got their own magazine in winter 1942. The same team produced a cowboy title, *Boys' Ranch*, for Harvey in 1950. The most successful kid gang was the Little Wise Guys, who gradually took over *Daredevil Comics* from the costumed hero who gave it its title. They were created by editor Charles Biro for Lev Gleason Publications.

Gleason and Biro also brought a new and very controversial slant to comic books with *Crime Does Not Pay*. Beginning in 1942, this comic book featured factual accounts of conflicts between criminals and the law. In a broad sense, this was the same theme the superheroes had explored. Conflict is, after all, the basis of plot, but *Crime Does Not Pay*, minus the fantasy element, really sharpened the impact. The tone was sternly, even dogmatically realistic, and grim details were never lacking. The story reprinted here, "Baby Face Nelson vs. The U. S. A." (No. 52, June 1947) represents this publication during its period of greatest popularity. The artwork is by George Tuska. It seems certain that the intention of this comic book was sincere; certainly its new approach was successful, as it gained huge circulation during the postwar years. Perhaps as a result of the mixed emotions it inspired, perhaps because comic books had been around long enough to gain general recognition, there were rumbling resentments against the industry as a whole. In 1950, the year following Harry Wildenberg's disparaging remarks, there was a congressional investigation of possible links between comic books and juvenile delinquency. The industry rallied to its own defense, and was given a clean bill of health. Opposition would rise again in a few years, with much more devastating effects.

Before discussing this second controversy, or the company whose insistence on freedom of expression brought it to a head, a look is in order at the gentler world of comics where dumb animals held the stage.

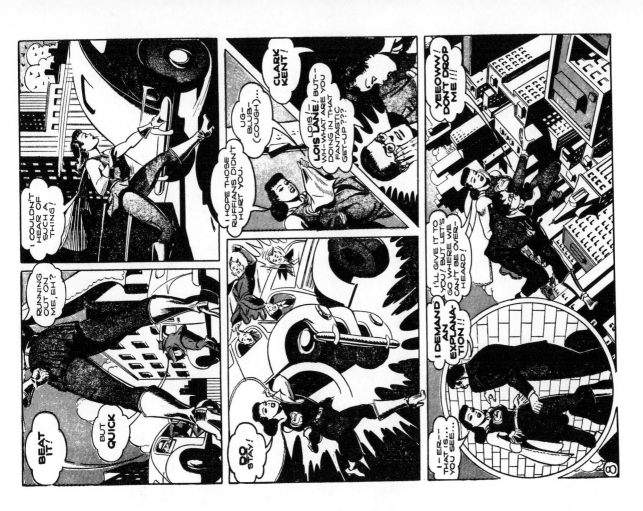

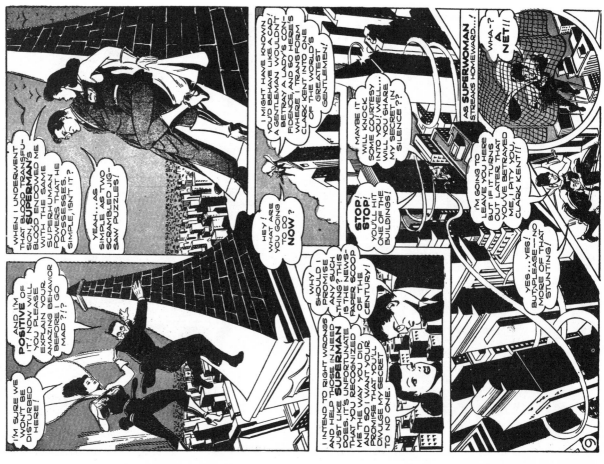

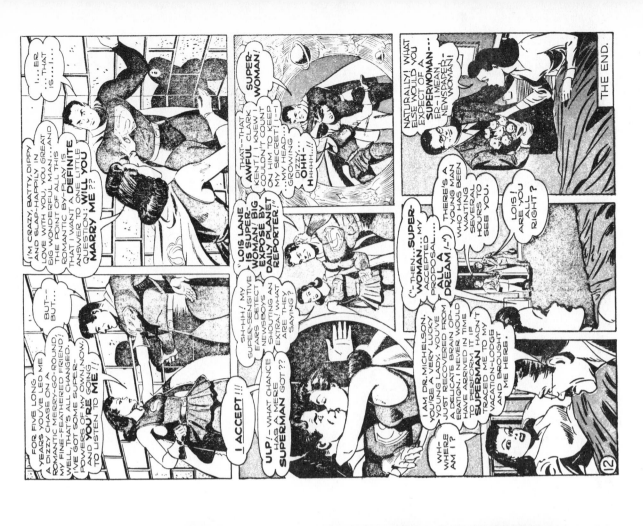

DEAD! THE THIRD KARLOVNAN OFFICIAL IN THREE DAYS -- ALL SUPPORTERS OF WORLD DEMOCRACY TREATIES!

WHAT? MISS BARLOVSKY, ACCEPT MY DEEPEST SYMPATHY! I AM SHOCKED AND GRIEVED TO HEAR IT!

OUT OF ZE WAY, BOTH OF YOU!

HERE IS ITS MATE, FOREIGNER -- DIE!

IT'S DREADFUL! COME WITH ME! I WILL INTRODUCE YOU TO RAMBIN, THE BANKER! HE IS ONE KARLOVNAN I TRUST!

HE IS, INDEED, A FIENDISH LOOKING LITTLE CREATURE! AND HE KILLED HIMSELF TO AVOID CAPTURE -- AND QUESTIONING! I WONDER --

The airport at KARLOVNA -- midnight -- and a flight of world-famous planes... those of the BLACKHAWKS -- drops down for a landing!

I AM VEREEN BARLOVSKY, BLACKHAWK! THANK YOU FOR COMING AT MY REQUEST!

I AM GLAD TO HELP THE DAUGHTER OF CHIEF BARLOVSKY... HIS POLICE WORK HAS AIDED ME OFTEN IN THE PAST! HOW IS YOUR FATHER?

THIS IS THE ONLY CLUE! IT WAS FOUND STUCK INTO HIS BACK!

SUCH A DAGGER I HAVE NEVER SEEN!

ANDRE SAFED DEM! QVICK, VE CAPTURE DIS UGLY BEAST!

YOU HAVE ME TRAPPED -- BUT YOU'LL NEVER TAKE ME ALIVE!

BLACKHAWK

KARLOVNA HAD A TRUE UNDERWORLD!

In the ancient sewers, beneath the stones of the streets, moved the weird dragon people who slew at night and defied even The BLACKHAWKS... the flying, fighting crew who encircle the globe in the cause of justice and freedom!

8

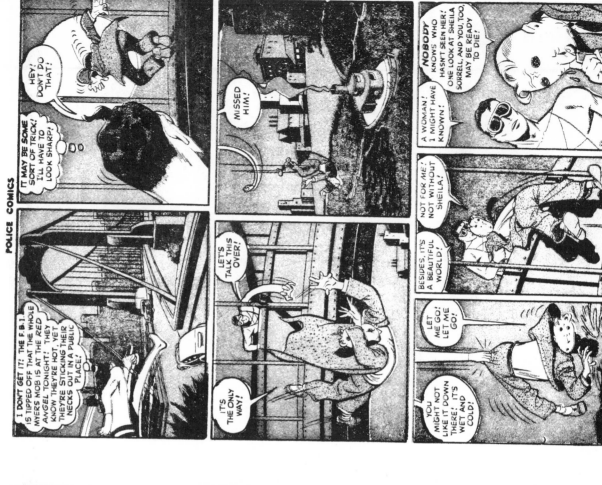

EVERYONE SUCCUMBED TO THE STRANGE, COLD BEAUTY OF *THE GRANITE LADY!* BUT IT TOOK *PLASTIC MAN* TO MELT HER HEART OF STONE!

THE GRANITE LADY

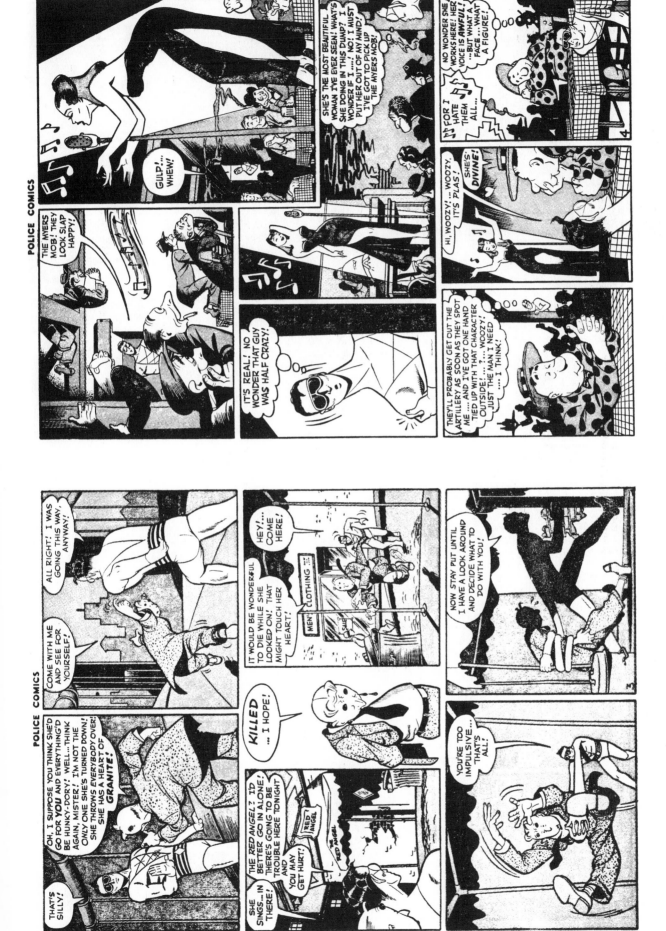

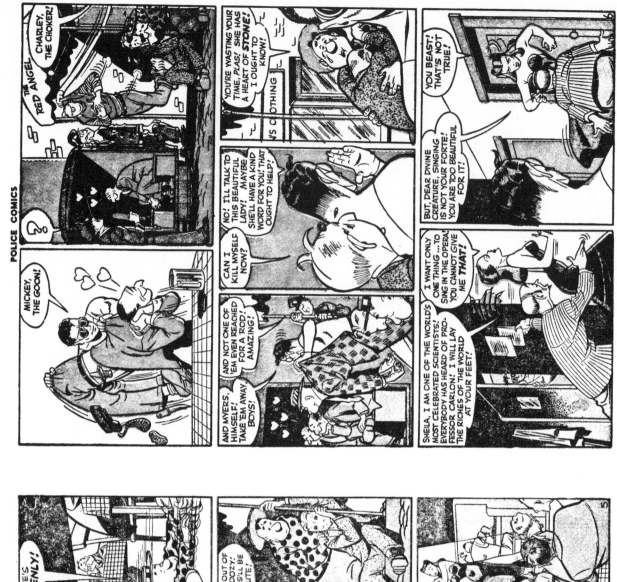

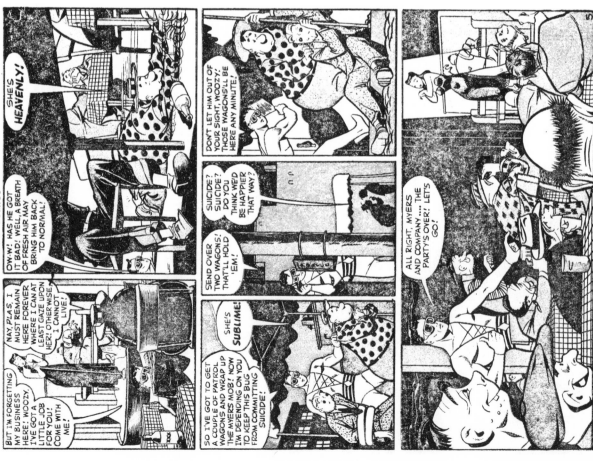

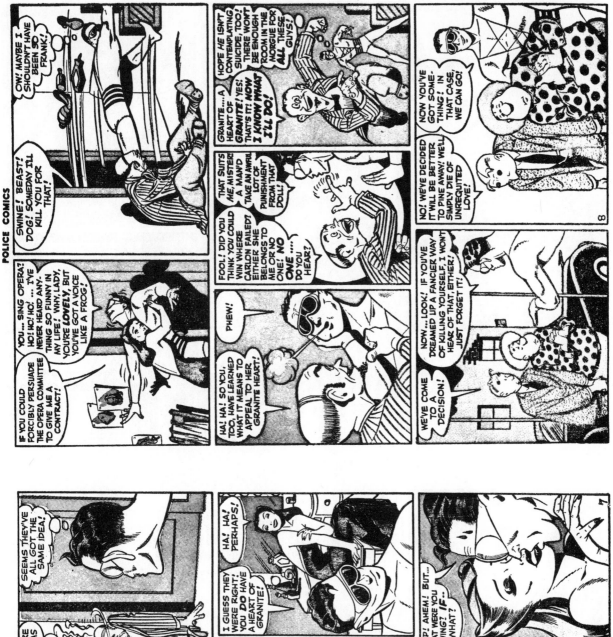

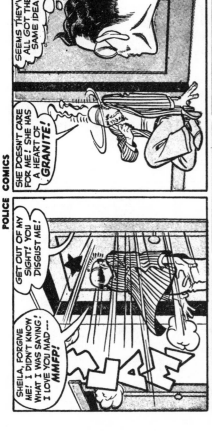

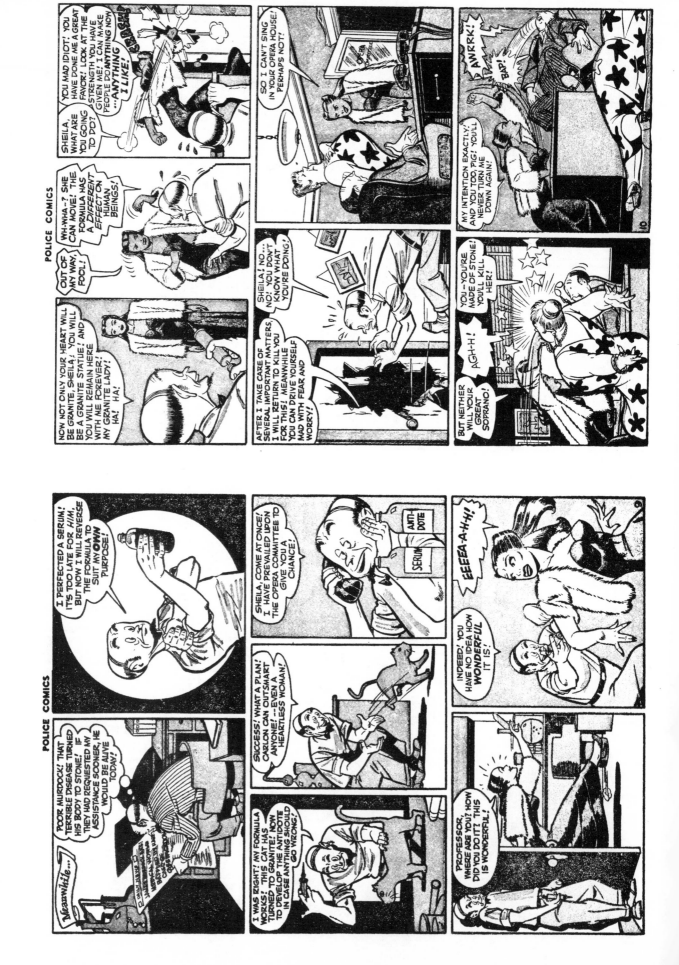

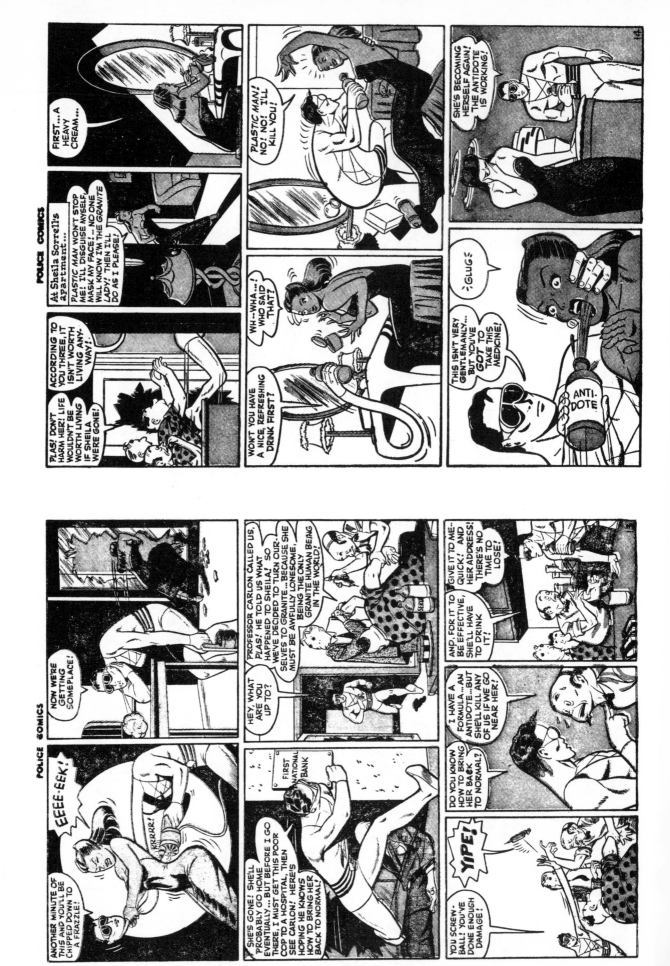

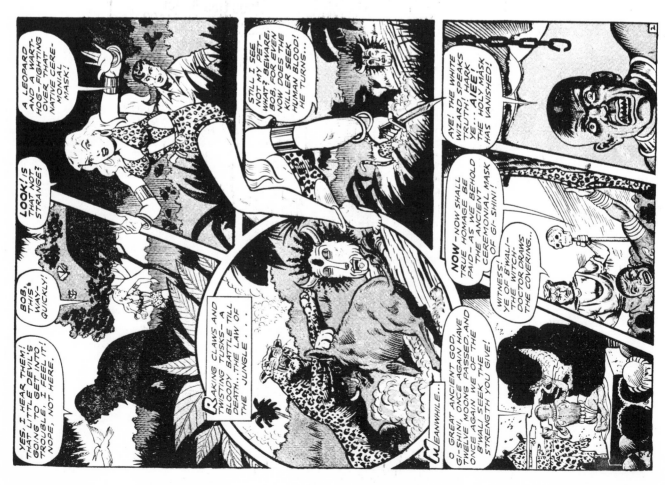

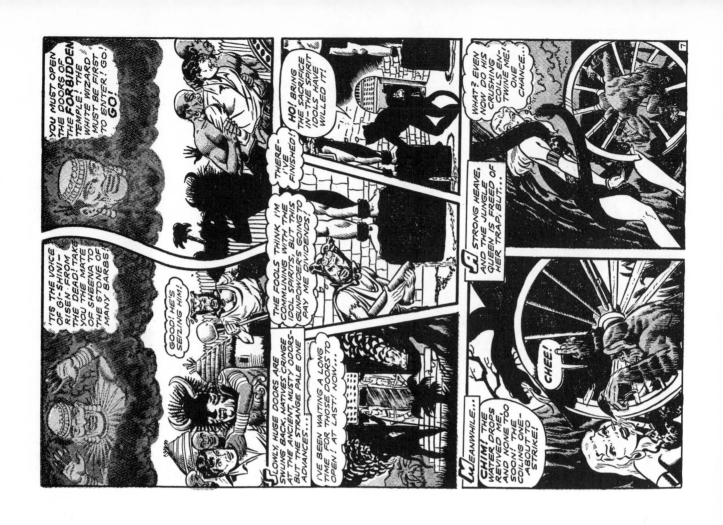

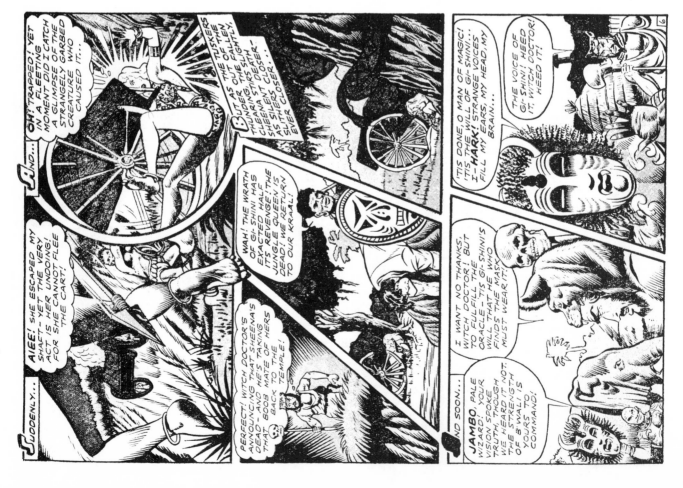

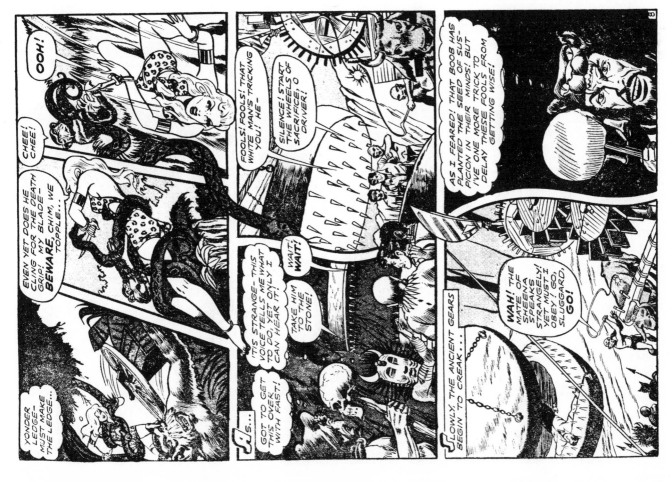

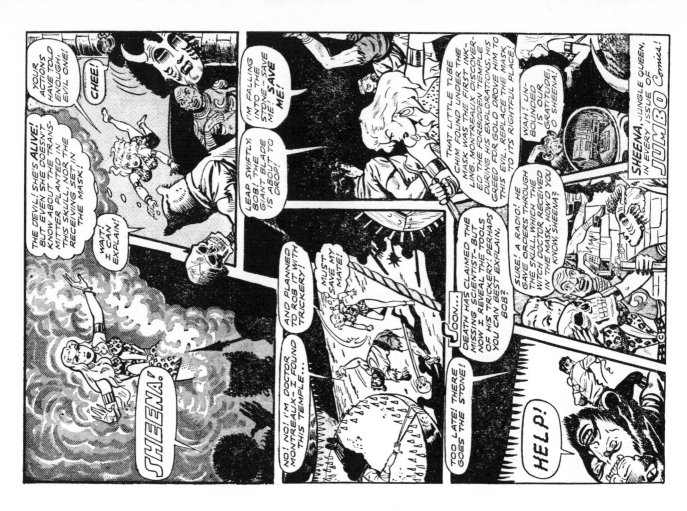

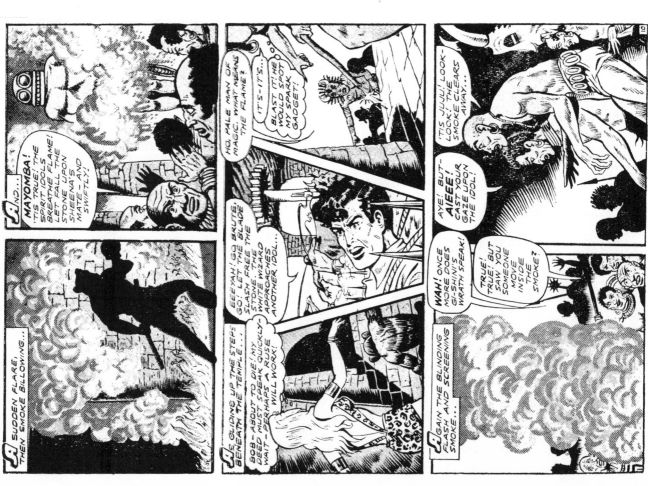

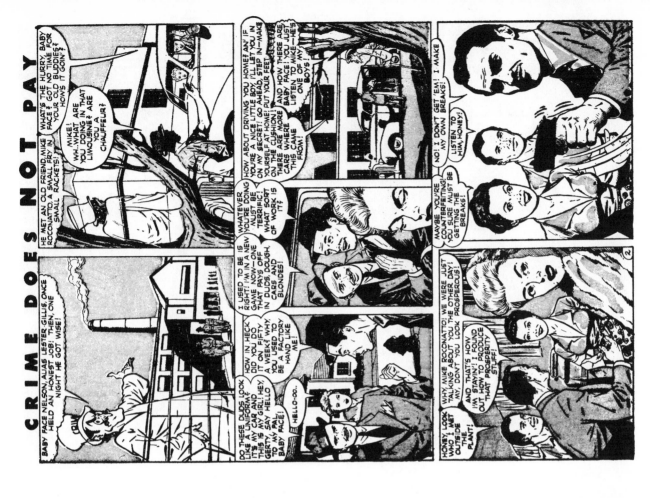

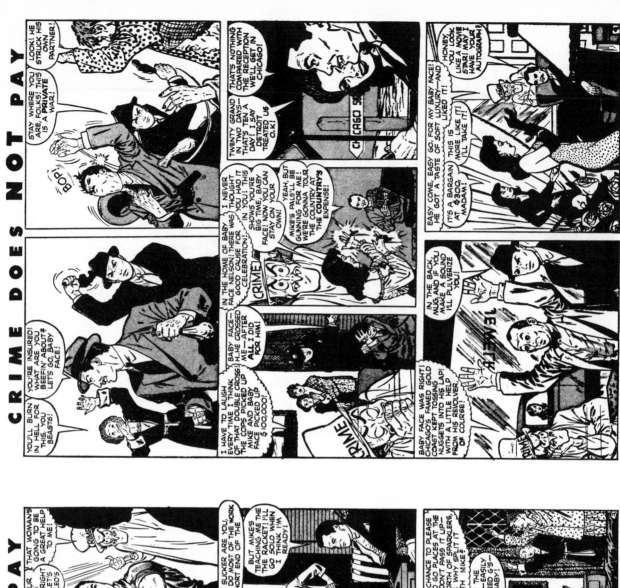

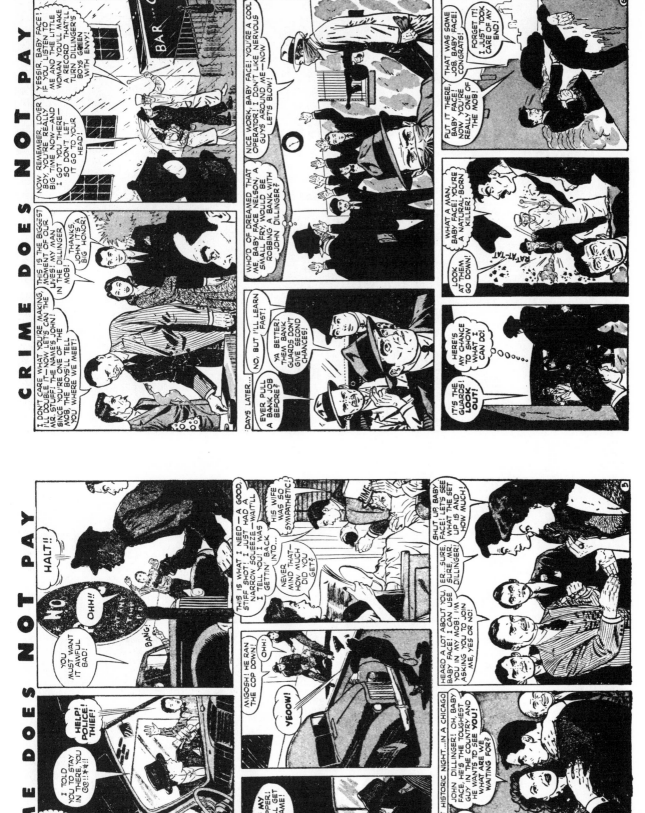

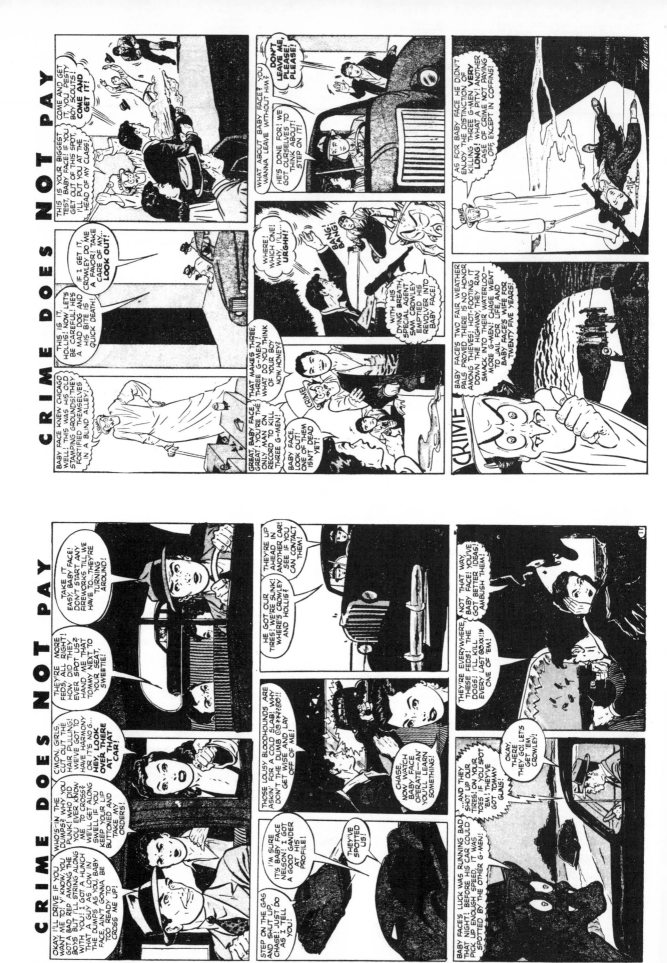

Chapter Three: Dumb Animals

Comedy involving human beings in domestic situations found scant representation in comic books, where the dominant element is generally some form of adventure-oriented fantasy. The humorous features which did succeed in capturing a large share of the growing comic book market nearly always concerned themselves with the anthropomorphic antics of animals. The adventures of such characters were obviously aimed at the youngest of comic book readers, but from time to time the animal creations achieved levels of imagination and insight which made them genuinely worthy of respect. The mere fact that beasts were performing in a human manner suggested by the obvious contrast that a level of satirical comment might be present; whether or not the potential would be realized depended on the tendencies and the talents of individual artists and writers.

The two humorous features to gain large followings without the presence of animal characters were variations on the kid gang theme. One was *Little Lulu*, a character created by Marge Henderson for the *Saturday Evening Post*, and translated into comic book form by John Stanley. The kids here were human, but the graphic style was representative of the effective simplicity of the animal comics. Dell Publishing's first *Little Lulu* comic book appeared in 1945, two years after the debut of John Goldwater's *Archie*, which attracted a large following by consolidating the market for a comic book with a teenage theme.

The range of animal comics extended from the sublime to the ridiculous, and both qualities had the potential for evoking laughter. The sources would include newspaper strips, especially one which has been offered the highest of accolades, George Herriman's *Krazy Kat*. However the most direct influence came from the movies where, with the development of the animated cartoon, most of the major animal characters would spring to life to inaugurate careers from which the later comic books came almost as a matter of course.

The man who got the whole show started was Winsor McCay. His newspaper strip, *Little Nemo in Slumberland*, began its short career in 1905. The incidents springing from the dreams of a small boy brought new vistas of imagination to the funnies pages, with an emphasis on vast panoramas and strange perspectives marking a distinct departure from the narrow stages on which its contemporaries took their stand. McCay's most influential achievement was not the strip for which he is so fondly remembered, but the production of the first important animated animal cartoon, *Gertie the Dinosaur*, in 1909. By tediously drawing and photographing thousands of pictures, McCay came up with a short film which he introduced personally in public appearances, standing in front of the projected image to create the illusion that his heroine was eating out of his hand. Gertie's other principal trick was to consume and then regurgitate the contents of an entire lake. Her appearance created a sensation, and a new branch of the motion picture industry had come into being.

McCay was to make nine more animated films, including at least one with a serious theme (a propaganda piece for the First World War), but none would have the impact of his initial effort, which contained, in its treatment of a personable, ludicrous beast, the prime ingredients that would inspire the most important and successful subsequent efforts. Credit for consolidating the concepts into a consistently marketable commodity should probably go to Paul Terry, whose first cartoon film appeared in 1914. He introduced Farmer Al Falfa, a human character born to be overshadowed by the hordes of demonic, fast-moving animals who were the plague of his rural existence. They proved to be so effective that Terry's postwar product undercut the original hero, taking the title of *Aesop's Fables* for the adventures of rotund black cats and spotted pups and the skinny little mice with whom they did constant battle. Mayhem was the order of the day, and the films traditionally closed with a scene of hot pursuit toward a distant vanishing point, followed by an irrelevant moral. The world of the earliest animated cartoons, like that of the first newspaper strips, was a cheerful chaos.

In 1917, William Randolph Hearst made an attempt to expand his comic strip holdings, such as *Mutt and Jeff* and *Bringing Up Father*, through a new company, International Film Service, which was designed to adapt some of his syndicate's most popular series into films. The project was abandoned in 1921, suggesting once again that people were not the ideal subject for movie cartoons. The one Hearst adaptation that might have had some significance was a version of *Krazy Kat*, but it seems to be lost beyond recall.

Fortunately, this was not the fate of the strip itself, which has been reported as Hearst's personal favorite, and has won praise as well from sources as diverse as President Woodrow Wilson and poet E. E. Cummings, whose appreciative introduction to the Kat has appeared in two separate collections of Herriman's classic strip. The Kat also inspired Gilbert Seldes to write the first major consideration of the comics as a respectable medium in his book *The Seven Lively Arts* (1926). The object of all this enthusiasm, a supreme celebration of the power of nonsense, began officially in 1916, and died, with its irreplacable author-artist, in 1944. It had evolved slowly from the bottom panels of *The Family Upstairs*, a treatment of the domestic squabbles of the Dingbat family begun for Hearst in 1908. Here an urban cat and mouse team had quarrels which were the equivalent of those engaging the attention of their human counterparts. In the final form, they acquired more distinct personalities, in part through the inclusion of a third character whose presence completed a perfect triangle, a structure on whose unshaking foundation was built almost thirty years of whimsical humor. On either side of the passive, poetical Krazy Kat stood the dogmatic champion of order, Officer Pupp, and the petty revolutionary, Ignatz Mouse. Ignatz demonstrated daily his contempt for the Kat and his hatred of authority by throwing a brick at Krazy's head, or at least making a valiant attempt to do so. Pupp responded by preventing such crimes when he could, and jailing the mouse when he could not. Meanwhile, Krazy's strange logic interpreted the brick as a symbol of love, and she viewed the struggles of her attacker and her defender as a "little game." The comedy theme of misinterpretation between two male realists and one (probably) female surrealist spawned endless variations which were the source of the strip's appeal. The very opaqueness of the endless, senseless syndrome seemed to demand some sort of explanation or interpretation, yet none was ever entirely satisfactory, which was perhaps the final source of satisfaction. A personal vision with overtones of universal truth, *Krazy Kat* displayed its dramas before the shifting desert landscapes of Coconino County, where the spare, primitive settings served to suggest an elusive symbolic significance. The Kat's exquisitely garbled dialogue had much the same effect, hovering as it did between idiocy and inspiration. As a combination of subtlety and simplicity, *Krazy Kat* has never been surpassed, and it has influenced, directly or indirectly, almost every one of the cartoons and animal comics which followed in its wake.

While Herriman made comic strip history, a young man named Walt Disney began work in 1920 on animated movies which were to have far more obvious repercussions. *Krazy Kat* was always the darling of intellectuals rather than a great popular favorite, but Disney's skill lay in an increasingly evident ability to gain acceptance from the widest possible audience. Beginning in a Kansas City garage, he produced a series of *Laugh-O-Grams*, and combined cartoon characters with an actual little girl in his *Alice* series in 1923. His first major animal character, Oswald the Rabbit, hit the screen in 1927, but he was soon overshadowed by Disney's favorite character, Mickey Mouse, who narrowly missed being named Mortimer.

Mickey took the public by storm with his third cartoon featurette, *Steamboat Willie*, released in 1928. This is the accepted classic, rather than the 1928 *Plane Crazy* in which Mickey made his debut, because it was the first animated cartoon to feature a sound track. This intensified the illusion of actual events to the point where Mickey Mouse rapidly became the center of a personality cult, the first "star" in the movies who needed no salary. In 1930, Mickey became the hero of syndicated newspaper strips, which were almost immediately reprinted in large black and white books by David McKay, thus making Mickey a pioneer in the development of comic books. His own *Mickey Mouse Magazine* was published by Dell beginning in 1935, the predecessor of Dell's *Walt Disney's Comics and Stories* which first appeared in 1940.

Mickey, who originally was a rambunctious little rascal with red shorts and big yellow shoes, soon developed into a complacent bourgeois householder with pleated pants and a pet dog, Pluto. He gradually became less the star of cartoons than a figurehead for the burgeoning Disney enterprises, and almost from the beginning, original comic book stories have shown him as a sedate, serious-minded detective working closely with the local police. Moving in to fill in the gap left by the mouse's lamentable gain of legitimacy was a new character, Donald Duck, who had stolen the show from Mickey with his appearance in *The Orphan's Benefit*. A limitless capacity for fury and frustration soon set the duck apart from the mouse, and somehow put him on the road to even greater heights of popularity. It seemed that what the public wanted was not a moral exemplar, even a cute one, as much as they wanted a cruder character who would express some of their own baser impulses. But this development was to take another turn. As we shall see, a different, less disturbing Donald would be developed for the original comic book stories which began in 1942—some time after newspaper strip reprinting had already begun as a feature of *Walt Disney's Comics and Stories*. Donald had acquired his own strip in 1938.

As the Disney Studios moved into feature production with the full-length cartoon feature, *Snow White*, another outfit moved to the fore as the source of animated animal featurettes. This was Leon Schlesinger Productions, which had begun in 1930 as the producer of *Merry Melodies* and *Looney Tunes*, two titles which doubtless owed their origin to the award-winning Disney series, *Silly Symphonies*. The musical format implied by these designations soon

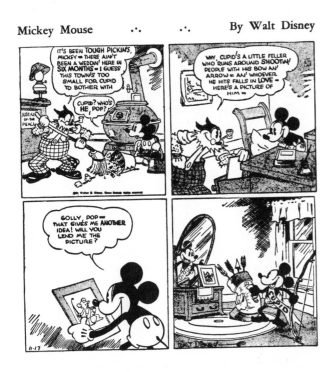

The mischievous Mickey Mouse of the thirties as he appeared in newspaper comic strips, which were reprinted as some of the earliest comic book collections.

gave way to a less tuneful series of animal heroes, who came into prominence once the original impact of the sound had worn off.

The first important character for the Schlesinger studio, which released its films through Warner Brothers, was Porky Pig, a stuttering, shaky, obese individual with an apparently rural background. Starting off as a bewildered juvenile, Porky lost weight as he gained confidence until he acquired a red sports jacket and a bow tie, indicating that he had arrived at a level of respectability similar to that already enjoyed by Mickey Mouse. The proof was provided by the film *Porky's Hare Hunt*, which confronted the pig with a nameless nemesis in the form of a renegade rabbit who ran him ragged and also got all the laughs. The rabbit, who was soon to be identified as Bugs Bunny, became the most popular animated animal of the forties. His spirited defenses of his home and his person, conducted with a wisecracking air of confidence, have been cited for making a contribution to boosting morale during the troubled days of the Second World War. Pale by contrast, Porky could not stand the competition, and a less sympathetic character, the self-centered Elmer Fudd, was introduced to battle the belligerent bunny, setting the pig free for further adventures of his own. Fudd was also to bear the brunt of the even wilder shenanigans of Daffy Duck, a lunatic rascal and enemy of civilization whose excesses surpassed those of the comparatively cool Bugs Bunny. To the neurotic Fudd, these two idols of millions were merely a "wascally wabbit" and a "dwatted duck."*

Like the Disney creations, all of the characters, and others from the same studio, were also presented in Dell comic books, but they made the transition less successfully than did Donald Duck, who had the good fortune to be blessed with an interpreter who had a real gift for plotting and character development. The *Looney Tunes* specialty was the perfect pacing and timing of slapstick effects which simply could not be transferred from one medium to another. Lost as well were the brilliant vocal characterizations of Mel Blanc. What was left for the comic books was fairly flat, and their durability is a tribute to their source. The *Looney Tunes* comic book got its start in 1941; *Bugs Bunny* had appeared at least on a one shot basis by 1939. The problem of determining exact dates for the birth of the various Dell animal comics is complicated by erratic numbering systems, and by early examples like *Four Color Comics*, which presented a different feature in each successive issue.

Dell drew on the animal creations of yet another studio for more of its comics. It inaugurated *New Funnies* in August 1942. Originally a mixed bag which included Pat Sullivan's Felix the Cat, who had begun in silent films, and Raggedy Ann, a children's storybook character, it soon devoted itself exclusively to the antics of characters originally produced for Universal Pictures by the Walter Lantz studio. Lantz had acquired the old Disney hero, Oswald the Rabbit, but gained wider recognition through two new creatures, Andy Panda and Woody Woodpecker. Their careers followed the traditional pattern: the lovable Andy was the star at first, but he was to be overshadowed by the manic Woody, whose raucous cry sprang from the mouths of countless child imitators, but could never be put in a comic book. Instead, the troublemaking bird was tranquilized and slipped into the suburbs, where his feuds with a doglike neighbor, Tackhammer, gave way to more responsible behavior when Woody was supplied with a niece and nephew named Knothead and Splinter. These two were a typical comic book addition—Porky Pig got one nephew (Cicero) and Mickey Mouse got two (Morty and Ferdie). But only in the Donald Duck stories of Carl Barks were the relationships between kids and adults to be treated with sympathy and imagination.

Dell made its other indisputably valuable contribution to the comics medium when it acquired the services of Walt Kelly. Beginning as an animator for the Disney studios, Kelly soon transferred his attention to comic books. His work is evident in renderings of Donald Duck for some of the early *Walt Disney's Comics and Stories*, but he did this rarely. He did have a long run drawing movie kids for *Our Gang*, and began to evolve his brilliant Pogo feature from an early series entitled *Bumbazine and Albert the Alligator*, set in Georgia's Okefenokee Swamp. Bumbazine, a human child who lived and communicated with the animals, was gradually upstaged by the beasts, especially after Pogo Possum was introduced as a minor character in 1943. Populated only with animals, the series became *Albert and Pogo*, and was the lead feature in Dell's *Animal Comics*. *Pogo Possum* began as a comic book in 1949, the same year that he became the hero of a nationally syndicated newspaper strip. He had previously appeared in the pages of the New York *Star*, a daily with a lifespan of less than a year. This is one of the infrequent cases of comic books supplying newspapers, and by all odds the most important, considering Kelly's distinguished career.

After early sequences featuring fairly typical animal antics laced with outrageous southern dialect, the strip evolved into a gently satiric mood, with the isolated swamp serving as a microcosm of modern American society. An array of fully realized individuals came into being: the solid, sensible possum, the bombastic alligator, the poetically inspired halfwit turtle Churchy La Femme, self-styled expert Howland Owl, the sentimental hound Beauregard Bugleboy, and Porkypine, the cynical softy. Pogo is the one stable factor in a group bent on reduplicating the insanities of the world at large, which reach the backwaters in strangely adulterated forms. Most of this is good-natured enthusiasm, but sometimes a darker note is struck. Kelly has moved with powerful effect into specific political caricature, supplanting his ordinary swamp villains like the roughneck Wiley Catt and the hypocritical Deacon Mushrat with creatures who have recognizable faces from the real world. The first of these was Simple J. Malarkey, a version of Senator Joseph McCarthy who showed up in 1953 and caused several newspapers to drop the strip. The courage displayed by Kelly in taking on a powerful opponent at the height of his influence made this sequence a high point in the history of comics. Later targets have included Nikita Khruschev and Fidel Castro, acceptable here but not abroad, and, most recently, Vice-President Spiro Agnew. Kelly's enthusiasm for ideas, his solid drawing and some delightful whimsy have made his strip one of the finest. And rather than turning his back on the strip's comic book origins, he has used them to good advantage by producing regular collections of the strips in book form.

Dell captured the lion's share of the animated animal market, but it was not alone. Another important publisher was the St. John Publishing Company, which handled the group of features which the Paul Terry studio had produced since the advent of sound films. These included the Terry Bears, Dinky Duck, and Gandy Goose, and the uninhibited Heckle and Jeckle, a pair of fast-talking magpies who were not above challenging the law and who occasionally ended up behind bars in their comic book adventures. At the opposite end of the scale was Mighty Mouse, champion of justice. Mighty Mouse was a takeoff on the superhero syndrome and had some genuinely amazing moments in the movies and the comics when performing in burlesques of old-time melodramas, opposing the villainous cat, Oil Can Harry. The principal titles for these characters were *Terry-Toons* and *Paul Terry's Comics*. Mighty Mouse had his strangest moment when he was chosen to star in the first three-dimensional comic book in October 1954. The process, called "3-D Illustereo," employed double printed drawings in orange and blue-green ink. When cardboard glasses with a red and a green lens were worn, the distance between the two colors produced an illusion of depth. The lenses served to cancel out one color and produce a separate image for each eye. The effect was fascinating, and widely imitated, but it proved too troublesome to last long.

The D. C. line also carried a few animal comic books in addition to its impressive stable of costumed heroes. The best of its animals was the *Fox and Crow* series, adapted from a relatively unknown group of Columbia Pictures featurettes. Their appearances in *Real Screen Comics*, which began in 1944, were impressive for the variations employed in treatments of

what was essentially a study of economic manipulation. As such, they provide an interesting counterpoint to the more widely known money myths promulgated in the Disney duck stories by Carl Barks.

To talk of the content of the "dumb animal" stories in this way may seem at first an overstatement, but there is a strong and persistent moral impulse behind all of the animal comics. While the lessons to be learned are never so obvious as they are in, say, the Greek fables, there is absolutely no doubt that at least part of the intent and effect is educational. That this intent was frequently confused or unconscious in no way makes it less genuine. Children learned about capitalism from Scrooge McDuck and about the degrading, amoral effect of too-easy money from Gladstone Gander (Gladstone's defining characteristic, of course, is his appalling good luck, but in the Disney comics this luck is almost invariably exercised in the acquisition of money. He becomes, in fact, an exemplar of the debilitating effect of inherited wealth: a wavy-haired, smug, dandified Gatsby). Similarly, the *Fox and Crow* series works an endless variation on the themes of victimization, gullibility, disguise and violence. Any child who ran a lemonade stand or tried to con his best friend out of a collection of baseball cards knew, without being told, what those stories were talking about. That the crow triumphs financially or intellectually in each story at the expense of terrible, bone-shattering beatings from the fox mitigates neither his enjoyment of the victory, nor the child's vision of guile proving itself superior to dumb force. At an age when children had little on their side except the ability to dissemble and a repertoire of alternate fantasy identities, and were surrounded by dumb adults or neighborhood bullies, these images released, quite simply, the power to do infinite things with minimal resources.

There was an important reason why these comics appeared in the forties and fifties—comics, that is, featuring not only animals, but animals like the Fox and the Crow, Uncle Scrooge and Gladstone Gander, who are preoccupied with money. The power and beauty of these images came less from their appeal to their preadolescent audience than from the fascination they held for their creators. The animals first of all provided a link with a vision of America that was rapidly disappearing: a world of small towns and barnyards that most of these men had known. Donald makes it clear in several stories that he "lives" fictionally in Burbank, but he is obviously from much further East. Ducks live in Missouri and Kansas, not in southern California. The comics business was precarious—fantasy-ridden and fantasy-mongering—and for the men who created these strips (as so obviously for the great Disney himself), the animal images were echoes of the collective past they had left behind. At the same time, it is not surprising that men who were pressed for deadlines, who lived by their wits, who were misfits in other occupations, who had lived through the Depression, should embody their preoccupations with money and how to get it in the figures of irascible ducks and shifty crows.

Walt Disney himself is the best example of the dual impulse behind these comics: rural nostalgia and economic necessity. He made himself rich and famous by exploiting and channeling his childhood frustrations and bourgeois fantasies. That he could call on similar backgrounds, aspirations and experiences from the men who worked for him is the point here. It is only temporarily amazing that out of such mixed motives emerged such enduring art, for the creators of these stories, apart from using figures that have sources in great antiquity (Aesop's fables, for one) were appealing to basic human emotions of insecurity and inequality.

The man who created the best stories for Disney, the long unsung figure who invented Donald's complex comics character, Uncle Scrooge, Gladstone Gander and that earthly system whereby skill and honesty *were* rewarded, the Junior Woodchucks, had a background similar in many respects to Disney's. Carl Barks, like Disney, came from a relatively poor rural background, this time in southern Oregon. Like Disney, he tried other trades and failed, finally deciding to become a cartoonist because he was working on a railroad riveting gang during the Depression and wanted an "easier" way to make a living. Again like Disney, he was primarily a very unself-conscious man, thinking of himself as a hack artist, unwilling or unable to interpret the figures once they left his drawing board. Disney was notoriously impatient with any attempt to read something into his stories; he disdained intellectuals and seems to have been nervous about examining the basis of his creations. A similar tone of self-deprecation and practicality characterizes some statements of Barks', who until a short time ago, when he was "rediscovered," labored entirely in obscurity, the Disney studio evidently unwilling to give out the name of any individual responsible for the comics—except, of course, Disney's.

But the recent attention paid to Barks' style and inventions appears to have made him reconsider, in a bemused way, the value of his own output. He was finally unlike the man whose name appeared at the top of comics he had created (it was meant to be Disney's signature, but he never signed his name like that), in that Barks *continued* to create. While Disney soon exercised only editorial control over the studio's output, Barks worked away in San Jacinto through the forties, fifties and into the sixties, making *Walt Disney's Comics* famous for the consistency of its style and the amazing verbal and visual detail of its stories. He was recognizable to the people who read

his stories by his craftmanship and by the sense of depth in his panels, and became known only as "the good artist," to distinguish him from the others, less involved, who would sometimes appear in the Disney comics and who later took them over when Barks retired. That phrase, "the good artist," originally intended to convey an artistic discrimination, has been repeated so frequently among his admirers since his emergence from obscurity that it has taken on moral overtones as well.

Donald Duck's character as it appeared in the early film cartoons was not entirely suitable for a role that would support a story dependent on something other than sight gags, so Barks progressively modified his comics character in the early forties. From the stage personality who exploded into sputtering rage at every irritation, and whose main expression was a wary truculence, Donald became under Barks a complex figure: still stubborn enough to try to oppose his whims to the more common-sense wisdom of his nephews, but now more given to fuming than ranting. His courage became more obvious and his curiosity or boredom was the spur that got many of the stories moving. Indicative of Donald's change of life was the fact that the stories during the late forties didn't depend, as did the ones at the beginning of the decade, on sight gags and pratfalls. Nor did they always revolve around the domestic conflicts between Donald and the kids (although Barks gives the game away in one story when Donald refers to himself as a "parent," the fiction of Huey, Dewey and Louie as nephews was maintained to avoid the embarrassment, obviously, of having to deal with a deceased or divorced Mrs. Donald). Instead, the metaphors of escape and rescue become predominant.

Sometimes it is Donald's fortuitous occupation as janitor or museum guard that initiates stories of travel and adventure that take him to the North Pole, Tibet, the Andes, Persia, Saudi Arabia; more frequently it is the pluck and obstinancy of a character who was introduced in 1947, Donald's sickeningly rich Uncle Scrooge. Scrooge is the most complex and contradictory figure Barks ever created; his character changed too during the forties. Originally he was rich, but not yet the richest duck in the world. He was scraggly and somewhat pitiful in the early stories, but as Barks saw another way to take some of the weight off Donald as a main character, Scrooge took on the **personality he kept for nearly twenty years; an em**bodiment, on the one hand, of the virtues of capitalism and Calvinism, willing to deny himself simple luxuries to avoid depleting his fortune, an exponent of hard work, yet a miser who, on the other hand, seems curiously addicted, not to the power of his sextaquillions, but to the sensual enjoyment he gets by burrowing in the stuff, throwing it into the air and letting it hit him on the head. Scrooge's description of his favorite activity occurs so frequently that it has the effect finally of both a religious litany and a child's song, and that paradox is a clue to his character.

He is seemingly senile, and yet of all the ducks the one most willing to face an enemy, the most childlike in his approach to danger and misfortune. He is miserly and greedy and must be tricked out of his money, even for good causes, but he explains that he loves the stuff because he acquired it in the mines, logging camps and deserts of his youth, and that he loves the *feel* of the coins and the rustle of greenbacks. His thrift and steadiness serve as foils to Donald's irresponsibility and to middle class life and as a grotesque reflection of Gladstone's luck—money flows to Gladstone out of sheer luck alone—and yet inasmuch as he seems lonely and unhappy, he is an example of the dehumanizing power of wealth.

It is the freedom Scrooge's money gives him that allows him to drag Donald and the boys on the most memorable of their adventures to foreign countries. Ironically Barks himself never traveled, and while we may see these Duck adventures as wish-fulfillment, it is even more surprising that they were stunning because of the quality of the details. Barks managed somehow to give a physical sense of each place: the chasms of the Andes, the sweep and solitude of the desert, the terror of the southern Atlantic in a boat. This quality of atmosphere, of physical depth to the drawings, was perhaps Barks' greatest figurative achievement in these comics, and it was a vision unavailable in any other comic series. Not only were details of dress, speech or architecture convincing, but there was a chilling realization of great scale, of a vastness of landscape or design (Scrooge's money bin is a prosaic and persistent example of this). In "Christmas in Shacktown," for example, an otherwise sentimental treatment of the spirit of Christmas, Scrooge's money drops through the bottom of his bin and is resting on a thin crust of rock beneath which is a pit of bottomless quicksand. That image was as disquieting as the image in another story of great caverns beneath the earth inhabited by the Terries and Fermies, ball-shaped creatures who make earthquakes by rolling against the pillars that support the crust. In each case, the interior spaces are only small parts of the story, but in Barks' world those chasms, caves and tunnels were real and vivid, a reminder of fragile separations and dark holes that the adventure-dominated comic books were to exploit explicitly.

Barks' world is finally a masculine world, and that fact links his stories to one tradition of American literature, its notorious sexlessness. Daisy Duck, Donald's garden party girlfriend, is no more than an infrequent, annoying interruption, and we have already noted how the stories themselves move away from domesticity to more elemental contests between the ducks and assorted villains—ghosts, giant animals and the elements themselves. Barks recreated in comic form the myths of the hunting of the whale, the taming of the west and the conquest of pride, central concerns of more "serious" and more famous American artists.

The serious theme of economic interdependence is treated humorously in the two animals stories reproduced here. The first is part of *The Fox and the Crow* series by James F. Davis from *Real Screen Comics* (September 1951, No. 42).

This piece is interesting because it feeds upon itself; that is, like the Romantic poetry of the early nineteenth century, it takes as one of its subjects the creation of its story. The story begins predictably enough: the crow quickly invents a scheme for chiseling the gullible fox. In this episode he seems motivated not by any real financial pressure, but by the need to justify his day by somehow swindling the fox. Throughout the fox and crow comics, there is a noticeable nobility about the crow's profession: he is not usually worried about the amount he swindles, but rather whether or not at the end he has somehow come out on top mentally. At the middle of the story he may be thousands of dollars ahead and at the conclusion be left only with five or ten dollars, but if it's the five or ten dollars he needed originally, he's satisfied.

The swindle today threatens to be harder than usual, however, because the fox remembers that he has been tricked by the same ruse before. He remembers not by recalling his past life, but by consulting his collection of the comic books in which he and the crow appear. This is a very interesting gambit, destroying as it does the illusion that these animals, or any other fictional creations, have lives of their own outside the art that embodies them. For the fox, reality only exists if he can find it in the back issues he owns. When the crow shows up in a costume that the fox hasn't seen, either in his "life" or in his reflected life in the books, he is convinced that a giant is at his door. The next logical step in such a universe would be to have the fox consult the very issue that he and the crow are currently appearing in: art within art.

This riff is actually a very subtle justification of and plug for the medium itself, similar in spirit to Harvey Kurtzman's forthcoming plea in the first twenty-five cent *Mad* magazine, "Please buy this magazine." In *The Fox and the Crow*, however, this message from the editors is unlabeled. Another facet here is that the crow's need to invent a new disguise is an image of the difficulty of the cartoonist's need to continually invent changing variations on such a slim formula. Again like the Romantic poets, the artist cannot think of a new story and so he will make *that* the subject of the piece.

A celebration of industriousness rather than ingenuity is provided by the Barks story from *Walt Disney's Comics and Stories* for March 1951.

Scrooge has rarely been so confident about the loss of his money as he is in this tale. The story begins with a listing of the virtues of rural work, the nephews happily shearing sheep and collecting eggs—punctuated by Donald's grumbling about the drudgery of having to work. Uncle Scrooge, of course, reprimands him, and the kids too are more "mature" and satisfied about the cosmic necessity of working than is Donald. As they frequently do, the nephews seem older and more responsible than their uncle, even referring to him in panel three as "that boy."

What follows from this beginning is a fable about capitalism, explicitly a lesson for the children about the disaster of daydreaming or loafing. But more serious than the overt content are the implications about the impossibility of equal distribution of wealth and about Marx's contention that he who controls the means of production controls . . . fill in the blank.

The logic of it is brilliant. Donald, lured away from his unrewarding job by the attraction of Gladstone Gander's famous luck and hoping that some will rub off on him, goes fishing. A tornado, of course, sucks up all Scrooge's money and deposits two million of it in the hands of the wastrels by the riverbank. Now the lesson starts. The wastrels hope to go see the world, but with the tornado having been profuse in its generosity everyone has a million dollars and nobody is working. Predictably the money ends up back in Scrooge's bins, brought there by the starving, ill-clad populace who need the basic essentials only Scrooge's farm is still producing.

These are disturbing images, images that call to mind not only the hoarding that went on during the Depression and the War, but the more recently awarded legal right of a landowner to repulse from his bomb shelter any desperate neighbor. "Guard those eggs, Dewey," Scrooge says, and although we may be happy to see Scrooge get his honestly earned fortune back and to see Donald and Gladstone punished for presuming to upset the balance, what is disturbing is that the economic balance is here made to look like a natural balance. It is a system that justifies Donald and the kids working in the fields at such wages that Scrooge can feel magnanimous at considering a ten cent raise; it is a system that mocks the middle class dreams of instant wealth as surely as it subverts the notion of public responsiblity. The only redeeming quality here that relieves Uncle Scrooge's smugness at having money and knowing he will always have it, is the injection of his childlike fascination with the feel and smell of it. Although the final panels lighten the mood of the moral, they are somehow inconsistent with the rest of the piece. Donald in fact has the last word: "Disgusting."

FOX and CROW

BEFORE I T'INK UP SOME REAL NASTY, UNDERHANDED CHISELIN' TRICK, I BETTER MAKE SURE FOXIE'S HOME.' AH! DERE HE IS.'

C.CROW

I'M HERE TO COLLECT.'

TO COLLECT? TO COLLECT WHAT?

MONEY!!

IF DEY GAVE DA NOBEL PRIZE FOR BEIN' A GREAT CHISELER, I'D WIN EVERY YEAR! *DIS* TIME IT ONLY TOOK ME A ZILLIONTH OF A SECOND TA T'INK UP A REAL KEEN ONE.'

SWOOSH C.CROW ZOOM

2

THAT'S SILLY! *YOUR* AIR IS OVER BY YOUR TREE; MY AIR IS *RIGHT HERE.'* I'M BREATHING MY OWN AIR.'

FOXIE, I DETEST DESE NEIGHBORHOOD ARGUMENTS.' DEY UPSET ME.' I T'INK DIS CAN BE SETTLED BY YOUSE ANSWERIN' A QUESTION.

FROM *THAT* WAY.'

CORRECT! RIGHT FROM MY *TREE.'* DAT MEANS MY AIR IS BLOWIN' OVER HERE.'

SO HOW MUCH IS AIR TODAY?

YOUSE CATCH ON QUICK! WE'LL-L-L-L-

$5⁰⁰ A BREATH.'

I DON'T OWE YOU ANY MONEY.'

SO WHAT?

YOU'RE BREATHIN,' AREN'T CHA?

SO IT'S MY AIR.'

OKAY, WHAT'S THE QUESTION?

FROM WHICH WAY IS DA WIND BLOWIN'?

STOP BREATHING? BUT I CAN'T *DO* THAT.' I'D *DIE!*

SO PAY UP FAST OR STOP BREATHIN'.'

WHAT A REVOLTIN' DEVELOPMENT *DIS IS,* WHAT STARTED OUT TO BE A SIMPLE LITTLE CHISELIN' SORTIE HAS ENDED UP IN *CALAMITY.* ME VERY EXISTENCE AS A *CHISELER* IS TREATENED, DAT FOX HAS A *COMPLETE HISTORY* OF *EVERY* CHISELIN' METHOD I EVER INVENTED!

IF YOU'RE PLANNING TO GO HOME AND DON ONE OF YOUR MANY *DISGUISES,* YOU'LL BE WASTING YOUR TIME, BECAUSE I HAVE EVERY ISSUE OF "REAL SCREEN COMICS" AND I CAN CHECK ON *ANY* COSTUME YOU EVER OWNED OR USED ON ME, *HA!*

SO...

HEH! HEH! DIS I'VE *NEVER TRIED! STILTS,* NOW ON WIT' DA LONG COAT AN' I'M ALL SET!

I'LL NEVER GIVE UP! NEVER! HE CAN'T STOP ME! EVEN THOUGH HE HAS DA SACRED SECRETS OF ME TRADE, I'LL CREATE *NEW ONES!* AND I'LL DO IT *NOW* TOO!

YIII! A GIANT! A 15-FOOT GIANT!

RAP
RAP

$5.00 A BREATH! SAY-Y-Y! JUST A *MINUTE!* HMMM. ONE MOMENT! I'LL BE RIGHT BACK.

MAKE IT SNAPPY! YOUSE HAVE ALREADY BREATHED $50.00 WORT' A ME AIR!

I *THOUGHT* SO! HERE IT IS, THE *VERY* SAME THING!

LOOK AT *THIS,* CROW! WHAT *IS* IT?

AN ISSUE A DA COMIC YOUSE AN' ME ARE IN!

EXACTLY! AND IT SHOWS THAT YOU PULLED THIS AIR CHISELING STUNT ON ME BEFORE!

NOW *SCRAM,* YOU *FRAUD!* THE AIR BELONGS TO *EVERYONE!*

SPLASH

I TOUGHT DAT CHISELIN' IDEA CAME AWFUL EASY! I'LL GO BACK HOME AN' GET ONE A ME COSTUMES AN'—

HOLD IT, CROW! ONE MORE THING! IT'S A WORD OF WARNING, SO TO SPEAK!

ZOOM

REAL SCREEN COMICS

REAL SCREEN COMICS

Chapter Four: The E.C. Revolution

It must have been the dream of a million boys who were growing up with comic books that one day they could take a place in the industry that was fulfilling their fantasies. Sooner or later, some of them would make it, moving into staff slots as artists, writers, or editors, but there was probably an accompanying air of disillusionment in their eventual success, because they were moving into a business as well as a dream world. By 1950, comic books had been established for a decade; that they should have taken on overtones of the establishment was inevitable. Jules Feiffer's book, *The Great Comic Book Heroes*, gives a personal account of his experience with the growing calcification of a business that was becoming increasingly businesslike. Youthful enthusiasm gradually gave way to adult resignation, as comic book men realized that their job was not to develop newer and more gorgeous inventions for the four-color pages, so much as it was to breathe new life into time-honored formulas. In Feiffer's words, "the men

who had been in charge of our childhood fantasies had become archetypes of the grownups who made us need to have fantasies in the first place."

Of course, good and enthusiastic work continued to be done in various places, and each year new readers would rediscover the built-in appeal of characters like Superman and Batman. The work of Carl Barks was continuing brilliantly in the Disney books. But second-string artists were taking over many of the best titles, and some important losses had been sustained in the industry's post-war slump, most significantly among the heroes of the Timely group, which will be discussed in chapter seven. Lev Gleason's documentary crime comics, the last innovation in the field, had declined from their peak of popularity in 1947. The time was ripe for new concepts, and the market was ready for a new look. The question of who could provide this renovation was to be answered by one of these boys who grew up to work on comic books, one who was able to overcome the inertia of the industry because of a unique advantage: he didn't go to work for a publisher—he began at the top.

This man was William Gaines, son of M. C. Gaines who, as has already been noted, had had a varied, and somtimes innovative, career throughout the early days of comic books. One story states that he had created the very format of all these publications, and he has also received credit for getting the germinal *Superman* feature onto the newsstands. He undeniably headed the All-American comic book line, working in partnership with D. C. to produce some of the most famous superheroes of the forties. He sold out his interest to the parent company as the war was closing, getting a high price for his valuable paper contracts just before the Allied victory ended the shortage of newsprint. He then inaugurated a new company, E. C., or Educational Comics, and it was through this firm that his son and successor realized the most revolutionary group of comic books ever produced.

The early years at E. C. were not too promising. Most of the comic books were variations on the standard themes already available, and frequent title changes indicate that they were not enjoying wide circulation. There was one unusual development, a series that seems to have been the elder Gaines's pet project: *Picture Stories from the Bible, Picture Stories from American History, Picture Stories from World History*, and *Picture Stories from Science*. These efforts to inject culture into the world of comic books were printed and reprinted in single and annual forms under both the D. C. and the E. C. banners. They were sincere and reasonably successful, but a certain stiffness in the style made them less than attractive. Reverence has never been a major comic book commodity. In particular, the minimal artwork by Don Cameron eliminated most of the dramatic appeal of Bible stories to produce images relatively pedestrian, considering their supernatural potential. These comic books did have the distinction of receiving endorsements from a variety of religious leaders, including Dr. Norman Vincent Peale.

For the most part, though, the titles produced by E. C. in the late forties were mining the traditional vein. There were a number of juvenile-oriented animal types, including *Tiny Tot Comics, Land of the Lost, Animal Fables, Dandy Comics*, and *Animated Comics*, the latter of which featured "Bouncy Bunny in the Friendly Forest" and lasted only one issue. An equally short run was enjoyed by the adventures of *Blackstone*, the magician detective. Title changes indicated circulation problems as in the transformation of two humor titles to the western-flavored *Gunfighter* and *Saddle Justice*. The latter took six issues to turn into the odd combination of *Saddle Romances*, which was good for just three appearances.

The most important single character during this early period of groping was a super heroine, Moon Girl, drawn by Sheldon Moldoff, who had been the original delineator of Hawkman during the All-American period. Moon Girl lasted through eight issues under three titles, *Moon and the Prince, Moon Girl*, and *Moon Girl Fights Crime*, before her comic book dissolved into *A Moon, A Girl, Romance*. (The company also had another nonwestern love offering, *Modern Romances*.)

The comic most indicative of coming trends was *International Comics*, which became *International Crime Patrol*, and then just *Crime Patrol*. The stories of lawbreakers began to take on an increasingly grotesque cast, prefiguring what William Gaines would announce to the public and the industry as a "new trend" in comic books. The last two issues featured tales introduced by a character called the Crypt Keeper, who then took over the magazine in the spring of 1950, when the April issue became *Crypt of Terror* (later *Tales from the Crypt*). Launched simultaneously with *Crypt* was *The Vault of Horror* (formerly *War Against Crime*), and a month later *Gunfighter* became *The Haunt of Fear*, completing the trio of extraordinary horror comics which formed the backbone of E. C.'s new trend.

But there were other titles in the new trend. Launched in May 1950 were two science-fiction titles, *Weird Science* (picking up from *Saddle Romances*) and *Weird Fantasy*, whose numbering followed the order of the love comic that had once been *Moon Girl*. A war and action book, *Two-Fisted Tales*, exploded into the E. C. line in November 1950, to be joined by *Frontline Combat* in July 1951. Two suspense titles, *Crime Suspenstories* (October 1950) and *Shock Suspenstories* (February 1952) seemed, for a time, to round out the line, and insure the company's dominance in the field of hard-hitting, uninhibited entertainment. These titles alone, with their impeccable artwork, imaginative plotting, and literate scripts, would have been enough to assure E. C. a high place in any history of comics, but there was more to come. October 1952 saw the birth of *Mad*, the most extraordinary comic book ever to appear, and one unparalleled in its effect on the national consciousness. It was the first really original humor publication since the *New Yorker* had appeared in the twenties and soon spawned a sister publication, *Panic*, inaugurated in February 1954.

It may be said without qualification that the new trend at E. C. (defined on cover logos as "entertaining" comics) created reactions more intense than anything that comic books ever produced. They were loved by some, and hated by others, but they were not to be ignored. Comic books came of age in these pages, which were created not to pacify the mind of some theoretical child out there in newsstand land, but rather to give writers and artists a free hand in extending the limits of the medium in all directions. Never were so many comics read by adults, whether they sought entertainment or an opportunity for indignation. The atmosphere fostered by William Gaines and nurtured by his editors, Albert Feldstein and Harvey Kurtzman, was one in which imaginations were not only stimulated but jolted.

Their treatment of the horror comic was a case in point. Of course, frightening characters and situations had existed previously in the heroic type of comic book, especially perhaps in the Timely and Quality lines. The sources of certain heroes like Batman, the Spectre and the Spirit had macabre overtones, and the villains designed to curdle the blood of readers and protagonists alike are numberless. Yet there was always an element of reassurance in these tales, which would invariably end with the menace destroyed, and virtue triumphant. Moreover, the presence of a continuing hero absolutely demanded that the forces of evil would go down in defeat, since any other con-

clusion would have ended the series for good. Thus, suspense, one of the most important of plot considerations, was seriously dampened in order to maintain a commercially successful publication, and it took only a short time for fans to realize that the hero was too valuable to the publishers to ever really come to a bad end.

The effect of the E. C. line was to eliminate this restrictive format, and the decision to do so was a bold one, since it also meant eliminating the concept of a continually featured character, a factor presumed to guarantee a steady audience. Instead, stories of high quality would have to be presented in order to develop a market without the traditional come-on. It is a tribute to the men behind these comic books that they were able to pull it off.

As has been intimated, the three horror titles—*Tales from the Crypt*, *The Vault of Horror*, and *The Haunt of Fear*—were the most consistently popular of the E. C. line. They owed their success, perhaps, to the theories and practice of Edgar Allan Poe, who had

THE OLD WITCH

THE VAULT-KEEPER

THE CRYPT-KEEPER

©1952 by Fables Publishing Co., Inc.

NOW...IF YOU JOIN...YOU GET THE BULLETIN...FREE!

ER... YOUR NAME AND ADDRESS WAS LISTED IN *THE E.C. FAN-ADDICT CLUB BULLETIN*. YOU...YOU GOT *BACK ISSUES?!*

YES, FANS... *YOU, TOO*, CAN BE *LUCKY LIKE MELVIN, HERE!* *YOU, TOO*, CAN COMPLETE *YOUR COLLECTION OF E.C.'S! YOU, TOO*, CAN JOIN THE

E. C. FAN-ADDICT CLUB

AND RECEIVE YOUR *MEMBERSHIP KIT* (WHICH INCLUDES A FULL-COLOR 7½ x 10½ ILLUMINATED *CERTIFICATE*, A STURDY WALLET *IDENTIFICATION CARD*, A SNAZZY EMBROIDERED *SHOULDER PATCH*, AND A STUNNING ANTIQUE BRONZE-FINISH BAS-RELIEF *PIN*)... PLUS A *FREE* SUBSCRIPTION TO THE *E. C. FAN-ADDICT CLUB BULLETIN!*

©1954 by Educational Comics, Inc.

Before and after: the faces of E. C.'s horror hosts, as originally created by editor Feldstein (left) and later elaborated by artists Ingels, Craig, and Davis (right). Between them, an ad for the first fan club centered around a company rather than a character.

THE OLD WITCH

THE VAULT-KEEPER

THE CRYPT-KEEPER

©1953 by Fables Publishing Co., Inc.

called for short stories planned to achieve a single effect and ceasing when the effect had been achieved. The result was a series of downbeat or offbeat endings which stopped the story dead at the moment of greatest impact, providing simultaneously a definite chill and the satisfaction of seeing an unpleasant character get a suitable comeuppance. There was also a healthy dose of black comedy, as the tone of the narrative suggested a certain glee in the development of events too outrageous in their morbidity to be taken altogether seriously. This was reinforced by the fact that the plots were constructed so that the source of horror was also the source of justice. Corpses not content to rest on their lilies had a strong motivation for walking around, sparked as they were by the same spirit which fired Elizabethan revenge tragedies. Thus readers were lured into identification with what they also feared, leading to a unique kind of catharsis.

Serving as a master of ceremonies on each trip into weird worlds was one of a trio of ghoulish characters, each associated with one of the three magazines. Originally delineated by writer and editor Al Feldstein, the Crypt Keeper, the Vault Keeper and the Old Witch (hostess of *Haunt of Fear*) were to find permanent portrayers in the pens of Jack Davis, Johnny Craig and "Ghastly" Graham Ingles. These were the three artists who set the pace for the horror titles, although a number of others were featured, with Jack Kamen and George Evans the most regularly represented.

The ghost-hosts had a significant function in providing a sense of aesthetic distance between the shocks they presented and the readers to whom they presented them. Their jeering dialogue, replete with outrageous alliteration and even more outrageous puns, succeeded in making the most bloodcurdling situations somehow laughable. Their tone was reminiscent of the works of that master of sarcasm and satire, Ambrose Bierce, although their most immediate predecessors were the radio announcers who hosted shock shows like *Inner Sanctum* and *The Hermit's Cave*. All the scripts were actually written by Al Feldstein, after plot consultations with editor Gaines, but the device of the authorial persona was so successful that it was carried over into all phases of the publications, including the letters pages, in which correspondents would direct their comments directly to the ghouls, who would invariably answer in character, and were perfectly capable of making snide remarks about their "employers," the editors, who would respond in kind with parenthetical wisecracks. The schizophrenic nature of these exchanges helped to set the tone for the entire E. C. line, in which ordinary concepts of behavior and decorum were reversed with an unholy enthusiasm.

And yet, at the core of the stories was a dis-

cernible sense of morality. Uninhibited exhibitions of the ugly effects of a hunger for power were provided by Jack Davis and his Crypt Keeper. An incredibly fast worker who filled more pages at E. C. than did any other artist, Davis brought a gritty naturalistic quality and a gift for anatomical distortion to his labors in the crypt. His numerous stories concerning the grim details of capital punishment left no doubt about how unpleasant it could be. A unique group of tales drawn by Davis concerning blood sport used a simple reversal to make important points in arguments which we might consider from the standpoint of current concern with ecology. In one, "Gone Fishing" (*Vault of Horror* No. 22), the gory details of angling were exploited to full effect in a debate between a fisherman and his humanitarian companion. The story ended as the sportsman took a bite of a candy bar which proved to be a hooked piece of bait, attached to a line which dragged him to a watery doom. Another such story, "The Trophy" (*Crypt* No. 25), apparently an editor's favorite, was later redrawn by Davis for *Three-Dimensional Tales from the Crypt of Terror*, and anthologized in the sixties for one of two collections for Ballantine Books. The story concerned a hunter, with a fondness for mounting animal heads, who met his comeuppance when a maniac in a forest gave him the same sort of treatment. Quoth the madman, "I don't call it murder! I hunt for the pure sport of it! After all, they're only human beings!" In "This Little Piggy" (*Haunt* No. 14) a soldier in India with an irresistible fondness for roast boar ended up on a steaming plate with an apple in his mouth.

If the Davis specialty was the struggle for survival, Johnny Craig and his Vault Keeper featured strange versions of the battle of the sexes. Typical stories depicted domestic or romantic situations which degenerated into terror as one or the other of the purported lovers was revealed as a murderer or a monster, with the mate on the receiving end of the mayhem. This was an extreme but not altogether inappropriate counterbalance to the standard mass media presentation of love as a guarantee of a happy ending. Such stories took on overtones of satire when depicted in Craig's careful drawings. He had a knack for creating clean-cut, commercial characters who looked like they stepped out of a magazine advertisement, and the contrast between their appearance and their activities gave the Vault Keeper's offerings an added level of significance. Craig was never more effective than he was in "Till Death" (*Vault* No. 28), a little epic about a young plantation owner whose wife was revived as a zombie after succumbing to a tropical fever. She was unfortunately not immune to decay, and his life became the nightmare of one exposed to what must have been the ultimate in "body" odor. The Vault Keeper's puns involving the name of a well-publicized deodorant soap made it clear to initiates that there was more to the story than met the eye. Was the story in bad taste? Possibly, but an effective device for depicting a rotten marriage—and a strong commentary on the growing tendency among toiletry manufacturers to encourage fears of offending in order to boost their sales.

If Davis brought to his work the vigorous skill of an all-round illustrator, and Craig the particular irony of an artist with a commercial bent (he would later have his own advertising agency), the one who expressed the greatest ghoulishness of all was Graham Ingles. If ever a man was born to draw horror comics, it was the alterego of the Old Witch, who took particular delight in signing his eerie efforts with the pseudonym "Ghastly." A master of morbidity, a visual poet of the macabre, Ingels infused his visions with an unequalled intensity of feeling. The quality of his line seemed to evoke decay, not only in his monsters, but in his apparently normal characters, and even the backgrounds. When working in a grim tale with no obvious supernatural elements, Ingels still evoked a sense of the fragility of the mortal condition that hit home in spite of, if not because of, the fact that he was often assigned scripts in a somewhat sentimental strain. For instance, "Oh! Henry!" (*Vault* No. 37) concerned the conflict between an old-lady shoplifter and a hardened cop. He saw to it that the served her sentence despite her sob-story about a paralyzed husband, which the policeman later discovered to be true, after a visit to her home revealed a corpse in a wheelchair. This sort of material went a long way toward dispelling any notion of the value of maintaining a "tough guy" pose. The importance of the horror story, especially in the graphic comic book form, is that it makes the ugliness of certain activities quite apparent. Being repelled by a fiction is certainly preferable to learning a hard truth by experience.

The most astounding of the Ingels stories, and the one which the Old Witch gleefully noted as the greatest producer of a reader response, was "A Little Stranger," reproduced here from *Haunt of Fear* (No. 14, July 1952). This tale was indeed a little stranger than even the average Old Witch offering, and it popped up in the same issue in which she announced that the E. C. staff was hard at work on a new magazine, which turned out to be *Mad*. The atmosphere of outrageous humor which made Harvey Kurtzman's brainchild possible is quite apparent in this story, which replaces the E. C. standard of the hellish marriage with the sincere and affectionate relationship of two hellish characters, and shows that things worked out beautifully, despite the efforts of society to keep them apart with wooden stakes and silver bullets. The stock figures of the werewolf and the vampire had by this time been so thoroughly exploited in fiction, in films, and certainly in these

very comics, that they had become familiar friends to the readers. The real magic of Zorgo and Elicia is not in their traditional powers, but in their ability to transcend even the traditional means of their destruction, and to build something which, in the staggering denouement, proves to be the source of the very comic in which their history unfolds. Coming as it did in the middle of the magazine's run, and presented as it was with no advance warning, "A Little Stranger" must be the most bizarre origin story in the history of comic books.

While the horror titles took the public by storm, *Weird Science* and *Weird Fantasy* remained the poor relations. House ads in the other magazines consistently proclaimed "E. C. is proudest of its two science-fiction magazines," but circulation remained a problem. Eventually, in March 1954, the two titles were combined into one, *Weird Science-Fantasy*. Even this did not provide real relief, and the price of the magazine was raised to fifteen cents in order to meet costs. This was to become the standard price of comics in the sixties, but the 1954 newsdealers apparently would not stand for it, and *Weird Science-Fantasy* reverted to a dime. If the science-fiction continued to be published at a loss, it must have been because it was too good to die.

And so it was. There had been science-fiction comics before, notably *Planet Comics*, but nothing like these. They bypassed the whole feeble and standardized concept of "good guy" versus "bad guy" melodramatics which serious students of the genre dismissed as "space opera." Here instead were tales about unexplored possibilities and probabilities which were employed, not to provide a new setting for the same old fist fights, but rather to afford an opportunity for speculations about the human condition. This perspective was the same kind of sophistication that had elevated the prose in the field into something worthy of serious consideration, but it was rare indeed to find it in comic books. Perhaps this is why the audience was never too large, but it made up in enthusiasm what it lacked in size.

The editor and writer was again the indefatigable Al Feldstein. Principal artists included Wallace Wood, Joe Orlando, Jack Kamen, and Al Williamson. As in the horror comics, Feldstein began as an important artist, but soon forced himself out of the running to concentrate on the writing and editing. The only rest he got was the result of an arrangement with the distinguished fantasy writer Ray Bradbury, who had a number of his stories adapted to the comics format by Feldstein. These included some horror tales as well as science-fiction, but the latter were more impressive, based as they were on Bradbury's more mature work.

A typical example of the sophistication of plotting in the science-fiction comics was shown in the Wallace Wood story, "A Weighty Decision" (*Weird Science* No. 13). The cliche of a beautiful girl stowaway who appears on a rocket flight to provide romantic interest has been used so often that it generally passes without question. Here concern with scientific probability left the pilot's foolhardy fiancee in an awkward position, since her additional weight load jeopardized the safety of the voyage and, as the only useless passenger, she was tearfully ejected to avoid total disaster. Wood's artwork, as usual, was beyond reproach. As he came to the fore in E. C.'s science-fiction line, it became apparent than an extraordinary talent was at hand. His attention to detail, his skill in delineating the human form, and the imagination employed in depicting the unknown, placed him in the front rank of comic book illustrators. A number of fans and critics consider him the top man in the field.

Al Williamson, perhaps the most distinguished of Wood's cohorts, had a style reminiscent of Alex Raymond, the creator of *Flash Gordon*. The subtle texture of his artwork was based on his ability to suggest shapes without a constant reliance on hard outlines. The result was an extraordinary impression of depth which worked to good advantage in speculative stories of unexplored vistas of time and space. Joining the E. C. ranks in 1952, Williamson performed subtly and brilliantly in a variety of tales, with an adaptation of Bradbury's time travel piece, "A Sound of Thunder" (*Weird Science-Fantasy* No. 25) certainly one of the most outstanding.

It would be impossible to do more than suggest the incredible variety of stories that were imagined by Gaines and Feldstein for their science-fiction line. What distinguished these stories, as has already been pointed out with regard to E. C.'s horror line, was that each of the four pieces in each issue was a unique and self-contained effort. The general theme of the science-fiction pieces, if one might be extracted, was the fallibility of humanity and its capability for fouling things up which would be retained despite the most fantastic technical progress. "The Loathsome" (*Weird Science* No. 20), a tale of a mutated little girl, was one of many which explored the perils of atomic experiments. "The Inferiors" (*Weird Science-Fantasy* No. 28) told of a space mission discovering the remnants of a race which had destroyed itself to avoid an irreversible process of degeneration. The hideous result which justified the mass suicide would have been development into the "vile" creature, man. Other tales examined prejudice in interplanetary settings.

One issue, *Weird Science-Fantasy* (No. 26, December 1954), bypassed fiction to present a documentary of the unidentified flying object phenomenon. This special "flying saucer report" was subtitled "E. C. Challenges the U. S. Air Force." In view of the troubles which the firm was experiencing with various

authority figures and groups, this "challenge" was a bold maneuver, one which may have alienated many at a time when E. C. needed all the friends it could get. Yet questioning the veracity of government conclusions on some controversial saucer sightings was perfectly in keeping with the uninhibited and uncompromising quality which was E. C.'s stock trade.

The two short science-fiction pieces which appear here, "The Expert" and "The Ad," labeled "E. C. quickies," are from *Weird Fantasy* (No. 14, July 1952). They are not exactly typical of the product, but they do reflect the basic theme of human fallibility when confronted with unexpected discoveries. The zany comedy also anticipates the coming of *Mad*, which was to be the firm's most lasting contribution. Finally, they exemplify the unusually close relationship which existed between the staff and the readers of these comic books. While most other titles tried to give the impression that they created in some exquisite vacuum, E. C. delighted in giving its public a look behind the scenes at another constructed scene representing the reality of business. During the same period, "Kamen's Kalamity" (*Crypt* No. 31) showed Jack Kamen cracking under the strain of constant horror assignments, and was illustrated by Kamen himself. Later Jack Davis would portray Harvey Kurtzman as a homicidal undertaker (*Crypt* No. 39). The give-and-take of the letters column in all the magazines reflected the same spirit of self-satire.

"The Expert" and "The Ad" were drawn by Joe Orlando, a talented artist who was described in one column as part of the "Wood-Orlando school." His steady, solid work for numerous publications over the years has demonstrated a chameleon-like quality which enables him to absorb a format and rapidly become an important contributor. His subjects here are editors Bill (Gaines) and Al (Feldstein), familiar enough to readers to need no introduction as they tear their hair over production problems. The elements of parody in these pieces, together with the concept of an advertisement for a nonexistent product, are signposts to the future of E. C. and constitute the most accurate predictions to be offered in these forward-looking publications.

With the benefit of hindsight, it is easy to see all the trends at E. C. as the forerunners of the specific satire and parody which have made *Mad* such an outstanding achievement. What is remarkable is that Harvey Kurtzman, who conceived *Mad*, and has since gained a reputation as one of the most ingenious and imaginative humorists in the country, should have first come to public attention as the writer and editor of the grimly realistic E. C. war comics, *Two-Fisted Tales* and *Frontline Combat*. While the nasty events in Feldstein's fantasy titles were so extravagant that laughing them off often seemed an appropriate reaction, the early Kurtzman work stood out from the mass of comic books in its steadfast refusal to be taken lightly. The message was "war is hell," and the medium delivered it. There was a specific reaction here against the gung-ho presentation of mortal combat as something which the good team invariably won with no difficulty. Kurtzman has been quoted by critic John Benson: "I did then feel very strongly about not wanting to say anything glamorous about war, and the only stuff that had been done was glamorous war comics."

The range and depth of the material offered in the two war magazines was staggering. Dedicated research and dramatic presentation recreated the battles of history and headlines with high intensity. Probably Kurtzman summed it up best himself in his farewell message for the last issue of *Two-Fisted Tales*, which succumbed with issue No. 41, February 1955, to the pressure inspired by the new Comics Code (to be discussed in the next chapter): "We cannot help but look back with nostalgia upon our experiences in connection with *Two-Fisted Tales*; our sessions at the great New York Public Library (a treasure-house of rare old history books), where we relived the wars of the past. We have sprung the catapults with the Army of Caesar . . . weilded the glaive and the bill-hook at Agincourt . . . touched fuse to harquebus with Cortez . . . and primed and loaded the flint-lock with General George Washington at Pell's Point. We charged into the Valley of Death with the Light Brigade . . . we watched the Texicans massacred by the Mexicans at the Alamo . . . saw the first shot lobbed from a mortar into Fort Sumter . . . followed Teddy Roosevelt, his Rough Riders and his Gatling Guns up San Juan Hill and flew in Baron von Richtofen's blood-red Fokker over the valley of the Somme."

Chief artists on these war titles (besides Kurtzman himself) were Davis, Wood, and John Severin, whose sister Marie was an outstanding colorist for the entire E. C. line. Severin, working in a deceptively simple technique in which suggestion and solid layout took the place of the elaborate renderings which were the E. C. trademark, was in many ways the backbone of the war staff. Three successive issues of *Two-Fisted Tales* (37, 38 and 39) used his artwork exclusively. (Severin also worked in collaboration with Bill Elder, who inked Severin's pencilings on a number of stories before coming into his own as a master parodist of cartooning styles.)

Kurtzman was dead serious about his war pieces which, whether fact or fiction, were distinguished by scrupulous research. The readers came to expect such accuracy as a matter of course, and were quick to pick up on the slightest error, the spotting of which always received acknowledgment in the letters column. Kurtzman worked very closely with his artists, always laying out the panels himself to assure the correct composition and angle for the proper effect.

The amazingly cinematic technique in which successive panels show the same scene with slight but significant variations is particularly his own. This technique was also employed with size variations to reproduce the effect of a zoom lens.

Amidst an impressive array of action pieces (some of the stories in *Two-Fisted Tales* concerned themselves with aspects of adventure like exploration or pioneering), none had a greater impact than Kurtzman's "Big If," reproduced here from *Frontline Combat* (No. 5, May 1952). This is the same issue in which the editor responded to a letter criticizing the grim tone of the publication with the remark "There is a need for people to realize the utter horror and futility of war." This story has perhaps less of the colorful detail which distinguished Kurtzman's typical tale, and certainly does not hold the record for number of corpses in one of his stories, but is notable for the way its very starkness strips away the glamour of massive encounters in war to reveal the ironic senselessness behind them—the final price to be paid for war. Here the individual participating in battle is shown, in the plot and the graphics, to be alone and the victim of fate, though protected by an army. No dismembered corpse from E. C.'s *Haunt of Fear* was ever as terrifying as the implacable progress of "Big If." In creating the industry's finest war comics, Kurtzman also created the first antiwar comics, and so played an important part in educating a new generation about mankind's oldest curse.

It seems a far distance from this tragic tale to the freewheeling comedy of *Mad*, but the fact that Kurtzman edited such apparently dissimilar publications simultaneously is a clue to what they had in common: righteous indignation and contempt for hypocrisy. If the most obvious meaning of *Mad* was "crazy" (confused by the absurdities of modern existence), the connotation of anger was never entirely absent.

Mad was to achieve its greatest fame as a purveyor of parody and satire, but it took a few issues for the format to become established. The original concept, revealed on the editor's page of the first issue, was "A comic book! Not a serious comic book . . . but a COMIC comic book! Not a floppity rabbit, giggily girl, anarchist teenage type comic book . . . but a comic mag based on the short story type of wild adventure that you seem to like so well." In other words, the original *Mad* based its material on the style which had already been established by the rest of the E. C. line. Stories like "A Little Stranger," "The Expert" and "The Ad" indicate that there was not far to go. Just a slight weight would tip already loaded scales into the world of the "way out." Probably the most impressive piece in the first issue was "Blobs," drawn by Wood. This was a science-fiction takeoff which was only a little weirder than the *Weird* stories, and depicted a world of the future so technically advanced that human beings had become big-headed creatures with atrophied bodies who made their way through luxurious lives on powered pushcarts. A breakdown in the central power source at the end of the piece left them helplessly crippled and covered with spider webs. Humorous details in the drawing and script made for comic effect, and set the tone for the early issues, which existed in a strange limbo halfway between previous E. C. titles and the *Mad* that was to come.

Wallace Wood, Jack Davis and Bill Elder were to be the principal *Mad* artists, each doing one of the four stories per issue for the twenty-three that appeared in the color comic book format, but the first *Mad* parody was drawn by Severin, who delivered "Melvin" (*Mad*'s favorite "Christian" name) in the second issue. This was a version of the Tarzan saga which might technically qualify as a parody of the comic strip, although Tarzan had captured so many media that the object of the parody was not exactly clear. Gags about the difficulty of swinging from vines and the hero's tendency to deliver his famous cry as "Hoo Ha!" characterized this pioneering effort. The third *Mad* saw Elder at work on "Dragged Net" (he would draw a more accurate version of the popular television crime show for the eleventh issue) while Davis offered up "The Lone Stranger." Both stories were delineated in the artist's own style, and apparently based on radio broadcasts.

The first story to come across in the definitive *Mad* style was *Superduperman*, lovingly delineated by Wood for the fourth issue. Although it was Bill Elder who finally acquired the greatest reputation for his ability to render other comics in the pages of *Mad*, it was Wood who established the trend in an unbroken succession from issues four through eleven, following his first effort with "Black and Blue Hawks" (*Blackhawk*), "Teddy and the Pirates," "Smilin' Melvin" (Mosely's *Smilin' Jack*), "Bat Boy and Rubin," "Little Orphan Melvin," "G. I. Shmoe" (*G. I. Joe*), and "Flesh Garden" (*Flash Gordon*). Whereas Elder would succeed due to his uncanny ability to imitate the style of the artist he was mocking, Wood drew the characters in his own way, supplying enough of the original detail to make the source apparent. Which technique the reader found more effective was largely a matter of taste. Both were devastating. Wood did two more comic takeoffs, "Prince Violent" (*Mad* No. 13) and, for the twenty-third issue, "Gopo Gossum," a version of *Pogo* which rang down the curtain on the *Mad* comic book.

Starting with the tenth issue, Elder began his attack on comics with "Woman Wonder," a version of the super heroine which succeeded on the satirical level although it was closer to his own style than that of Harry Peter, the artist of the series. Elder came into his own with "Starchie" (*Mad* No. 12) which

gave the impression that it had actually been drawn in a moment of madness by an *Archie* staff artist. Following in quick succession were "Manduck the Magician" (Lee Falk's *Mandrake*), "Gasoline Valley," "Bringing Back Father," "Mickey Rodent," "The Katchandhammer Kids," and "Poopeye."

The fact that *Mad* was offering its own versions of other comics, both from newspaper strips and from comic books, was doubtless the key to its success. Although the parodies were outnumbered by other types, they set the tone for the entire publication. This was not the first time such a device—one comic presenting another—had been employed; the most obvious predecessor was Al Capp's character Fearless Fosdick. There had been similar efforts, albeit generally crude ones, in various college humor magazines (in fact *Mad* was to be described by one of its staff as a professional version of such magazines); also a whole school of narrowly defined parodies in the first "underground" comics—the pocket-sized, pornographic, eight-page comic books—depicted popular characters in a variety of sexual activities. Yet none of these efforts really account for the success of *Mad*, which was unprecedented in its flavor and tone.

Rather than just using the standard characters, the *Mad* technique exposed them. The characters became self-conscious commentators on their own formats, which they talked over with themselves, their peers, and the readers. They were aware of the fact that they existed in a narrow frame, and seemed to resent it. Thus "Mickey Rodent" could hatch a plot to regain the popularity he had lost to "Darnold Duck," and the "Gasoline Valley" folks watched their own aging process with fascination. "Superduperman" was aware of the Superman lawsuit against Captain Marvel, and had his adventure defeating "Captain Marbles," who had given up battling crime to become a mercenary. "Poopeye" fought versions of characters from other comics to establish himself as the most powerful of all, and the "Katchandhammer Kids" passed from their youthful pranks to become adult gangsters.

Other characters experienced role reversals which illuminated their standard bahavior. Thus the shady "Batboy" spent his story searching for an outlaw who was finally revealed to be himself ("For you see, Rubin, I am no furshluginner ordinary Batboy! I . . . am a vampire Batboy!"). The autocratic leader of the "Black and Blue Hawks" struggled ruthlessly to uncover a revolutionary plot which he found, too late, to be the work of his own disgruntled followers. "Woman Wonder" was finally undone by a villain who turned out to be her frustrated fiance, and she ended up thoroughly domesticated.

There were also versions of current movies, and literary material like "Shermlock Shomes" and "Alice in Wonderland." Famous poems like "The Raven" and "Casey at the Bat" were reproduced verbatim in narrative blocks, while the accompanying illustrations provided ludicrous counterpoint.

Jack Davis, whose technique was least altered by the mutation-manufacturing atmosphere of *Mad*, tore into the pervasive pattern which characterized the relation between two other arts in "Book! Movie!" (*Mad* No. 13), a study of the contrast between a sordid popular novel and its whitewashed movie version. Portions of the book treatment were obscured by a censorship stamp because, as Kurtzman's text explained, "if we duplicated a typical modern novel in this comic book, we'd be run out of town on a rail." The statement contained more truth than poetry, and the story was part of E. C.'s campaign to retain at least as much freedom for the comic book as their efforts had already earned. Davis continued to illustrate this argument in the sixteenth issue with "Newspapers," which demonstrated with only slight exaggeration how lurid the contents of an average tabloid could be. "Even as we speak, grown-ups of America battle tirelessly to destroy evil reading matter that is corrupting youth! However, behind their backs looms unchallenged evil reading matter that is corrupting grown-ups!" In such a manner was the war waged against the repressive forces who sought to control comic books. Unfortunately, *Mad* readers were not the people who needed convincing, and the censorship body, the Comics Code Authority, was formed in the same month (October 1954) that this story appeared.

The days of E. C.'s uninhibited new trend were numbered, but the kicks kept coming until the middle of 1955. Perhaps the highpoint of the *Mad* comic book was reached with the brilliant seventeenth issue. Here was "Bringing Back Father," a version of the McManus strip in which Elder's imitation alternated page by page with a version by B. Krigstein which showed the brutalized Jiggs reacting to his wife's slapstick with real resentment and real injuries. He finally hired a gang of thugs to re-establish himself as the head of the family. Jack Davis drew "What's My Shine," which courageously depicted the Army-McCarthy hearings as a television panel show. In taking on real and powerful politicians, *Mad* established another comic book landmark.

Precedent breaking political satire from the seventeenth *Mad*.

Basil Wolverton, a cartoonist who had distinguished himself by drawing "the world's ugliest girl," contributed a whole gallery of them as contestants in the "Miss Potgold" beer and beauty contest. Best of all, Kurtzman and Wood came up with "Julius Caesar," a piece which used the then current film version of Shakespeare's play as a springboard for a treatment of *Mad*'s own techniques.

This story, reprinted here, reflected some resentment at the fact that *Mad*, like the E. C. horror comics, had inspired a throng of imitators, Only one was an E. C. product, *Panic*, edited by Feldstein, and Feldstein himself has been reported as admitting that it was not up to the original. Of course, he was in a position to give it only a small portion of his time, as he was involved with so many other projects. It was at least, as house ads stated, the "best imitation of *Mad*," and employed the same staff artists, minus Kurtzman, who drew the early *Mad* covers and some inside pieces. The introduction to "Julius Caesar," which employs the names of imitations as part of the prose, creates an air of exhaustion which is maintained through the last panel, in which the story actually destroys itself. The devices enumerated for successful "lampoons" do not constitute a complete list, but no single piece ever captured the essence of *Mad* as well as this multi-level effort in which the weapon of satire was turned against the satirist's own head, and iconoclasm gave way to pure nihilism.

The sophistication of this story makes it serve as a suitable stopping point for this study of the company which did more than any other to explore the outer limits of a medium which was, in theory, boundless. But by ranging wide, they stepped on more than a few toes, and eventually ran into a brick wall. An examination of that wall, and of the ideas and individuals behind it, will be the subject of the next chapter.

MISS BEDNEY FLUNT

MISS FLUDNEY BENT

MISS FLUNTNEY BLENT

MISS PHILODENDRON POTGOLD
(WHO JUST HAPPENS TO BE GORGEOUS NIECE OF MR. MELVIN POTGOLD, OWNER OF POTGOLD BEER.)

MISS FLENTNEY BUNT

MISS BLENTNEY FUNT

MISS FLINTNEY BONT

MISS BONTNEY FLONT

©1954 by Educational Comics, Inc.

A few of the hideous entrants in *Mad*'s "Meet Miss Potgold" beauty contest, as depicted by Basil Wolverton, who has been credited with influencing the style of today's underground catoonists.

OF COURSE, WE WERE ONLY *KIDDING* IN THAT FIRST "E.C. QUICKIE"! WE GOT THE *STRAIGHT DOPE* A COUPLE OF MONTHS LATER WHEN WE RAN...

THE AD!

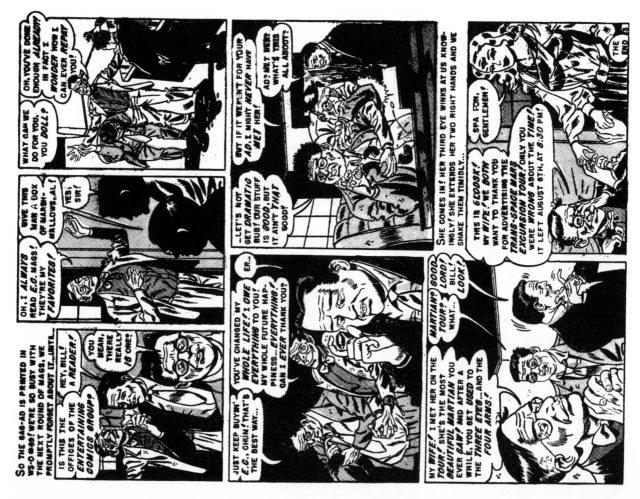

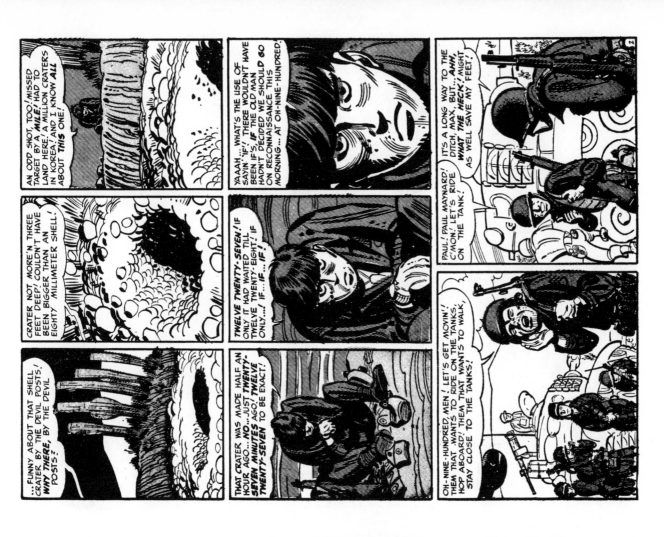

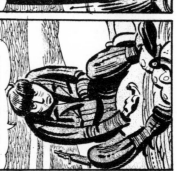

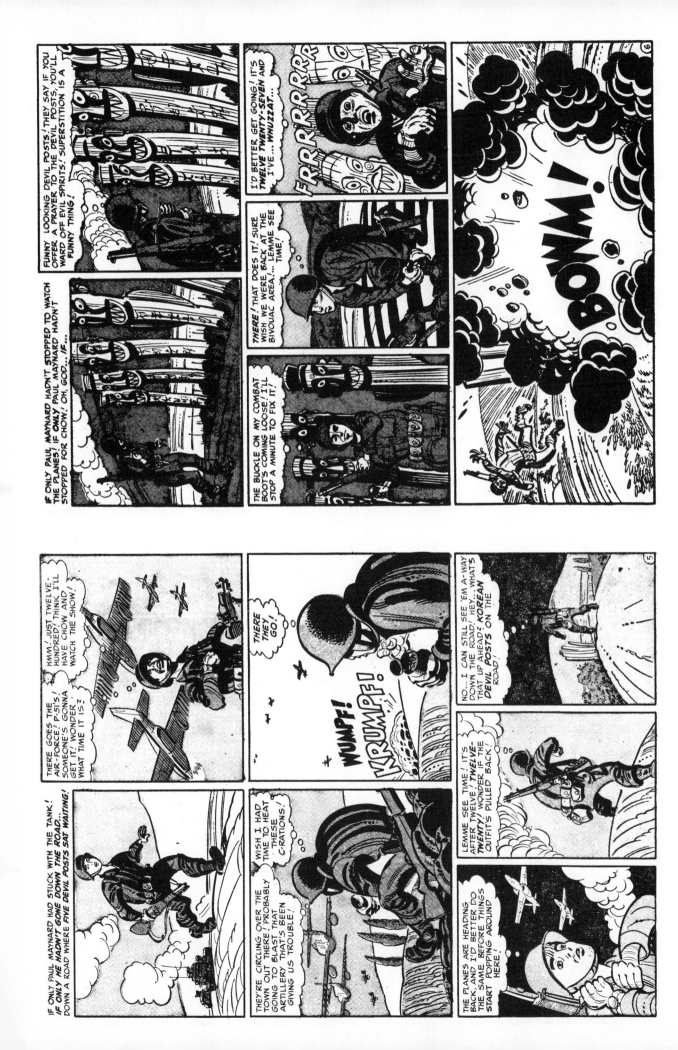

PROOF... OF 8 BRANDS TESTED, PANIC IS BEST IMITATION OF MAD

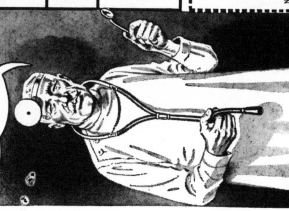

> YES, EXTENSIVE TESTS BY THE E.C. RESEARCH BUREAU HAVE PROVEN CONCLUSIVELY THAT *PANIC* LEADS EIGHT OTHER BRANDS IN IMITATING *MAD!* *PANIC* USES MORE OF *MAD'S* ARTISTS, MORE OF *MAD'S* PRINTERS, MORE OF *MAD'S* POTRZEBIE AND FURSHLUGGINER THAN ANY OTHER *MAD* IMITATION!

	PANIC	BRAND A	BRAND B	BRAND C	BRAND D	BRAND E	BRAND F	BRAND G
BEST IMITATION	■							
FAIR IMITATION								
POOR IMITATION								
ECCCCHHHHH		■	■	■	■	■	■	■

©1954 by Educational Comics, Inc.

"IF PAUL MAYNARD HADN'T STOPPED TO BUCKLE THE COMBAT BOOT!.. COULD'VE WALKED FIFTY MORE FEET IN THE TIME IT TOOK TO BUCKLE THAT BOOT!"

"IF PAUL MAYNARD HADN'T STOPPED TO LOOK AT HIS WATCH!... COULD'VE WALKED TWENTY-FIVE FEET IN THE TIME IT TOOK TO LOOK AT WATCH!"

"IF PAUL MAYNARD WALKED FASTER...OR SLOWER, OR DIDN'T WALK AT ALL! OH, LORD..."

"IT WAS ONLY A STRAY MORTAR SHELL! COULD HAVE LANDED ANYWHERE! IF ONLY THAT SHELL SPLINTER HAD GONE *FIVE MORE INCHES* TO THE RIGHT..."

"OR IF PAUL MAYNARD'S HEART HAD ONLY BEEN FIVE INCHES TO THE LEFT... OR IF PAUL MAYNARD HADN'T EVEN BEEN BORN!"

"IF... IF... IF... (SOB) ... IF... IF..."

BEFORE THE TOWN OF X___ IN KOREA, A ROW OF ANCIENT WOODEN DEVIL POSTS GRIN DOWN /...WOODEN GRINS FROM ONE WOODEN EAR TO THE OTHER... GRIN DOWN UPON THE BODY OF PRIVATE PAUL MAYNARD, KILLED IN ACTION! AND MAN'S DESTINY GOES MARCHING ON!

END

BUGHOUSE — Dear readers!... We interrupt this next story for a special announcement!... I, your MAD writer am going to the

CRAZY — Today... there are so many lampoon type comic books on the newsstands, the competition is driving me

EH! — But competition is the American way and although we are inclined to shrug off our competitors with a mere

FLIP FLIP — ...the fact is, twelve comics books during the calendar month grind thirty-two lampoon stories at a

GET LOST — Now, lampoon material is very limited, and when lampoon writers cannot get any more of this material they will

MAD — And so, I... your MAD writer hereby announce that there is no more material left... and that's why I'm going

MADHOUSE — Here I am, with no more material to finish this book!... However... there's one idea left that might save me from the

NUTS! — ...One idea that hasn't been attacked by the lampoon comics, although lord knows they've done everything from soup to

PANIC — And what the lampoon comics have not lampooned are the lampoon comics!... Ha! You think I clutch this wretched idea from sheer

RIOT — Not so! To watch the standard gag situations and routines appearing in our different books at the same time is truly a

WILD — With the following story we propose to take our brush and our ink... we propose to enter our own back yard and run

WHACK — So as we adjust our neck on the chopping block, our final word is... there is nothing at which we're not willing to take a

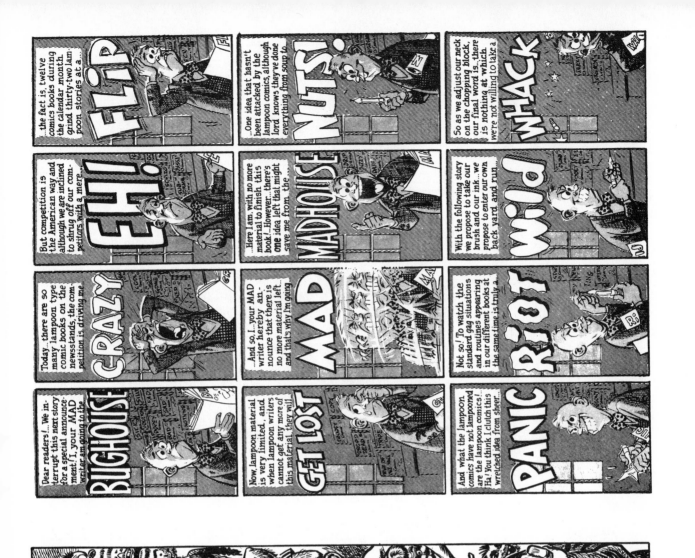

Chapter Five: The Comics Code Controversy

The year 1954 was a troubled one. It was a time of witch hunts and blacklists, name-calling and back-biting. A number of industries and organizations were roughed up during this period, which was characterized by the investigative activities of Wisconsin's Senator Joseph McCarthy. The comic book took its place among the suspicious characters who were to be exposed to an intensive scruntiny, and some radical changes were made as a result. Styles and contents were changed, characters and titles were dropped, and a number of major companies disappeared without a trace. All this was accomplished in an effort to "clean up" the comic book, which was under attack by those who viewed it as exclusively a medium for children, and one which would have to be altered to conform to very narrow concepts of mental hygiene. Unfortunately, and probably not coincidentally, these moves occurred during a period when the comics were just achieving new heights of sophistication in concept and execution, especially through the efforts of the E. C. line. The result was a setback for the art of comics, which was forced into essentially infantile patterns when its potential for maturity had only begun to be explored. There was some hysteria in the comics controversy, and more than a little intellectual snobbery. It was still too early for a serious defense of the medium; apparently nobody would stand up and be counted as a friend of what was so widely assumed to be childish nonsense.

There were three principal agents of the comics controversy. The first was a book that contained a strident and impassioned attack on comic books, Frederic Wertham's *Seduction of the Innocent*. Released in the spring of 1954, this polemic created a wave of public indignation, which had its peak when comic books reached the floor of the United States

Senate where they were investigated, significantly, by a subcommittee on juvenile delinquency. The government finally did nothing about the comics controversy, presumably reasoning that the medium was entitled to the same latitude as other forms of printed matter. Yet the simple fact that there was an investigation gave more momentum to the comics critics.

The industry, the second agent, finally reacted, perhaps in an effort to avoid legislation against comic books, perhaps simply to clear its increasingly blackened name. Most of the major publishers banded together in October to create the Comics Code Authority. This was an organization which set up an elaborate if rather vaguely worded list of restrictions with which all subscribing publications were expected to comply. In exchange for this cooperation, the comic books were permitted to display on their covers the seal which read "Approved by the Comics Code Authority." Those without the seal could easily be boycotted, or perhaps refused distribution. The individual who was to pass judgment on each comic book was former New York City Magistrate Charles F. Murphy.

The goal of the Comics Code Authority was painfully obvious. The Authority actually stated in its propaganda bulletin, now fifteen years old but still available, that the Authority "at its inception adopted as the cornerstone of its program the most stringent code in existence for any communications media." It proudly proclaimed itself the most oppressive force of censorship on the American landscape, and nobody batted an eyelash. In addition, it even managed—ironically—to provide indignant comic-lovers with a scapegoat: Dr. Wertham. The irony is that while Wertham was the most clever and coherent of the comics critics, he most certainly was not connected with the Authority figures who concocted the Comics Code. In fact, what he was to write about the Code as we shall see, was no less harsh than what he wrote on the comics. Unfortunately, it was not so well publicized.

In theory, the code was designed to protect the comic book business. No doubt it had this effect insofar as the seal did placate members of the public who had become incensed over the allegedly noxious contents of comic books. But can it have been an accident that so many companies ceased publication shortly after the code went into effect? What in theory had been designed to protect the industry had in practice the result of killing off a number of major contributions. A comparative handful of companies were left in charge of the field; the rest were either unwilling to change or unable to produce a marketable product within the code's narrow framework. Lost even in the surviving comic books was a certain enthusiasm and the wild imagination which had given the medium most of its finest moments.

The third agent in the controversy were the mothers of America. Inspired by Wertham and incited by the code-creators, the feminist movement took its first great political stand since the grim reality of the Depression had crushed their giddy dream of prohibition. In keeping with a grand tradition, the women chose to work outside the law. While legislators and philosophers pondered the significance of a new and powerful means of communication, an army of mothers took to the streets. Bridge clubs turned overnight into vigilante committees, pressuring newsdealers into suppressing what somebody had found offensive.

The potent force of outraged womanhood was the purse-string power behind the threat of newsdealer boycott that strangled complex distribution lines and finally started the castration of comic books. Doctors might point the finger of suspicion, and vultures might wait in the wings, but only a militant power-bloc could stem the rising tide of printer's ink.

It is possible to be more than a little suspicious about the value of the whole comics controversy. The attack was perhaps more sincere than sensible, and the defense was more successful as a business maneuver than as an artistic stand. The success of the code concept made it a simple matter to squeeze presumably objectionable publications off the market without ever proving them to be in any way illicit or illegal. Although there was a brief flurry of local legislation, it is extremely doubtful that any of it would have held up if the code had not made it unnecessary. Such excesses as the comic books committed could have been discovered in any other medium, and could hardly have been prohibited by constitutional legislation. Assuming this to be true (and there is no concrete evidence to the contrary), the code which was ostensibly created for industry "self-defense" proved, in a number of cases, to be suicidal.

The code seal made it all too simple for distributors and dealers to distinguish between "good" and "bad" publications, and thus to defend themselves from harassment by those citizens who had been incited into a state of ill-informed indignation. Freedom of the press came to be a less important consideration than freedom from pressure, and the concept of a seal of approval allowed everyone to forget the comics controversy in a hurry. It is notable that three members of the press who attacked Senator Joseph McCarthy nationally before he was censured by his colleagues were Walt Kelly, Herblock, and Harvey Kurtzman. All were cartoonists; all were censored. And nobody noticed. Except millions of kids. Those perenially concerned with the problem of youth soon found new targets like television and rock and roll music, but not before the world of comic books had undergone some permanent and unfortunate changes.

Harvey Kurtzman has some prophetic gifts, and it was pretty certain that he had seen the handwriting on the wall by the time he did the cover for the sixteenth *Mad* comic book, which was dated for the same month (October 1954) in which the Comics Code Authority announced itself. This cover was a mock-up of a newspaper front page, tabloid style. The two "photos," rendered in Kurtzman's cursive simplicity, showed an artist (Elder) being dragged away by the men in the white coats, while a writer (Kurtzman) evades the bluecoats on a street corner, still surreptitiously peddling his magazines to a group of grinning kids. The screaming headline reads: "COMICS GO UNDERGROUND!" In light of recent developments which have brought that label into new prominence—where today's underground cartoonists describe their own and each other's morbid fantasies with relish—it seems fair to suggest that the man was a dozen years ahead of his time.

Gaines' E. C. publications were the principal fall-guys for the repressive forces which operated under a guise of liberal humanism. Nobody claimed to be attacking liberty; they all claimed they were protecting someone else's children. From what?

There were various strands in the horror against which the critics leveled their attacks. One was the *Mad-Panic* syndrome. As a wet blanket of massive media had settled on the mid-century horizon, citizens began to notice that the lives they portrayed for each other in the media were hopelessly false. Thus were planted the seeds of the modern sensibility. Communications overkill had created a jaded audience, and the unconditioned children were the first to grow numb. Midst flashes of three-dimensional chess and non-Euclidean geometry, the cross-referenced multi-level comic book had been born. By employing ever-increasing elements of parody and satire, E. C. succeeded in creating, with *Mad* and *Panic*, comic books that were actually about the process by which ideas are created and destroyed. The kids, intuitively aware of the processes of the media, recognized immediately that *Mad* and *Panic* were equally aware. Grownups were horrified, especially when they discovered their jaded offspring devouring this apparent garbage as if it were milk and honey. It had been bad enough for some when Al Feldstein, with incredible productivity under pressure (he wrote a story a day for more than five years), ultimately exposed the pathology of the mystery and fantasy themes he reworked for comics like *Weird Science* and *Vault of Horror*. When he and Kurtzman moved in on the respectable mass media, it was too much.

In its few short years as a comic, *Mad* had recircuited the stereotyped programs of American culture. Comics, popular fiction, literature, the fine arts, movies, radio, television, advertising, crime, politics, sports, economics and even *Mad* itself fell under Kurtzman's snickering spotlight. Those targets missed by *Mad* were eagerly impaled by Feldstein's *Panic*. No potential victim escaped. Some of the mocked smiled ruefully, but others writhed in indignation.

Voices still whisper in undertones that *Mad* might have been happier had Kurtzman and Elder never spit in the face of a certain buck-toothed creature with a granite grin topped by carrot-colored criss-cross marks. Such suggestions may mean nothing, but it is interesting to note that John Goldwater, the spearhead of the Comics Code Authority, was in his spare time the owner and manager of that perennial champion of tasteless conformity, Archie. Billed as America's typical teenager, he has remained steadfastly behind the times. When *Mad* parodied his career as "Starchie," he was transplanted from the cardboard world of suburban one-upmanship into the blackboard jungle. After unreal adventures among Elder's famous metropolitan junkyards, Starchie was jailed for running a high school protection racket. Goldwater was presumably not amused. This much is clear: the Comics Code Authority which he headed inspired marketing pressure which drove certain comic books out of business.

Still, the man who started the short-lived but far-reaching controversy, and who supplied the ammunition with which the business men staged their bloodless coup, was Dr. Frederic Wertham, and he must bear much of the responsibility for the subsequent reign of the inane. Wertham had been senior psychiatrist for the Department of Hospitals in New York City from 1932 to 1952, and directed mental hygiene clinics at Bellevue Hospital and elsewhere. The fact that he had spent so much time among disturbed juveniles seems to have colored his view of all children, whom he depicted as teetering on the brink of mental disaster. His book, *Seduction of the Innocent*, was written in a sensational style and touted by the publishers as "the most shocking book of the year." His insistence on the essential innocence of youth and the awesome power of comic books sometimes suggested a remarkable naivete. For instance, he cited the case of a lad who had offered to break his sister's arm, and concluded: "This is not the kind of thing that boys used to tell their sisters. To break people's arms, or to threaten to do so, is one of the comic book devices." This unlikely assertion exemplifies Wertham's technique, which rarely offered concrete proof concerning the allegedly deleterious effect of comic books. Instead, he juxtaposed the concept of the comic book with unpleasant incidents or attitudes to suggest relationships between the two which were largely theoretical.

Most of the 397 pages of *Seduction of the Innocent* were devoted to an attack on what Wertham called "crime comic books." This obviously included within its scope the entire school inspired by the success of Lev Gleason's *Crime Does Not Pay*, which had reached a peak of popularity in 1947, when the publishers claimed a following of seven million readers. The transparent allegorical face of Gleason's narrator character Crime, who drove gunmen gleefully to their doom, had even begun to appear in advertising comic strips as Mr. Coffee Nerves and Mr. Tooth Decay. But Wertham used the term "crime comic books" to designate any type of comic book in which crime was depicted, regardless of style or setting, thus extending the negative implications of the "crime" tag until it included almost the entire industry. References to "so-called Western comics that actually featured crimes" indicate Wertham's tactics.

The importance of the "crime" label can hardly be overemphasized. The documentary-style crime comic books depicted without restraint the gang-life of the Depression and the psychopathic aberrations of the postwar liberation. In a medium where fantasy was the standard fare, the crime comics exposed some unpleasant truths about our society. Their honesty, we may assume, made them unpleasant. In any case, they came under attack for causing what they were actually only reporting, even as bearers of bad tidings might be executed by resentful rulers.

Horror comic books were also under fire. They were not particularly emphasized in *Seduction of the Innocent*, but repercussions from the book's general condemnation took specific form when E. C. publisher William Gaines was summoned to testify before the Senate subcommittee on delinquency, generally referred to as the Kefauver hearings, in honor of the presiding senator. Somehow Gaines was singled out from the mass of inferior imitators that had followed E. C. into the horror field, and given the difficult task of defending the genre before a group who were apparently unsympathetic toward the entire medium. The most widely reported exchange between Gaines and the committee centered around one of Johnny Craig's covers, featuring a severed head. The picture in question was attacked and defended on the basis of its comparative "bad taste." Certainly there was pressure on Gaines, who described his experience as "traumatic," and just as certainly his company was exposed to unfavorable publicity by his very presence at the hearings. Yet the fact that the debate was over taste rather than legality indicated how weak the case was against even the wildest comics.

The fact that Wertham's accusations against comic books were based on the medium's presumed ability to suggest and to stimulate behavior made any specific refutation a virtual impossibility. Opinions might be offered to counter his opinions, but concrete proof regarding the cause and effect relationship was bound to be elusive. And nobody could match Wertham's dedication, which found perhaps its most remarkable manifestation when he devoted a chapter of his 1966 book, *A Sign for Cain*, to a specific attack on horror comic books, naming the titles that had disappeared more than a decade before. It may not have occurred to the Doctor that he was beating a dead horse, but the new book did not have the impact of *Seduction of the Innocent*, even though it emphasized the same narrow view of art as force which is more likely to corrupt than to produce catharsis.

Wertham's basic charge was that comic books led children to crimes of lust, violence and anarchy, and that they accomplished their insidious program by depicting such events in public places. Sad to say, the E. C. images and Lev Gleason's images of brutal realism were not the only ones that were washed overboard in the Doctor's teapot tempest. Other idylls that sank in the storm included those bastions of pulp fantasy, Fiction House and Quality Comics. Lost beneath waves of indignation were such mighty creations as the Spirit, Plastic Man, and Sheena, Queen of the Jungle. Characters like Wonder Woman and the Blackhawks survived, but, robbed of their fantasy-life eroticism and their futuristic ethics, they staggered slowly and sadly toward the sinking sun.

Ultimately time would prove that nobody could clean up the comics. The unclean kept cropping up like fungus. Even code-approved comics soon evolved new ways of symbolizing Dr. Wertham's trilogy—sex, violence and anarchy. Every art form is always expressing these concepts, for it is a duty as well as a curse. When we call these concepts by their respectable titles of "love," "death" and "freedom," we recognize their true significance as our most meaningful triad of spiritual mysteries. The comics made the fatal error of expressing these dreams openly in an oppressive atmosphere where the established opinion-makers favored careful observation and dissection. And so they fell from favor for a while.

Yet they remained remarkably willful. Soon after the code had taken effect, Dr. Wertham took a stand in his original corner, the *Saturday Review of Literature* (April 9, 1955). He wrote, in his usual blunt style, "At present it is far safer for a mother to let her child have a comic book *without* a seal of approval than one with such a seal." The title of this article was "It's Still Murder," and Wertham's implicit argument was that the code had really done nothing to remove the crime from comic books. All it had done was to disguise the actions in a hypocritical aura of good taste where the ghastly effects of heartless cruelty were never realistically depicted. Murder looked more like a game than ever under the new, self-awarded seal of approval.

What Wertham had advocated at the conclusion of

Seduction of the Innocent was a rating system which would have left serious comics on the stands, but for sale only to those over sixteen. This sounds comparatively fair. It would have given kids the dumb animals, and probably kept in business freethinkers like Gleason, Quality, Fiction House and E. C., because they commanded sophisticated audiences. As it was, much of the creative talent was gradually forced out of the business, and the field was taken by the mindless face-kickers and panacea-pushers whom Wertham had found most despicable. As if this were not an ironic enough conclusion to his crusade, it became clear that both friends and foes of the comics held Wertham responsible for the Authority.

Wertham must have felt sick. He had spent years trying to destroy a monster, but the result was that he somehow animated another, and one which stole his thunder in the bargain. The pious physician lit the flame that sparked book-burnings. Small wonder that he, too, began to feel burned.

Still, he deserved his share of the blisters he raised, for *Seduction of the Innocent*, as has been implied, was in all regards an extremely questionable book. Members of his own profession attacked him in professional journals for subverting scientific ethics to promote a shaky thesis. This was tit for tat, as Wertham suggested to readers of *Seduction of the Innocent* that any psychiatrist condoning comics (there were many) was motivated by the desire to receive a consultant's fee.

In fact, attacks on other psychiatrists occur frequently in Wertham's books. *Seduction* was just one of a series. He didn't strike gold until he noticed his juvenile patients reading comics (just like every other American kid), but his earlier studies of "unseduced" deviates demonstrate the same dogged conviction that every doctor who crossed swords with Wertham was making a serious mistake.

Probably the most spectacular of Wertham's previous efforts, one which provides a useful perspective for his study on comics, was a collection of case histories entitled *The Show of Violence*. It is still quite a show. In fact, any attempt to summarize the work is doomed to failure. Fortunately, a few copies have been preserved by librarians. Like its successor, it is now out of print, a condition which serious students of psychology can only regret. *The Show of Violence* offers some interesting clues regarding his basic approach and the source of his unquestionable public appeal, which was to prove a central element in the comics controversy. Of course, all his works are "science," and thus above reproach, but it is interesting to note, for example, that research teams have yet to uncover a library copy of *Seduction* in an unmutilated condition. In every case, some of the good Doctor's carefully selected illustrations have been removed by some student of suppression who felt obliged to study it more intimately.

In terms of horror, the stories in *Show of Violence* (unfortunately not illustrated) leave Wertham's comics catalog far behind. These are tales of persons Wertham examined or treated who were or became murderers. The first is the wife of a homosexual who fed her son and daughter acid, strangled them, and then jumped out of a window. Another considers a gentleman who strangled a ten-year-old girl and ate her. X-rays revealed that he had also permanently embedded twenty-seven needles in his own crotch. A third concerns a young widow who took an ax to her children because she was convinced they would interfere with her proposed career as part of a dance team. She also set fire to them. One lived anyway. No trouble is spared to present the gory details. This is, in short, the kind of book bored psychology students pray for, exciting if not exactly edifying.

The most spectacular case in *Show of Violence* concerns a sculptor who strangled a beautiful model and her mother, then stabbed their boarder in the head seven times with an ice pick. These murders are described fully and repeatedly, but that is not the half of it. It seems that this artist had been a patient of Wertham's for some time, and had previously distinguished himself by making a partially successful attempt to amputate his own penis. This act, with its medical results and implications, is discussed and analyzed in exquisite detail for eighty-four pages.

This incident of emasculation is more sordid than anything described or even suggested in any of the comics Wertham attacked, and is covered with more specific anatomical references than any injury ever inflicted on any character in any comic ever imagined. If anybody had printed Wertham's chamber of horrors as a "funny book," he would have been ridden out of town on a rail.

Yet the Doctor, by subtle manipulation of his audience's most dread desires, was finally able, by employing a similar melodramatic approach in *Seduction*, to elevate himself for a year into the mighty universe of the ladies' luncheon-club circuit. How did Wertham bring about the uprising of America's mothers? He used mainly one magic word. And the magic word was "sex."

Using his knowledge of morbid deviation, Dr. Wertham attempted to analyze fantasy-projections as though they were real people. Thus Batman and Robin, two crimefighters who shared the same quarters, were analyzed as homosexuals, despite the clear lack of overt evidence. If they had been actual men, they could have won a libel suit. As it was, Wertham dug up a homosexual who admitted that he would have been willing to trade places with either of the "Dynamic Duo." This passed for proof. What inspired the original idea must remain the Doctor's secret. Similarly, he branded Wonder Woman and her cohorts as lesbian sadists because some of the villains they slugged were men. Of course, if they slugged other women it was even worse. And males who leaned on females were the most reprehensible of all.

Wertham was one of the first to realize that Freudian terminology was so extensive that any possible pattern of human behavior could be analyzed as a disorder. Stories with predominantly male characters were accused of creating homosexual atmospheres, while predominantly female casts were hotbeds of lesbianism. If the sexes were evenly distributed, the comic in question lay open to the most damning charge of all: they induced pre-adolescent heterosexuality, the same shameful concept on which Freud was nearly crucified by his Victorian colleagues. With a three-pronged attack like this, no comic was safe. It is equally true that these attacks could be leveled against any narrative ever devised, but it would only have worked against comics, because they were the low men on the cultural totem pole, the great unwashed of the fourth estate. A few writers quietly refuted Wertham (not a difficult task for any competent critic) but nobody shouted his indignation from the rooftops.

Wertham was able to further incite women by pointing out that most of the female characters in comics came equipped with breasts, which he branded "headlights" on the strength of information received from a juvenile delinquent. He reworked this simple anatomical fact until it appeared that some fiend in the comic industry had not only invented these shocking objects but also all male interest in them. Passages could be cited *ad nauseum*. He even included a chapter called "Bumps and Bulges," considering at length the negative effects which these nasty "headlights" might have on girls approaching puberty. The Doctor's concern with proper adolescent pectoral development shines through these passages like a beacon.

The sophistication of the sixties and seventies may have weakened the role of the psychiatrist as the divinely appointed guardian of the human spirit, but in 1954 it was still possible for one to create a mild form of hysteria in some of his readers by using words like "blood" and "burglary" in the same sentence with the phrase "children's comic books." Wertham even mentioned "sado-masochism" at a time when even knowledge of the concept was considered virtually verboten. In the anxiously bourgeois atmosphere of the McCarthy era, even the idea that a person had any sort of sexual identity tended to have a frightening charge to it. In such a repressed atmosphere, too, Freudian exposes also had a certain market value as erotic stimulants, exploiting the same material they were ostensibly exposing.

Seduction also got in a few licks by relating comic books to the rising tide of public concern over juvenile delinquency. This, according to most accounts, had decreased proportionally since the war, but Wertham, using the simple statistics, was able to convince his readers that kid crime was on the rise. No need to ask who he blamed. He cited a few examples of comic book stories in which methods of crime were described (imagine a body of literature without such stories), and branded the comics textbooks of terror. In an era where scapegoats were at a premium, the suggestion proved irresistible.

From these concerns—sex and juvenile delinquency—Wertham raised his army.

In retrospect, the most disgraceful feature of Wertham's book is the manner in which he used illustrations. These were isolated panels removed from their context to promote Wertham's prejudices. A drawing of a jungle-man was enlarged greatly to reveal a tiny triangular patch of ink which Wertham convinced the ladies was nothing more or less than a representation of their own shameful sexual organs. Helpful captions for other selections included "Children told me what the man was going to do with the red-hot poker," providing a spurious suggestion which the complete story would never have supported. (Only in books by people like Wertham were people portrayed who mutilated genitals.) While generally avoiding the naming of names, Wertham printed wild drawings by two of E. C.'s top artists, Elder and Davis. None of these reproductions was credited, and the good Doctor was able to employ the talents of these men to provide himself with some marketable material while simultaneously trying to place the artists he exploited among the unemployed. There was also a beautifully rendered study of Phantom Lady in bondage, a state which contradicted Wertham's assertion that she was a sadist. Possibly the drawing was just too attractive to leave out. The carefully chosen illustrations proved fodder for the reader's fantasies—but were packaged so that he disguised his real interests under a display of righteous indignation. The picture section was a masterstroke. It is as true of *Seduction* as of the comics Wertham attacked that more people pondered the pictures than pored over the pious prose.

Undoubtedly Wertham's favorite selection was his demonstration of what he insisted on calling "the injury to the eye motif." This motif turns up again and again like a bad penny throughout *Seduction*. It's hard to know why. No doubt injuring people's eyes is nasty, but among the countless acts of violence occurring in crime and adventure comics, it seems grotesque to emphasize it so strongly. Perhaps it represents some symbolic function known only to the medical profession or, more likely, only to the enlightened Wertham. Sigmund Freud considered the issue when he branded Oedipus (the classic eye-gouger) as a literary example of the incestuous guilt-complex. For the master, the bloody eye-socket was a symbol of sexual shame. For the pupil, it was an opportunity to exploit the unconscious guilt of his own followers. It is as if a student of the theater were to equate the entire school of Elizabethan drama with the scene of Gloucester's blinding in *King Lear*.

It would have been bad enough had Wertham been content to raise the issue. What he actually did was worse. The picture he chose came from a story entitled "Murder, Morphine, and Me" in *True Crime* comics. When he wrote his book, this then already defunct magazine was eight years old. More to the point, nobody in the comic book had an eye injured. What Wertham found was one panel from a *dream sequence* in which a female dope-pusher dreams that a junky threatens to take revenge for his destruction by sticking his empty syringe into her eye. The next panel shows her waking up safe and sound, all organs intact.

Of course, Wertham did not cite his source for this picture, since it would have deflated not only his beloved "motif" theory, but his contention that comics incited crime as well. No kid who read this factual story would be inspired to try morphine. The caved-in faces of the desperate junkies are studies of horror, rivaled only by the acid-etched spook stories of E. C.'s Graham Ingles. Furthermore, the comic went on to describe the devious channels by which drugs reach the street. The heroine finally reforms when she discovers that the kingpin of the dope empire is the respectable businessman she trusted and admired. Not the kind of thing we want our children to hear about, even if it might keep them off the needle. (It is interesting to note that Wertham's other principal shocker, a shot of crooks dragging victims behind a speeding car, was taken from the same 1946 issue of the same magazine. His research was not exactly exhaustive).

In all, his success with his women's army derived principally from the fact that he was able to exploit the battle between the sexes which had entered a new phase during the war years. At that time, women had dominated the marketplace while their men were protecting them overseas, and competition for power and profit became desperate when the veterans returned.

When, to take literary examples, heroines like Scarlett O'Hara and Forever Amber were committing symbolic castrations right and left—see Gershon Legman's classic study, *Love and Death* (1949), the book that probably got Wertham started*—it was inevitable that an analyst like Wertham would have tremendous success. It was child's play for him to convince American women that American men were after their eyes, and after their kiddies as well. (He even invented the concept of the "Medea complex" to justify women who slaughtered their children in order to express their spirituality.) Of course, all the male murderers in Wertham's book were monsters, except maybe the one who took cold steel to his own reproductive organs. It's not too bad to be a killer if you're willing to pay the piper.

Wertham summed up his position pretty well in an early sentence: "Comic books with their words and expletives in balloons are bad for reading." This is the complete sentence, and anyone with a high school education can diagram it into its component parts. Remove the modifiers and you get the message: ". . . books . . . are . . . bad . . ."

Children awoke in dismay to discover than what they looked on as an enjoyable pastime had become, for no apparent reason, a shocking sin and the legitimate prey of parents who had turned into book-burners. It may be that they did not forget what happened in 1954, even after they grew up. Certainly, it was worse than a horror comic.

The Code saw to it, in any case, that the horror comics died. The words "terror" and "horror" were not allowed to appear on the cover of any comic book. The word "crime" was similarly condemned. These were the only three words ruled out of bounds. By a strange coincidence, E. C.'s two biggest money-makers, the magazines that made experiments like *Mad* possible, were *Crypt of Terror* and *Vault of Horror*. Lev Gleason's most popular entry was *Crime Does Not Pay*. Almost enough to make you stop and think.

The Comics Code dictated the style and content of virtually the entire medium. It would be more than a decade before it would be seriously challenged, and more than fifteen years before its rigid restrictions, still very influential, would be subject to even the slightest liberalization.

THE STANDARDS OF THE COMICS CODE AUTHORITY AS ORIGINALLY ADOPTED

CODE FOR EDITORIAL MATTER
General Standards   Part A

1) Crimes shall never be presented in such a way as to create sympathy for the criminal, to promote distrust of the forces of law and justice, or to inspire others with a desire to imitate criminals.

2) No comics shall explicitly present the unique details and methods of a crime.

3) Policemen, judges, government officials and respected institutions shall never be presented in such a way as to create disrespect for established authority.

4) If crime is depicted it shall be as a sordid and unpleasant activity.

5) Criminals shall not be presented so as to be rendered glamorous or to occupy a position which creates a desire for emulation.

6) In every instance good shall triumph over evil and the criminal punished for his misdeeds.

7) Scenes of excessive violence shall be prohibited. Scenes of brutal torture, excessive and unnecessary knife and gun play, physical agony, gory and gruesome crime shall be eliminated.

8) No unique or unusual methods of concealing weapons shall be shown.

9) Instances of law enforcement officers dying as a result of a criminal's activities should be discouraged.

10) The crime of kidnapping shall never be portrayed in any detail, nor shall any profit accrue to the abductor or kidnapper. The criminal or the kidnapper must be punished in every case.

11) The letters of the word "crime" on a comics magazine cover shall never be appreciably greater in dimension than the other words contained in the title. The word "crime" shall never appear alone on a cover.

12) Restraint in the use of the word "crime" in titles or sub-titles shall be exercised.

General Standards   Part B

1) No comic magazine shall use the word horror or terror in its title.

2) All scenes of horror, excessive bloodshed, gory or gruesome crimes, depravity, lust, sadism, masochism shall not be permitted.

3) All lurid, unsavory, gruesome illustrations shall be eliminated.

4) Inclusion of stories dealing with evil shall be used or shall be published only where the intent is to illustrate a moral issue and in no case shall evil be presented alluringly nor so as to injure the sensibilities of the reader.

5) Scenes dealing with, or instruments associated with walking dead, torture, vampires and vampirism, ghouls, cannibalism and werewolfism are prohibited.

General Standards   Part C

All elements or techniques not specifically mentioned herein, but which are contrary to the spirit and intent of the Code, and are considered violations of good taste or decency, shall be prohibited.

Dialogue

1) Profanity, obscenity, smut, vulgarity, or words or symbols which have acquired undesirable meanings are forbidden.

2) Special precautions to avoid references to physical afflictions or deformities shall be taken.

3) Although slang and colloquialisms are acceptable, excessive use should be discouraged and wherever possible good grammar shall be employed.

Religion

Ridicule or attack on any religious or racial group is never permissible.

Costume

1) Nudity in any form is prohibited, as is indecent or undue exposure.

2) Suggestive and salacious illustration or suggestive posture is unacceptable.

3) All characters shall be depicted in dress reasonably acceptable to society.

4) Females shall be drawn realistically without exaggeration of any physical qualities.

NOTE: It should be recognized that all prohibitions dealing with costume, dialogue or artwork applies as specifically to the cover of a comic magazine as they do to the contents.

Marriage and Sex

1) Divorce shall not be treated humorously nor represented as desirable.

2) Illicit sex relations are neither to be hinted at or portrayed. Violent love scenes as well as sexual abnormalities are unacceptable.

3) Respect for parents, the moral code, and for honorable behavior shall be fostered. A sympathetic understanding of the problems of love is not a license for morbid distortion.

4) The treatment of love-romance stories shall emphasize the value of the home and the sanctity of marriage.

5) Passion or romantic interest shall never be treated in such a way as to stimulate the lower and baser emotions.

6) Seduction and rape shall never be shown or suggested.

7) Sex perversion or any inference to same is strictly forbidden.

CODE FOR ADVERTISING MATTER

These regulations are applicable to all magazines published by members of the Comics Magazine Association of America, Inc. Good taste shall be the guiding principle in the acceptance of advertising.

1) Liquor and tobacco advertising is not acceptable.

2) Advertisement of sex or sex instruction books are unacceptable.

3) The sale of picture postcards, "pin-ups," "art studies," or any other reproduction of nude or semi-nude figures is prohibited.

4) Advertising for the sale of knives, concealable weapons, or realistic gun facsimiles is prohibited.

5) Advertising for the sale of fireworks is prohibited.

6) Advertising dealing with the sale of gambling equipment or printed matter dealing with gambling shall not be accepted.

7) Nudity with meretricious purpose and salacious postures shall not be permitted in the advertising of any product; clothed figures shall never be presented in such a way as to be offensive or contrary to good taste or morals.

8) To the best of his ability, each publisher shall ascertain that all statements made in advertisements conform to fact and avoid misinterpretation.

9) Advertisement of medical, health, or toiletry products of questionable nature are to be rejected. Advertisements for medical, health or toiletry products endorsed by the American Medical Association, or the American Dental Association, shall be deemed acceptable if they conform with all other conditions of the Advertising Code.

Chapter Six: The New Comic Books

The Code had a profound and depressing effect on comic books. A great number of publishers, unable to produce their colorful product within its broadly defined restrictions, and equally unable to get distribution without a seal of approval, abandoned their comic book lines for good.

It is true that there were two publishers who apparently felt that their integrity was so firmly established that they could afford to forego being sanctioned by a quasi-official board of review, and they refused to submit their comics. One of the companies was Dell, the majority of whose titles were of the clearly inoffensive animal type. Another was the Gilberton Company, which produced the Classics Illustrated line of literary adaptations. Begun in 1941 by Albert Kantner, this was one of the most sincere attempts to elevate the medium for educational purposes. Gilberton may have been resentful of the Code and Dr. Wertham because of a passage in *Seduction of the Innocent* which cites a comic book adaptation of

Shakespeare's *Hamlet* for adding a ludicrous expletive to Hamlet's dying speech. An examination of the Gilberton version, still in print, reveals that no such addition was actually made. The fact that two companies with such patently pure intentions chose to stand outside the Code was a significant indication that it was not as pure or powerful as it might appear, and continued sales of the Dell and Gilberton products showed that it was possible—at least for some—to ignore the Comics Code Authority and still stay in business.

Nevertheless, an important obstacle had been raised against efforts to bring to comic books a range of subjects enjoyed by more established modes of expression.

E. C., the company against which the Code's restrictions seemed to have been most obviously designed, rallied bravely. Rather than just capitulating, Gaines dropped his New Trend titles, and inaugurated a different though ultimately unsuccessful series, the

"New Direction" comic books. Launched simultaneously in March 1955 were *Impact, Valor, Aces High, Extra, M. D.* and *Psychoanalysis*. All of these were designed to meet Code requirements, and carried the seal of approval on the later issues. *Piracy*, another New Direction title, began a little earlier in October 1954, and the line was completed by a somewhat subdued *Panic* and by *Incredible Science-Fiction*, which continued *Weird Science-Fantasy*. Editing all these titles but one was the ubiquitous, prodigious Al Feldstein. *Extra* had artist Johnny Craig as editor for its stories about newspapermen covering crime. *Valor* and *Aces High* continued the E. C. war tradition, the latter concentrating on aerial combat. *Impact* featured a variety of stories employing the surprise ending which was already an E. C. specialty. The two unlikely entries, *M. D.* and *Psychoanalysis*, concerned themselves with the medical profession. In what was presumably an effort to produce something morally uplifting and socially redeeming, there emerged two of the most restrained and static comic books in history. Yet the high quality of writing and illustration was still in evidence, and managed to maintain interest even within a remarkably restricted framework. In fact, some of the medical mishaps encountered in these pages seemed, within the subdued context, grimmer than the extravagant gore served up by the Crypt Keeper and his cohorts.

The New Direction comics had a short life, bowing out for several reasons at the end of 1955, the same year in which they started. One of the reasons concerned *Mad*, which was to have a much more successful career. *Mad* No. 23, the last of the comic book series, concluded with an "important announcement" from the editors, which read, in part: "We're expanding *Mad* into a regular big twenty-five cent magazine with pictures, printed lettering, covers, and everything, gang. Boy, what exciting plans. Mainly since this may put us out of business, we're sick to our stomachs with excitement. Exciting plans are now under way to turn *Mad* into a regular large-sized adult magazine. For the past two years now, *Mad* has been dulling the senses of the nation's youth. Now we get to work on the adults." In short, the E. C. forces had decided to bypass the restrictions of the Code, transforming their most impressive effort into a new format which, despite its origin and overtones, would not ostensibly be a comic book. The new, larger-sized, black and white, sixty-four page *Mad* No. 24 appeared in July 1955. This was, among other things, a return to the original length of comic books, which had declined through the years to fifty-two and then to thirty-two pages. Kurtzman, continuing as editor and chief writer, offered another "important message from the editors," this time on the first page. Four figures knelt in supplication under a balloon con-

taining the words "Please buy this magazine."

They need not have asked. *Mad* was to make the transition brilliantly, and become one of the most popular and influential mass circulation magazines in the country. Along with Hugh Hefner's sexy *Playboy*, it was one of the only two magazines produced in the fifties that were successful innovations (excepting, of course, the reader service of *TV Guide*). Whether or not it should still be considered a comic book is a moot point. The first magazine issue of *Mad* generally avoided the characteristic speech balloons in favor of a combination of drawings and text which suggested a parody of *Life* magazine. Later issues would again feature the balloons more prominently, but explanatory blocks of print continued to remain an important addition. The standard piece became an article expounding on its subject rather than a story which exposed it. Movie parodies continued to be a prominent feature, but the comic parodies came to occupy less space, probably because, as the "Julius Caesar" piece suggested, material was being exhausted. The most impressive new idea to emerge from the first magazine was in keeping with its new apparently legitimate status. Advertisements began to appear in the inside and back covers, and since industrialists were not about to be welcomed by such an iconoclastic publication, these ads were parodies, rendered with the same uncanny accuracy which had distinguished the earlier treatment of comics. Elder, Davis and Wood continued as chief artists.

Following the new *Mad*, E. C. tried another experiment to transfer some of its more serious material into a different format. The result was dubbed "picto-fiction," and it included four titles, *Shock Illustrated, Crime Illustrated, Terror Illustrated* and *Confessions Illustrated*. These included stories in the old E. C. vein, but they were not comic books. Rather, they were pieces of prose fiction, set in type, and profusely illustrated by the staff artists. They lasted for only a couple of issues.

Shortly after *Mad* became a magazine, a disagreement developed between editor Kurtzman and publisher Gaines. There have been various versions of exactly what transpired—from both sides and from several other sources. In general, it seems that Kurtzman made a request for a larger share of stock in the enterprise, which Gaines refused. To Gaines, the request indicated a desire for financial control, which he was reluctant to relinquish. To Kurtzman, the request indicated a desire for editorial control, without which he was reluctant to continue as editor. Whatever the interpretation, the final result was that Kurtzman left *Mad* for good. The versatile Feldstein was called in by Gaines, and became editor with the twenty-ninth issue. It was partly as a result of this shift that the flagging New Direction line of comic books were dropped, and E. C. became a one-publication enterprise.

Under Feldstein, *Mad* was to abandon some of its earlier intensity to achieve a broader base of support. New writers and artists were recruited, and the product began to reflect the fact that it was no longer the work of a lone hand. Outstanding among the new contributors were the gifted caricaturist Mort Drucker, and cartoonist of the grotesque, Don Martin, billed as "*Mad*'s maddest artist." While the new magazine was becoming established, Gaines consolidated his position by arranging for publication by Ballantine Books of five collections of the best material from the comic books: *The Mad Reader, Mad Strikes Back, Inside Mad, Utterly Mad* and *The Brothers Mad*.

A figurehead for the *Mad* was established in the form of a grinning imp who, if his hair were removed, might have passed in a dim light for the Yellow Kid. After some confusion (he was briefly known as Melvin Cowsnofski or Mel Haney), he was dubbed Alfred E. Neuman, the "What? Me worry?" kid, and has graced the cover of almost every *Mad* for the last fifteen years.

The magazine's right to parody the mass media was apparently firmly established when *Mad* won a case brought by composer Irving Berlin in 1964. Judge Irving R. Kaufman of the U. S. Court of Appeals ruled that *Mad*'s brand of mockery did not infringe on copyright. His judgment read, in part: "While the social interest in encouraging the broad-gauged burlesques of *Mad* magazine is admittedly not readily apparent, we believe that parody and satire are deserving of substantial freedom—both as entertainment and as a form of social and literary criticism." More and more, the magazine's targets have tended to take the taunts in their stride, recognizing perhaps that their appearance in its pages is a sort of backhanded recognition of their influence on the public. It is not unusual for the subject of satire to write in to express amusement over the coverage (which is, at least, some sort of publicity). The fact that the magazine has become somewhat more tolerant may also help to account for this sort of reaction. Some of the early savage spirit has submerged itself into an atmosphere where fun and a certain affection for human foibles are now the norm. Yet it is remarkable how often *Mad* continues to make valid points, and over its long career it has, by its very presence, brought the qualities of skepticism and awareness to succeeding groups of readers who, in these days, need all the help they can get.

As for Kurtzman, after leaving *Mad* his next step was a move to what must have looked like greener pastures—a new publication, *Trump*, which began with an issue dated January 1957. The publisher was Hugh Hefner, whose success with *Playboy* and admiration for Kurtzman's work led him to expand his operation to include the most expansive and luxurious satire publication ever attempted. Higher quality paper and more sophisticated printing made it possible to reproduce elaborately rendered color pictures just as the slick magazines did. The Kurtzman charisma brought Bill Elder and Jack Davis into the enterprise, and the results were spectacular. Highlights included an elaborate parody of *Sports Illustrated* magazine, illustrated by Davis, and an impeccable Elder takeoff on Al Capp's popular strip, entitled "L'l Ab'r."

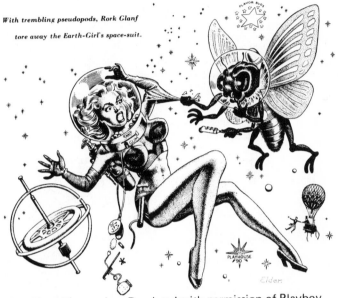

With trembling pseudopods, Rork Glanf tore away the Earth-Girl's space-suit.

©1957 by Trump, Inc. Reprinted with permission of Playboy Enterprises, Inc., successor in interest to Trump, Inc.

Bill Elder parodies science-fiction pulp magazines for *Trump*.

Unfortunately, this noble effort was to last for only two issues, which seems especially regrettable in view of the fact that the problem that led to *Trump*'s end had little to do with the contents of the magazine or even with the public reaction to it. Apparently the decision to fold *Trump* was based on factors operating at a considerable distance from the actual life of the publication. Finances were involved, but only as they reflected certain attitudes in banking circles and certain difficulties in the magazine publication industry. The failure of *Collier's*, once among the most popular magazines in the country, convinced Hefner's bankers that the time was not ripe for expansion of his enterprise, and *Trump*'s demise was the result of a general decline in funds for this sort of investment. Through no fault of its own, *Trump*, despite its merits, never really had a chance to prove itself.

Undaunted, the Kurtzman forces rallied again after a brief interval, producing the first issue of *Humbug* in August 1957. The publishers were Humbug Publishing Company, a redundant title which hid a bold experiment. *Humbug* was owned and published by Harvey Kurtzman and the artists who composed its staff. Despite the tense atmosphere which had killed off *Trump*, this group determined to put its own bank accounts on the line in order to promote the brand of satire to which its members were committed. The devoted staff artists included Elder, Davis, and two new stalwarts, Al Jaffee and Arnold Roth, both of whom had editorial positions. The captionless cartoon sequences of R. Blechman were a regular feature. The price of *Humbug* was fifteen cents, and the size was smaller than a standard comic book, which unfortunately made the magazine difficult to discover on crowded newsstand displays. The printing was black on white, with the addition of one pale color overlay per issue. The overlay was blue, yellow, red or green, and gave to drawings and backgrounds a pleasant, subtle pastel effect which has never been duplicated.

The tone of *Humbug* was set by its title, which of course owed its origin to Charles Dickens' classic cynic, Ebeneezer Scrooge, who, along with his partner Jacob Marley, was occasionally included as a

DANCING. Record players when plugged into TV phonojacks, tuned to wrestling, set fine rock and roll mood.

©1957 by Humbug Publishing Co., Inc.

Advice on mixing media from *Humbug*'s Jaffee.

member of the staff. Scrooge was featured in a drawing by Davis on the cover of the Christmas issue (No. 6), and inside in a version of *A Christmas Carol*, illustrated with unholy zeal by Arnold Roth. This piece distinguished itself by its humorously sympathetic treatment of Scrooge, who emerged as the only sensible character in a cast of sentimental stooges. So with *Humbug*, which stood out by its refusal to respect any thoughtlessly conventional view of the world. What other magazine would use its first issue to present a two-page seminude pinup of Teamster boss Dave Beeck? Readers themselves were occasionally the victims, as in the ninth issue, where the introduction to an article stated: "The following four pages are like nothing you have ever read in a magazine before." The pages were blank.

The magazine had many objects for its satire. Perhaps the principal target was television, which had risen up during the fifties to become a prime unifier—and depressant—of the national consciousness. *Humbug*'s attacks against the tube included not only specific programs but also general trends in programming and viewer reaction. In more than a few of these pieces, the illustrations took on the shape of the television screen. A regular feature was the "Humbug Hero of the Month," chosen by "Scrooge" and "Marley" from public figures who had performed in an outstanding, if not exactly notorious manner. Most of the magazine's material was extremely topical, and, as with the movie and television treatments, had more of an impact when it was first printed than it does today.

Perhaps it also demanded a greater level of awareness than most readers were able to bring. As Kurtzman wrote in the first issue, "We won't write for morons. We won't do just anything to get laughs... We won't sell any magazines." *Humbug* had an extremely devoted following, but seemed to lack mass appeal. As an independent enterprise, it also had some problems getting distribution. The letters column was full of complaints from eager fans who were

Harvey Kurtzman

Al Jaffee

Arnold Roth

Will Elder

Wally Wood

Jack Davis

©1957 by Humbug Publishing Co., Inc.

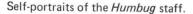
Self-portraits of the *Humbug* staff.

Bill Elder recreates the films of the thirties for *Humbug*. Above: the 1931 Universal production of *Frankenstein*.
Below: the Marx Brothers meet Queen Victoria in an illustration for Alex Atkinson's "Night at the Castle."

unable to get their hands on more than a few issues. After nine issues, *Humbug* increased its size and price to become a standard-sized, twenty-five cent magazine, minus the color tinting. This effort apparently served to confuse confirmed readers without attracting the new ones for which it was intended, and *Humbug*'s eleventh issue was its last.

The most impressive pages in the magazine were the work of Bill Elder, who was achieving a remarkable rapport with Kurtzman. Elder became the prime exponent of the editor's style. His advertising parodies continued to draw blood with their remarkable accuracy, and his movie treatments revealed an authentic gift for caricaturing celebrities. His version of the "all star cast" in "Around the Days in Eighty Worlds" (*Humbug* No. 2) included an array of personalities which grew increasingly unlikely with each addition, resulting in a cumulative effect which was truly staggering. Possibly his finest piece was a four-page version of the classic Boris Karloff horror film, *Frankenstein*, in the seventh issue. The care with which he rendered obscure actors like Colin Clive and Edward Van Sloane showed a certain mad integrity. Probably only a few people even noticed how accurately certain details had been presented, but the artist's devotion was undeniable.

With the demise of *Humbug*, in October 1958,

Kurtzman had again lost a forum for his pungent satire. He rallied with the release of a paperback collection of his own original comics, called *Jungle Book*.

But 1958 also saw the birth of a new magazine which, despite its unlikely title, was to be the foundation for a string of publications that would not only provide Kurtzman with a new, influential, and comparatively long lasting forum, but would also be a major factor in weakening the iron grip of the Comics Code Authority.

The man behind these maneuvers was James Warren, whose first publication, released in 1958, was *Famous Monsters of Filmland*. A Philadelphia advertising man, Warren posed on the cover of the first issue with a pretty model. He was wearing a Frankenstein mask. The subject of the magazine was the history of horror films, and illustrations were provided by stills from the movies. It seemed the sort of thing that would be, at best, a one-shot publication, but Warren persevered, and the magazine is still healthy today, more than a dozen years later. At a time when others were running scared, he had sensed the public's appetite for horror, and moved in with his magazine to fill the gap left by the death of this type of comic book. It had been roughly four years since the death of the great E. C. trio of horror comics.

The editor of *Famous Monsters*, Forrest J. Ackerman, is an expert in the field of the fantastic, and he brought to his work both considerable knowledge and good-natured enthusiasm. His writing kept the tone of the magazine light, employing a humorous touch which found its ultimate expression in horrendous puns. Although this attitude engendered some resentment among those whose attitude toward film is an academic or reverential seriousness, it worked perfectly with a primarily juvenile audience, who apparently felt less awe than affection for the assorted antisocial fiends who stalked through the pages.

Famous Monsters received simultaneous support from two other media sources during its early days, as motion pictures and television spawned a new wave of interest in the same subject. A package of Hollywood's greatest monster movies, labeled "Shock Theatre," was released to nationwide television through syndication, while two film producers, American-International and Britain's Hammer Films, captured large audiences with new films in the same gory category. Thus it was demonstrated quite clearly that there was an authentic and continuing market for material of the blood-curdling variety, despite the moralistic critics who had cut off the comic book supply of horror as though it were an isolated and controllable phenomenon. Eventually Warren would be the man who would crack the Comics Code by publishing new horror comic books, but this move was still some years away.

Meanwhile Warren Publications issued some variations on the *Famous Monsters* style, magazines covering other aspects of motion picture entertainment: *Spacemen, Wildest Western,* and *Screen Thrills Illustrated.* The last had the longest life, and was the most relevant to the subject of comics, as it regularly featured text and photographs documenting the appearance of various comic book heroes in motion picture serials. These included *Superman* (1948), *Atom Man Versus Superman* (1950), *Batman* (1943),

Batman and Robin (1949), *Captain Marvel* (1942). *Spy Smasher* (1942), *Captain America* (1944), and, the last of its type, *Blackhawk* (1952). Also featured were articles on serial adaptations of newspaper comic strip heroes, with special emphasis on Universal Internationals trio of outstanding efforts, *Flash Gordon* (1934), *Flash Gordon's Trip to Mars* (1938), and *Flash Gordon Conquers the Universe* (1939). The fact that these colorful magazines folded, while *Famous Monsters* did not, indicated how solid was the market for horror material.

But Warren was not ready yet to expand his interests in this field. He did, however, inaugurate a title which presented some interesting experiments in the field of comics, and provided a new home for the harried forces of what has been called "Kurtzmania." The first issue of *Help!*, edited by Harvey Kurtzman, was dated August 1960. The title was presumably inspired by the first *Trump*, which featured the word on its cover in one of Kurtzman's typical pleas for support. The magazine was outstanding in its use of photography, its habit of featuring celebrity entertainers, and its introduction of some young cartoonists who would, in a few years, become the nucleus of the underground comics movement.

Help! (subtitled "For Tired Minds") was to achieve a strong impact through the use of covers which featured prominent comedians and television personalities in ludicrous poses. The deciding factor in inducing these individuals to associate themselves with the publication was presumably the respect which Kurtzman had earned as one of the country's most innovative and imitated humorists. Among those who graced the covers of *Help!* were Ernie Kovacs, Jerry Lewis, Mort Sahl, Dave Garroway, Jonathan Winters, Tom Poston, Hugh Downs, and Jackie Gleason. The cover for January 1965 featured four well-known faces in a new guise: a photograph of the long-haired Beatles retouched so that they appeared bald.

The magazine still featured drawing, with the work of Bill Elder and Jack Davis very much in evidence, but what set it apart from previous efforts was a reliance on the photograph as a source of visual humor. Standard items in every issue were movie stills and news photos enlivened by comics-style speech balloons which had the effect of giving the subject a satiric twist. A classic example showed Nikita Khruschev and Fidel Castro locked in a political embrace, while Castro's balloon spouted the message, "Later, you mad fool!" Occasionally the balloons had risque overtones, or the movie stills contained partial nudity. This emphasized the fact that *Help!* was intended for a group older than the usual comic book audience. Never stooping to exploitation, the magazine nevertheless enjoyed a wide latitude in its treatment of the absurdities of our culture.

The most significant use of the photograph in *Help!* took the form of the "fumetti," which had enjoyed wide popularity for some years in Italy. This was the first important American use of the technique which employed photos in sequence, rather than artwork, to tell a story in comic book style complete with speech balloons. The difficulties in creating a piece, which include many of the problems of motion picture production, were brilliantly explored in Federico Fellini's comedy film, *The White Shiek*. Despite the problems, the *Help!* crew produced them regularly, beginning in the third issue with "On the Coney," scripted by cartoonist Ed Fisher. This was a parody of Nevil Shute's tale of nuclear destruction, *On the Beach*, but later pieces abandoned such "adaptations" in favor of strictly original material with a satirical slant. Settings occasionally took the staff as far afield as Mt. Snow, Vermont (for a treatment of ski society), and the Virgin Islands, for a spoof on skin-diving spies. The casts of these fumettis (the translation is "puffs of smoke") were generally unknowns, but included from time to time such recognized talents as Dick Van Dyke, Orson Bean, Tom Poston, Phil Ford and Mimi Hines, Jack Carter, and Henny Youngman. One of the best of these pieces was "Beatsville, U. S. A." (*Help!* No. 6), written by assistant editor Gloria Steinem.

"There's this ball, see? And they throw it. I think the whole thing is a sophisticated type of keepaway."

©1963 by Help Publishing Co., Inc.

Left: Beatniks and baseball from the *Help!* feature "Jack Davis Meets the Mets."
Below: Two panels from a typical *Help!* fumetti. Jane Counter and Bill Bonner appeared in this story by science-fiction writer Algis Budrys from *Help!* No. 23. The problems involved in rephotographing prohibit a more extensive presentation of this unusual comics form.

©1965 by Help Publishing Co., Inc.

Starring humorist Roger Price, the creator of "droodles," this tale seemed to be satirizing bohemian snobbery at a drug-infested gathering, until it was revealed that all the participants were actually undercover agents for various law enforcement agencies. Detective Price, his face registering exquisite dismay, was dragged away by the attractive policewoman he had attempted to warn about his own raid, ready, if a little too late, to become a "beatnik" himself. Another first-rate piece was "Christopher's Punctured Romance" (*Help!* No. 24), in which a tired businessman succumbed to the undeniable charms of his own daughter's shapely "Barbee doll."

Help! also served as an introductory course in the history of humor and satire, as editor Kurtzman searched through the past to reprint some of the finest work achieved by writers and artists of earlier decades. Reprinted in these pages were drawings by pioneers like Bud Fisher, Milt Gross, Winsor

McCay, T. S. Sullivant, H. M. Bateman, Will Eisner and Milton Caniff. Prose from the past included works by such writers as Charles Dickens, H. G. Wells, Saki, and Ambrose Bierce. At the same time it un-

©1965 by Help Publishing Co., Inc.

©1965 by Help Publishing Co., Inc.

©1965 by Help Publishing Co., Inc.

Early work from *Help!*'s "Public Gallery" by fledgling underground cartoonists Lynch and Williamson.

locked the storehouses of the past, *Help!* opened its pages to its readers with the introduction of its "Public Gallery," which solicited original contributions from aspiring cartoonists. Appearing for the first time here was the early work of Jay Lynch and Skip Williamson, who would emerge a few years later as the mainstays of one of the best of the underground comic books, *Bijou Funnies*.

Help! introduced the work of Robert Crumb, the most successful American underground cartoonist, with these studies of Harlem landscapes. Below, right: Crumb views Bulgarian consumers.

Occupying a larger number of pages were Robert Crumb and Gilbert Shelton, who were full-fledged contributors to *Help!* before they became the two most widely known cartoonists of the modern underground movement. Crumb's first appearance was on the letters page for February 1963, where he urged Kurtzman to keep up the good work. The first Crumb cartoons appeared two years later in *Help!* (No. 22, January 1965), where a visit to Harlem produced a group of poignant and evocative sketches. *Help!* No. 25 had him assigned to illustrate his trip to Bulgaria, where the pervasive gloom inspired some somber drawings with ironic captions. More representative of his current production were a pair of pieces about a nameless beast who was a prototype of the later Fritz the Cat.

Gilbert Shelton bowed in November 1962 with an adventure of his ludicrous "superhero," Wonder Warthog. Employing the basic pattern of the Superman story, Shelton originally created "the Hog of Steel" for the *Texas Ranger*, a college humor magazine. This repulsive hero became a *Help!* regular, achieving per-

Help! featured the first national appearances of Gilbert Shelton's ludicrous Wonder Warthog, who appeared (above) as a champion of American industry and (below) defeating a more traditional adversary in "The Return of the Masked Meanie."

haps his finest moments in the broad burlesque encounter with the Masked Meanie, who was eradicated about as thoroughly as possibly by the vindictive Hog. Another adventure concerning a motorcycle race reflected Shelton's early interest in such subjects (which eventually led him to feature Wonder Warthog in *Drag Cartoons*, a comic magazine edited by Pete Millar which was unique for the variations it employed on the single subject of cars and racing).

Beset by difficulties which were manifested in a publishing schedule varying from monthly to bimonthly to quarterly and back again, *Help!* was folded by publisher Warren in 1965, after a run which

gave Kurtzman one of his longest stints as an editor. Kurtzman and Bill Elder then moved on to Hefner's *Playboy*, where they now produce "Little Annie Fanny," a series of comic stories about a voluptuous scatterbrain who has a hard time keeping her clothes on. The slick magazine format provides the same opportunities as did the old *Trump*, with the result that these comics are actually full-color paintings, creating a sense of richness and depth unequalled in the history of the medium. Elder's spectacular work is matched by Kurtzman's unflagging wit, and the only fault to be found with Annie is that she does not appear more often.

THE ENEMY . . . *The first thing a Klansman must learn is that the enemy is often very SUBTLE. He is often able, through Godless Scientific Miracles, to assume any number of HEINOUS DISGUISES in order to gain the unwitting Sympathy of the good and simple people of America.*

In this example from a CASE STUDY, a Communist agitator from the North was able to assume the disguise of a CUTE PICKANNINNY and enroll in a white school where he began to INDOCTRINATE the children in ONE-WORLDISM and unholy MISCEGENATION. He is now on display at the Klan Museum.

Camouflaged as a gentle old nigra man, this INSIDIOUS MEDDLER was brought before a JUST TRIBUNAL. He was convicted of selling DOPE and HEROIN to children and was later sentenced to three years of swimming an Alabama river with 300 pounds of chains.

Many and nefarious are the schemes and PLOTS used to SUCK DRY the economy of the South while fattening the coffers of the JEW NIGRAS for the day when they move to take over the weakened country. The disguise above was found to be so realistic it could not be removed and the agitator had to be shot.

©1965 by Help Publishing Co., Inc.

Terry Gilliam attacks bigotry in a *Help!* article, "Buster, Have You Ever Stomped a Nigra?" which purportedly reproduced a Ku Klux Klan handbook.

Meanwhile, Warren had been hard at work on plans for a new venture. *Famous Monsters of Filmland* had proven to be his most durable publication, and a period of experimentation was inaugurated in 1964 through a series of new magazines to test the market for an adult comic book on the same subject. First the fumetti form was used to produce adaptations of horror films. Speech balloons were added to stills from the movies to produce three separate one-shot magazines which were, in effect, a hybrid of *Help!* and *Famous Monsters.* In November 1964, *Monster World* was introduced. This was a magazine much like its six-year-old predecessor, but it included one special feature, a *comics* adaptation of the 1931 film *The Mummy.* The adaptation did not use photographs but drawings by Russ Jones and Wallace Wood. This was the ground-breaker; horror comics, which had become the testing ground for the medium's freedom from unreasonable censorship, were now in print again.

The final result of these tentative steps was the first issue of *Creepy,* which began as a quarterly black and white comic book in 1965. A color cover by Jack Davis evoked memories of his early triumphs in the field, and the contents revealed a satisfying high level of artistic craftsmanship, including work by some of the best comic illustrators. The original editor was Russ Jones; he was soon replaced by the ingenious Archie Goodwin, who was already writing most of the scripts.

Reproduced here from the first issue of *Creepy* is "Success Story," written by Goodwin and drawn by Al Williamson. This delightful tale crosses the theme of supernatural vengeance with a telling spoof of perennial problems in the production of comics. A number of different jobs go into the successful comic strip or story, and the quest for credit can occasionally degenerate into controversy. Tales like this one have been circulated about more than one famous newspaper cartoonist, although recorded reports of chicanery have never included anything as extravagant as the murder of a trio of overworked assistants. Nevertheless, this is a look behind the scenes of the industry, and one in which the fantastic elements symbolize a level of reality. Included are caricatures of several *Creepy* contributors who will remain mercifully nameless, although resemblances have been noticed to the author, artist, and publisher of "Success Story," an inside joke which passed over the heads of most, if not all, of its readers. One face which can be definitely identified is that of the genial host, Uncle Creepy (drawn here by Davis), who opens and closes the tale.

Starting with the second issue of *Creepy,* Warren began featuring cover paintings by the masterful Frank Frazetta, who had previously displayed his superior skill sporadically in various publications without ever really being identified with any of them. The story he drew for the first issue may have been his last anywhere, for the overpowering glamour of his cover work brought him into greater prominence than had any of his earlier efforts, and his subsequent expansion has been in related fields like paperbound book covers. His strongly structured figures and subtle coloring have made *Creepy,* even at first glance, one of the most visually impressive of comic books.

Although there were muted mumblings in industry

organs by certain Code supporters, *Creepy* somehow got the distribution it needed to become self-supporting. Within a few months, it spawned a companion publication, *Eerie*. The first issue, inexplicably numbered as the second (there was never a number one), went on sale December 28, 1965. The host, Uncle Creepy's cousin Eerie, was as repulsively rotund as his relative was long and lean. Together, the two constituted a united front, employing the same editor (Goodwin) and most of the same artists during the formative period. Despite the tendency of the two figureheads to sneer at each other's offerings, the general uniformity of their efforts was especially emphasized during a period when contributions had slacked off, and the two titles were reprinting some of each other's best early stories.

The uncensored pages which these new comic books offered were an incentive which attracted outstanding talent. Here was the work of established masters, including some, like Johnny Craig (*The Vault of Horror*), who had been absent from the field for a decade. Here, too, were a few "moonlighters" like Steve Ditko (*Spider-Man*), whose success with the superhero school had not dampened his enthusiasm for more fearsome fare. Newcomers were equally welcome, and some soon established themselves as important contributors. The drawing of Tom Sutton, and somewhat later, Billy Graham, were most impressive in this category. It soon became apparent that a high level of performance was being encouraged by the lack of color, which had often been used elsewhere to compensate for weak drawings, or even to obscure good ones. Its elimination led to dramatic experiments in the use of techniques involving heavy brush work, ink washes, and even charcoal. The results constituted a significant advance in exploring the potential of the comic book, and justified editorial assertions that black and white art was often more conducive to the creation of a macabre atmosphere.

Some of the most consistently excellent illustrations in the new Warren comic books have been provided by Reed Crandall, represented here by "The Squaw." Crandall had achieved recognition for his fine work on the Blackhawk series (which was continued by D. C. after the Quality line folded), and he had also contributed numerous pieces to the E. C. line during its last two years. His use of painstaking fine-line shading gives the impression of an etching, and it proved to be most effective in black and white. The style is particularly appropriate for this period piece, adapted from a short story by Bram Stoker, the author of *Dracula*. The story, which originally appeared in *Creepy*, is reprinted from *Eerie* (No. 19, December 1968) to provide two views of Cousin Eerie, whose caustic comments open and close the action.

This tale of feline revenge is distinguished not only by Crandall's skill, but by the parallels between the fate of Hutcheson and the story he tells of the original squaw whom he had killed. The off-scene presence of this character who seems, by implication, to have instilled the cat with something of her own spirit, makes this one of the most telling treatments of the American Indian to appear in comic books. It has been almost impossible to show native Americans with any reality in the mass media; they appear inevitably as either stock villains, spineless stooges, or ridiculously hollow "noble savages." Here the significantly absent ghost of a slaughtered race hovers over the scene of a European torture chamber to exact blood payment from the foolish, fate-defying representative of the white man's senseless cruelty. The comparatively small irresponsibility which brings about Hutcheson's death is a function of the larger failing for which full payment is exacted.

The political implications of "The Squaw" (to say nothing of that pool of blood) were not recognized as acceptable under Code restrictions, which were challenged even more directly by an important but short-lived publication, *Blazing Combat*, a quarterly Warren comic book which bowed in 1965 between *Creepy* and *Eerie*. Also edited and written by Archie Goodwin, *Blazing Combat* offered frank war stories, illustrated by a staff which featured John Severin, Joe Orlando, Gray Morrow, Al Williamson, Angelo Torres, Reed Crandall and Alex Toth. The tales did not feature the easy heroics which had again become standard in comic books, inspired by a system which prohibited any depiction of brutality even if such prohibition meant distorting the truth. In *Blazing Combat*, the horrors of war were emphasized in pieces featuring the major conflicts of American history. Most significantly, this war comic book offered some views of Vietnam, a country where in 1965 our military presence was still being ignored by most of the public. This consideration of Vietnam preceded attention to the war in a number of supposedly more responsible and serious channels of communication.

The story which most honestly explored the futility of the Vietnam adventure was "Landscape," in *Blazing Combat* No. 2. Ignoring the obvious devices of focusing on an American serviceman, or even a member of the Viet-Cong, Goodwin chose as his protagonist a peasant farmer, representing the population which has little to gain from the promises of either side and much to lose from the punishment which both inflict on the land and the people. The progressive destruction of Luong's entire family may seem too pat, but who can say how often such events have actually taken place? Certainly stories of this sort rarely have taken place in comic books, and the graphically detailed violence displayed here by Joe Orlando sets "Landscape" apart as a landmark of conscience in a field where such considerations generally receive only scant attention.

Unfortunately, *Blazing Combat* was dead after four issues. It appears that dealers and distributors who could accept the frightening fantasy of the horror comics were unwilling to present these hard truths about current events. The magazine was not available in large numbers to the public for which it was intended, and could not be continued without unreasonable losses. But despite its short life span, the strength of *Blazing Combat*'s convictions made it one of the industry's finest moments.

Warren's next publication, some three years after the demise of *Blazing Combat*, continued the policy of challenging convention, but in a different area. The appearance of the first issue of *Vampirella* (September 1969) marked an impressive increase in the medium's use of erotically-flavored drawings. Plots continued in the vein of *Creepy* and *Eerie*, interspersing among the terror tales both science-fiction and the form of heroic fantasy adventures referred to as "swords and sorcery" stories. Although the tales did not deal specifically with any sexual activity, they were distinguished by a large number of shapely young women sharing among them a very small amount of clothing. Edited by Bill Parente (who had previously taken charge of its two forebears), this new comic book broke ground by demonstrating that the medium could enjoy at least a taste of the freedom in the area of sexual expression which had become commonplace elsewhere during the same period. By its continued success as the most liberated entry in the field of commercial comics, *Vampirella* is exerting an influence which, in combination with "Little Annie Fanny" and the underground movement, seems likely to break down the whole crippling concept that comic books are exclusively a child's toy, and must be constantly ground down to conform to the controls imposed on children.

Vampirella is a character as well as a title; she not only functions as hostess and the voice of the editor, but appears frequently in her own adventures, drawn by Tom Sutton. A voluptuous vampire, garbed in a brief clinging costume from which the middle is fetchingly missing, "Vampi" hails from the planet Drakulon where, as Forrest Ackerman's origin story explained, the entire population shares her condition. Moving to Earth to avoid a drought which had dried her home's rivers of blood, she has become something of a heroine by virtue of her encounters with less attractive and more menacing monsters. Sutton's claim as her definitive delineator has been occasionally challenged by Frank Frazetta, who painted her for the first cover and has contributed a few more drawings for house advertisements.

Perhaps the finest story to appear in this magazine to date is Wallace Wood's "The Curse" from *Vampirella* No. 9 (January 1971). Wood, who since the Code has worked sporadically for a number of titles, notably the new *Mad*, had demonstrated his devotion to liberalizing comic book contents by publishing eight issues of his own magazine, *Witzend*, a labor of love with miniscule distribution which afforded artists and writers a chance to print material deemed too strong for the mass market. His appearance in *Vampirella* is an impressive fantasy with a dreamlike quality which defies logical analysis. The monstrous hero with no apparent origin, the beautiful maiden and her menacing mother are archetypal figures, part of a cycle of illusion ending in a destruction which may be as false as the creation which brought it about. This is a story which, by suggesting more than it states, creates an authentic aura of mystery, giving the impression that Zara and Arachne may be two sides of the same consciousness, no more real than the images Zorg struggles against before retreating into the primal innocence which his human half had denied him.

The three Warren magazines—*Creepy*, *Eerie*, and *Vampirella*—now edited by the publisher himself, may vary in quality according to the skills of the writers and artists of each particular issue, but they constitute an important opportunity for the medium to grow into its full potential as a sophisticated art form. But, as these comics had in some measure anticipated the wild world of underground comics, another series—Marvel Comics—continued simultaneously to work the lode of the superhero theme and received massive recognition for the variations it mined.

END

ART BY REED CRANDALL/ADAPTATION BY ARCHIE GOODWIN

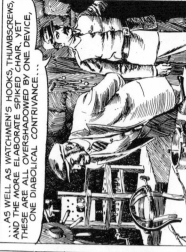

YOU NOW STAND INSIDE ONE OF THE GREATEST MONUMENTS OF MAN'S CRUELTY TO MAN...ALL THE WEAPONS IN THE RACK BEHIND YOU WERE USED BY THE HEADSMEN, THOUGH THEY FAVORED THE DOUBLE-HANDED SWORD...

...AS WELL AS WATCHMEN'S HOOKS, THUMBSCREWS, AND THE MORE ELABORATE SPIKED CHAIR, YET THESE ARE ALL OVERSHADOWED BY ONE DEVICE, ONE DIABOLICAL CONTRIVANCE...

...NEXT WE HAVE THE ACTUAL CHOPPING BLOCKS USED, AND BEYOND THEM THE USUAL COMPLEMENT OF RACKS, BOOTS, COLLARS, ALL MADE FOR COMPRESSING AT WILL...

...THE INFAMOUS *IRON VIRGIN OF NURNBERG!*

I'VE NEVER SEEN AN ANIMAL BEHAVE SO! AS THOUGH SHE COULD KILL YOU ...HER EYES LOOK LIKE POSITIVE MURDER!

'SCUSE ME, MA'AM, BUT I CAN'T HELP LAUGHIN'! FANCY A MAN WHO'S FOUGHT GRIZZLIES AND INJUNS BEIN' MURDERED BY A *CAT!*

AT THE SOUND OF LAUGHTER, THE CAT'S DEMEANOR CHANGED. SHE NO LONGER TRIED TO JUMP OR RUN UP THE WALL...

JEST LIKE A SQUAW!

SEE! THE EFFECT OF A STRONG MAN! EVEN THE ANIMAL IN HER FURY RECOGNIZES THE VOICE OF A MASTER AND BOWS TO HIM!

AS WE MOVED ON OUR WAY ALONG THE ANCIENT CITY WALL, EVERY NOW AND THEN WE LOOKED OVER, AND EACH TIME SAW THE CAT FOLLOWING US...

WE'RE GOIN' INSIDE, MISSY! RECKON YOU CAN GO BACK NOW AN' HAVE A PRIVATE FUNERAL FER THET PORE BUSTED YOUNG'UN OF YOURS!

YOU ARE QUITE FORTUNATE. THE TOWER IS ONE OF NURNBERG'S MOST INTERESTING ATTRACTIONS; TOURISTS FLOCK THROUGH HERE...BUT THIS MORNING, YOU HAVE IT ENTIRELY TO YOURSELVES!

SURE SORRY 'BOUT THET, BUT THE CRITTER'LL GET OVER IT IN TIME!

GUESS THAT THERE'S THE TORTURE TOWER WE BEEN HEARIN' SO MUCH ABOUT!

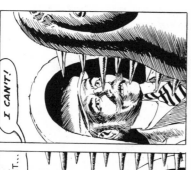
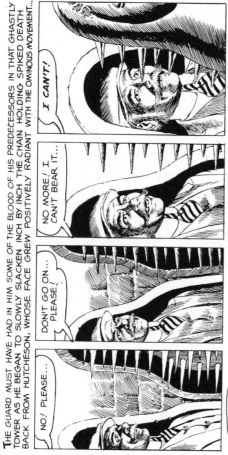

ART BY JOE ORLANDO/SCRIPT BY ARCHIE GOODWIN
Copyright ©1965 by Warren Publishing Co., New York City, N. Y.

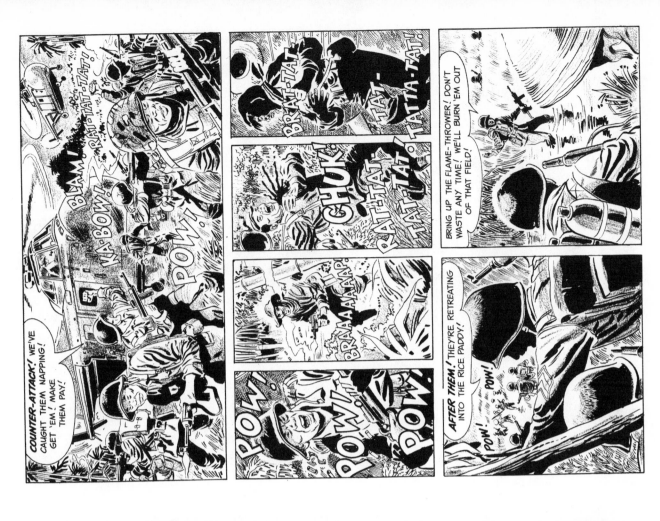

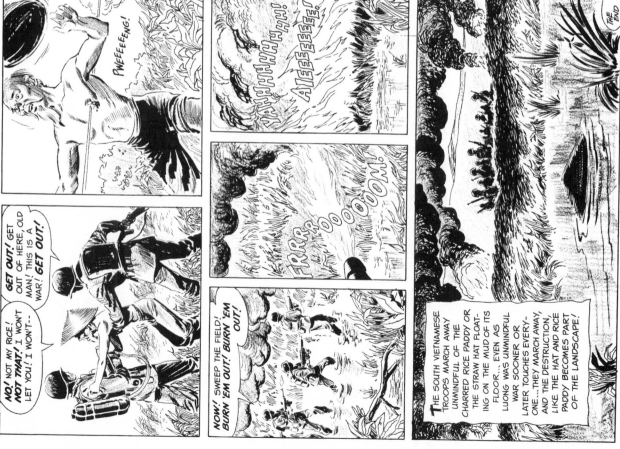

VERY WELL... I WILL DO IT... LET US GO...

ALL YOU NEED FEAR IS THAT YOU WILL BEGIN TO BELIEVE IN HER ILLUSIONS... APPARITIONS... AND I CAN HELP YOU TO AVOID THAT...

THE SWORD IS ENCHANTED... IT WILL KILL A WITCH, NO MATTER WHAT MAGICAL PROTECTION SHE HAS...

I WILL ATTRACT HER WHOLE ATTENTION TO ME, AND YOU WILL STRIKE!

BUT... WHAT CAN I DO? I AM NO WIZARD.

I MUST CALL YOU SOME-THING. HOW ABOUT ZORG? I LIKE THAT! WILL YOU HELP ME, ZORG?

WHAT IS YOUR CURSE? YOU DO NOT SEEM TO BE—

I WILL TELL YOU OF THAT WHEN IT IS TIME... BUT I KNOW THAT IT WAS THE WORK OF THE WITCH ARACHNE, WHO DWELLS NEARBY...

...AND, FEELING THE FEAR GROW IN HIS HEART, AND WITH GREAT MISGIVINGS, ZORG FOLLOWED THE GIRL PAST THE HOLLOW STARE OF THE EERIE SENTINEL...

NO, I AM NOT... BUT I LEARNED SOMETHING OF SORCERY FROM... MY MOTHER...

BUT NOW, NO MORE QUESTIONS! WE WILL SOON BE IN THE LAND OF ARACHNE... SO BE PREPARED...

...FOR MADNESS!

ONE MORE QUESTION, ZARA... ARE YOU A WITCH TOO?

PRESENTLY, THEY EMERGED FROM THE FOREST...

LOOK! UP ON THAT CLIFF!

IT IS A SIGN WE ARE ENTERING THE LAND OF THE WITCH... IT SERVES TO DISCOURAGE INTRUDERS!

HE SOON CAME UPON A CLEARING, AND...

COME... I HAVE BEEN WAITING FOR YOU...

NO, I...

I AM ZARA... YOU DO NOT KNOW YOUR NAME?

BUT... ENOUGH OF THAT FOR NOW... WE SHALL DISCUSS IT ALL WHEN WE HAVE EATEN...

THE WOMAN LED HIM INSIDE, AND BEGAN TO PREPARE DINNER, AS SHE WORKED, SHE TALKED... AND AS SHE TALKED HE BEGAN TO UNDERSTAND...

THEN... SOMEONE HAS SOMEHOW STOLEN MY MEMORY... MY IDENTITY... AND TURNED ME INTO THIS THING THAT I AM...

YES... YOU ARE THE VICTIM OF A SPELL, AN EN-CHANTMENT... AS I AM!

BUT I KNOW WHO IS RESPONSI-BLE, AND IF YOU WILL HELP ME, PERHAPS WE CAN DO SOMETHING!

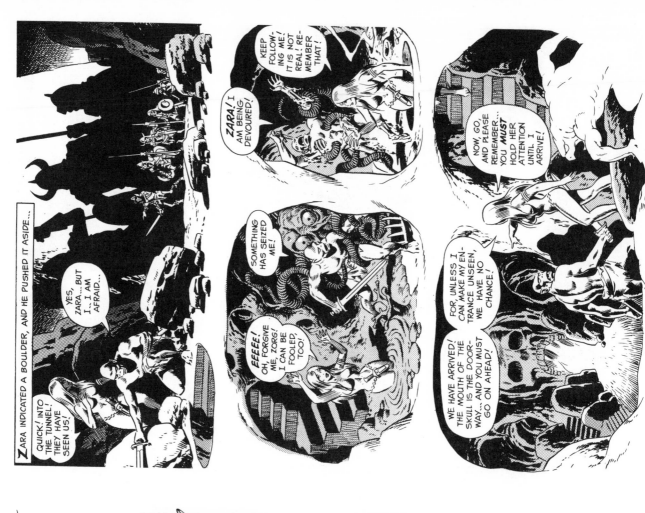

The following color section contains four stories discussed in separate chapters throughout the course of this book. The *Batman* story is mentioned in Chapter Two ("The Birth of the Comic Book"), the *Donald Duck* story in Chapter Three ("Dumb Animals"), the *Witch's Cauldron* story in Chapter Four ("The E. C. Revolution") and the *Sub-Mariner* story in Chapter Seven ("Mighty Marvel").

HOW'S THAT FOR COINCIDENCE! I BUY A MAGAZINE WITH *TWO-FACE'S* STORY IN IT-- AND A MOMENT LATER, HE COMES WALKING BY IN THE FLESH!

THE STRANGE CAREER OF TWO-FACE

HARVEY DENT WITH HIS FACE RESTORED BY PLASTIC SURGERY

HARVEY DENT AS HE LOOKED AFTER THE ACCIDENT WHICH TURNED HIM INTO *TWO-FACE*, THE DESPERATE CRIMINAL!

By

AND SO, A MOMENT LATER...

ALL RIGHT, YOU TWO! STAND WHERE YOU ARE!

HE SCARED ME! BY ACCIDENT, I LIT THE ...XPLOSIVE BEFORE THE CHARGE WAS SET! LET'S GET OUTTA HERE!

RUSHING BLINDLY OUT OF THE STORE, HIS FACE SEARED WITH PAIN, DENT HAILS A CAB WHICH TAKES HIM HOME, THEN, IN THE PRIVACY OF HIS BEDROOM...

LOOK AT ME! THE EXPLOSION HAS UNDONE ALL MY PLASTIC SURGERY--I HAVE BECOME *TWO-FACE !! TWO-FACE !! TWO-FACE !!*

ONE EVENING, IN DOWNTOWN GOTHAM CITY...

LOOK, DEAR! THAT MAN PASSING US! THAT'S HARVEY DENT, THE LAWYER-- THE MAN ONCE KNOWN AS *TWO-FACE!* FUNNY, I WAS JUST READING HIS STRANGE STORY IN THIS MAGAZINE!

SAFE-CRACKERS AT WORK! THERE WAS A TIME-- WHEN I WAS *TWO-FACE--* THAT I WOULD PASS A THING LIKE THIS RIGHT BY! BUT NO! AS A LAW-ABIDING CITIZEN, I MUST ACT!

YES, HARVEY DENT IN THE FLESH---AND COMPLETELY UNAWARE OF THE TWIST OF FATE THAT LIES WAITING FOR HIM JUST MINUTES AWAY!

TV SALES

SO INTENT IS HE ON CAPTURING THE CROOKS, DENT FAILS TO HEED THE DANGER-SIGNS! ALL AT ONCE...

MY FACE! MY FACE! OHHHH!

BOOM!

BATMAN WITH ROBIN

A HIDEOUS FACE, SPLIT DOWN THE MIDDLE! A HEART TWISTED AND WARPED WITH HATE! A BRAIN PACKED WITH DECEIT AND CUNNING! THESE ARE THE TRADE-MARKS OF ONE OF THE MOST AMAZING CRIMINALS EVER TO STALK THE GOTHAM CITY UNDERWORLD-- THE MAN CALLED *TWO-FACE!* NOW HE'S BACK! MORE DANGEROUS THAN EVER! BACK WITH A LUST FOR STRANGE REVENGE! AND FIBER OF THE GALLANT CRIMEFIGHTERS BATMAN AND ROBIN, THE BOY WONDER IN THE STORY CALLED

TWO-FACE STRIKES AGAIN!

BOB KANE

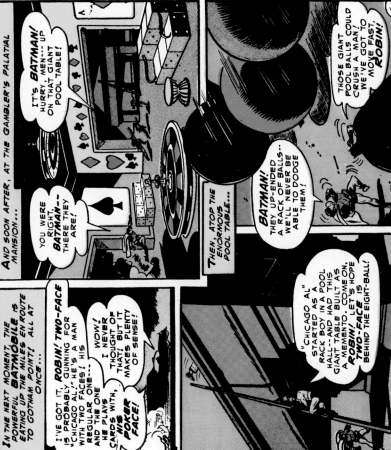

There are only four big estates out on Gotham point! We should be able to figure out which one would interest *TWO-FACE!*

But I know the people living there, and it doesn't make sense! There's Edgar Fanley, the author--Dr. Friend the surgeon--Chicago Al" Garver, the gambler-- and Nick Reo, the restaurant owner! Why would *TWO-FACE* attack one of them?

It's *BATMAN!* Hurry, men--- up on that giant pool table!

You were right, *BATMAN*-- there they are!

Then, atop the enormous pool table...

BATMAN! They up-ended a rack of balls... we'll never be able to dodge them!

Those giant pool balls could crush a man! We've got to move fast, *ROBIN!*

"Chicago Al" started as a pool hall-- and had this giant table built as a memento. Come on, *ROBIN!* let's look behind the eight-ball!

And soon after, at the gambler's palatial mansion...

Shortly afterwards, in the BATCAVE, as the police radio call arrests the attention of BATMAN and ROBIN...

A pedestrian reports seeing *TWO-FACE* and a car full of thugs speeding north on Gotham point road...

Some-one's spotted *TWO-FACE!* come on, *BATMAN!*

In the next moment the powerful BATMOBILE is eating up the miles en route to Gotham point!

I've got it, *ROBIN! TWO-FACE* is probably gunning for "Chicago Al." He's a man with two faces! His regular one-- and the one he plays cards with, *HIS POKER FACE!*

WOW! I never thought of that! but it makes plenty of sense!

Shortly afterwards, in the BATCAVE crime lab...

You see, Dick?? all of *TWO-FACE'S* latest victims had one thing in common-- in a sense they too were men with *TWO-FACES!*

Of course! so that's *TWO-FACE'S* newest wrinkle! He's apparently declared war on all the other *TWO-FACES* in Gotham City!

Now that we know how *TWO-FACE* is working, it narrows the field of possible future victims! We'll compile a list of all people who go through life with *TWO FACES!*

TARANDO--THE CLOWN WITHOUT MAKE-UP.

TARANDO THE CLOWN WITH MAKE-UP.

CHAS. FORD AS HE REGULARLY APPEARS.

CHAS. FORD, IN DEEP SEA DIVER'S HELMET.

ACTOR JOHN BENSON WITHOUT MAKE-UP.

BENSON IN HIS LINCOLN MAKE-UP.

Meanwhile, in his hideout, the bizarre Jekyll-and-Hyde criminal enjoys his initial triumphs!

Yes! I'm taking my revenge on all others whose lives depend on *TWO-FACES!* And now I'm ready to enlarge my operation by hiring a gang. If you're ready, we'll proceed with the interviewing!

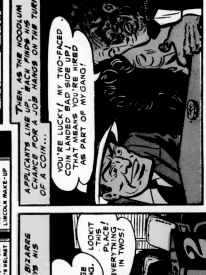

Then, as the hoodlum applicants line up, each finds his chance for a job hangs on the turn of a coin...

You're lucky! my two-face coin landed bad side up! that means you're hired as part of my gang!

Lookit this place! Everything in twos!

Next day, the twin-terrored criminal is ready to strike again!

AHHH! my new two-tone car! just the thing to carry us on our next job against a man with "TWO FACES!"

Say! I just thought of somethin', boss! you know who has two faces? *BATMAN!*

"Chicago Al"-- the big-time gambler?? don't get it! since when does he have two FACES?

Of course! don't you think I *KNEW* that?? the attack against *BATMAN* will be the *CLIMAX* of my crime wave! but first things first! our next victim will be "Chicago Al" Garver!

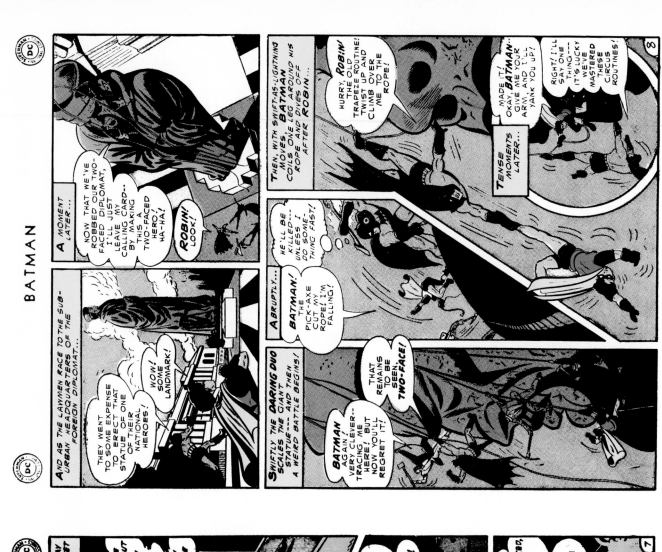

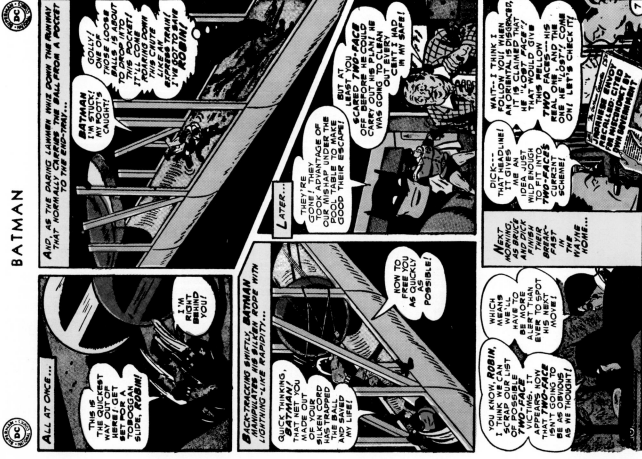

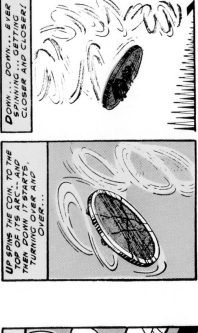

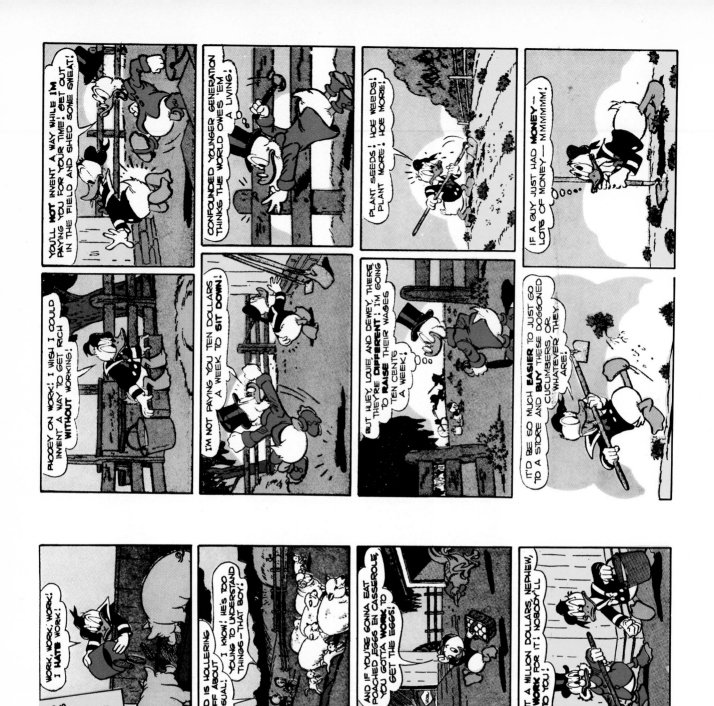

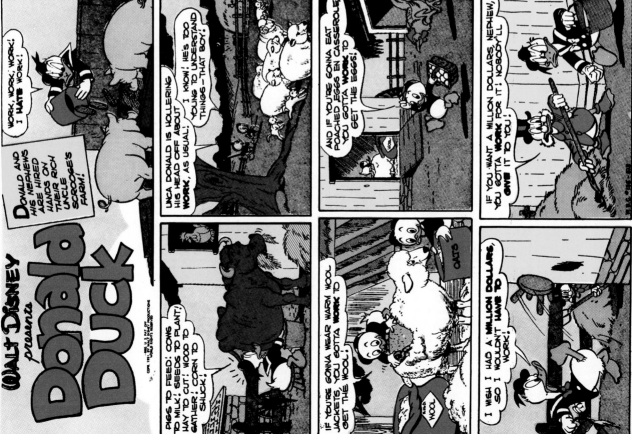

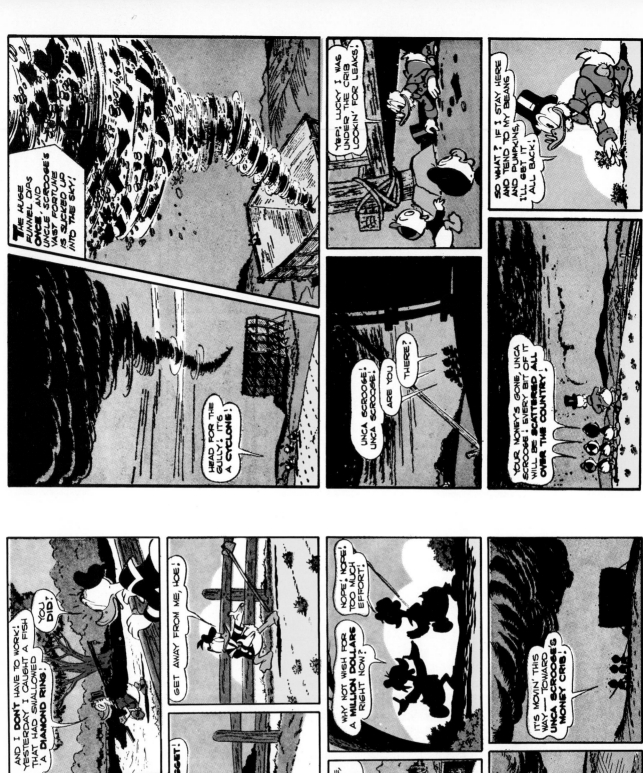

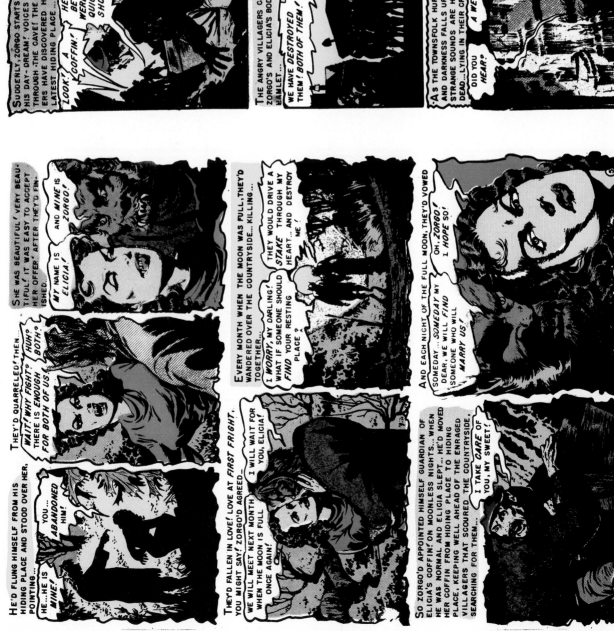

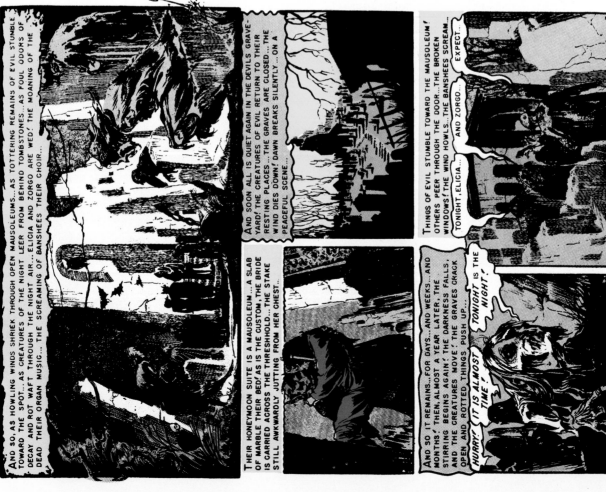

The SUB-MARINER MEETS A NEW ENEMY... FIRE!

CONTINUING OUR SEARCH INTO THE SUB-MARINER'S PAST, TO FIND OUT WHAT MAKES HIM WHAT HE IS --- (WE'VE LEARNED HOW HE CAME TO KNOW THE MEANING OF COURAGE -- HOW HE FIRST DISCOVERED HIS GREAT PHYSICAL STRENGTH -- HOW HE FOUND OUT HE COULD FLY THROUGH THE AIR LIKE A BIRD) -- NOW LET'S LOOK IN ON HIM AS, AGED SIXTEEN, HE JOINS HIS GIRL-COUSIN, NAMORA, AND THE EMPEROR'S STEPSON, PRINCE BYRRAH, ON AN EXPEDITION TO ADMIRAL BYRD'S ABANDONED SETTLE-MENT AT "LITTLE AMERICA" ON THE NORTH RIM OF THE ROSS SHELF ICE IN ANTARCTICA.... F-971

THERE IT IS! LIKE MOTHER SAID -- JUST A WHOLE BUNCH OF HALF-BURIED SHACKS SPREAD OUT ALL OVER THE ICE!

G-GOSH, NAMOR, DO YOU THINK THERE ARE ANY AMERICANS HERE NOW?

DON'T BE SILLY, BYRRAH! CAN'T YOU SEE THE PLACE IS DESERTED?

YOU'RE RIGHT, NAMORA! THERE'S NO ONE HERE-- MAYBE WE CAN LEARN SOMETHING ABOUT HOW AMERICANS LIVE!

COME ON, BYRRAH -- THERE'S NOTHING TO BE AFRAID OF! LET'S TAKE A LOOK AT THOSE BUILDINGS -- WHAT'RE THEY MADE OF, NAMOR?

MOTHER SAYS IT'S CALLED "WOOD" -- A SUBSTANCE THAT COMES FROM SOMETHING THE SURFACE-PEOPLE CALL "TREES" -- WE DON'T HAVE ANYTHING LIKE IT DOWN HERE IN THE ANTARCTIC, ALTHOUGH WE'VE SEEN SOME OF IT ON SHIPS THAT WERE SUNKEN DURING SCIENTIFIC EXPEDITIONS....

WELL, WHATEVER IT IS -- I'M GOING TO FIND OUT WHAT'S INSIDE THIS SHACK!

GEE, THEY DIDN'T EVEN LOCK UP WHEN THEY LEFT!

YOU GO AHEAD, NAMORA -- BYRRAH AND I WILL LOOK AROUND OUTSIDE....

SUFFERIN' SHAD! AMERICANS SURE ARE STRANGE PEOPLE-- WONDER WHAT THESE INSTRUMENTS ARE FOR? AND-- SAY, WHAT'S THIS---? OH-OH!!!

INADVERTENTLY, WHILE REACHING FOR THE PICTURE, NAMORA KNOCKS OVER A METAL CAN OF KEROSENE-- AND IT STRIKES ANOTHER METAL OBJECT AS IT FALLS!!

CLANG!

CLOSE BY, THE SUB-MARINER AND PRINCE BYRRAH WHIRL AROUND IN TIME TO SEE THE WOODEN STRUCTURE ENGULFED IN A SHEET OF FLAME!

GREAT PICKLED PENGUINS! WHAT'S THAT???

YIPE!

SUDDENLY--A BLINDING FLASH! A DEAFENING ROAR, AND--

HELP!!

EEEYII-IY!

BOOM!!

SECONDS LATER, THE NEARLY UNCONSCIOUS GIRL IN HIS ARMS, NAMOR LEADS OUT OF THE FLAMING BUILDING JUST AS ANOTHER TREMENDOUS EXPLOSION ROCKS THE ICE-BOUND SETTLEMENT!

EE-YIPE!

BAM!

NAMORA! NAMORA! WHERE ARE YOU? ARE YOU ALL RIGHT?

YES-- OVER HERE-- BEHIND THE SCREEN! BUT HURRY, PLEASE!

G-GOSH, NAMOR, I DON'T KNOW! I TOOK THE SIDE'S SPLIT OPEN! IT--IT SMELLS GOOD--LIKE FOOD! MAKES ME FEEL HUNGRY, AFTER ALL THE EXCITEMENT!

A MOMENT LATER, RECOVERED FROM THE SHOCK, AND AT A SAFE DISTANCE FROM THE FIRE....

WHAT IN THE NAME OF NEPTUNE HIT ME ??? HEY, NAMORA, WHAT DO YOU SUPPOSE IS IN THIS THING?

PROPELLED LIKE A BULLET FROM THE THUNDEROUS BLAST, A SMALL CYLINDRICAL CONTAINER HITS NAMOR IN THE BACK....

UGH!

AND SO, AFTER THEIR NEARLY TRAGIC EXPERIENCE, NAMOR AND NAMORA REALIZE THE MIRACLE OF FIRE--- THE EVIL AND THE GOOD OF THAT UNPREDICTABLE ELEMENT!

WHATEVER IT WAS THAT DESTROYED THE SHACK MUST HAVE DONE SOMETHING GOOD FOR THIS STUFF!

WELL, WHAT ARE WE WAITING FOR? LET'S TRY IT! MMMM-- GEE, IT'S GOOD! NOT COLD AND TASTELESS LIKE OUR OWN FOOD!

I DON'T KNOW WHAT IT IS, BUT I'M NOT STICKING AROUND TO FIND OUT! COME ON, NAMOR -- LET'S GET OUT OF HERE!

SHE'S TRAPPED! BYRRAH, COME BACK HERE, YOU COWARD! YOU'VE GOT TO HELP ME!

HELP! HELP! HELP!

NAMOR! BYRRAH! I-I CAN'T GET OUT OF HERE!

NO, BYRRAH! WAIT! NAMORA'S IN THERE! SHE MAY BE HURT!

TOTALLY UNFAMILIAR WITH FIRE -- NEVER HAVING KNOWN THIS ELEMENT IN HIS SUB-ANTARCTIC HOME -- THE YOUNG AQUAMAN CHARGES BOLDLY INTO THE ROARING FLAMES!

Y-E-YEOW! WHAT IS THIS STUFF? IT HURTS! I-I DON'T KNOW IF I CAN STAND IT!

NAMOR'S VOCABULARY CONTAINS NO WORDS FOR HEAT OR BURNS, BUT HE KNOWS ONLY TOO WELL THE MEANING OF PAIN!!

CRASH! UGH!

THE FLAMING TIMBER BOWLS HIM OVER--SENDS HIM CRASHING INTO THE ICY SEA! A MOMENT LATER....

OOOO, MY HEAD! I CAN HARDLY SEE --- BUT NAMORA'S STILL IN THAT SHACK!

THEN, TO HIS COMPLETE ASTONISHMENT, HE DISCOVERS THAT HIS WATER-SOAKED BODY IS NOW, INCOMPREHENSIVELY, IMPERVIOUS TO THE INTENSE HEAT!

THE--WATER SEEMS -- TO FORM -- A PROTECTIVE SHIELD -- AROUND ME!

BLINDLY, HE STAGGERS BACK TO THE RAGING HOLOCAUST....

GOT TO-- GET HER OUT-- SOMEHOW!

Chapter Seven: Mighty Marvel

The story of Marvel Comics begins early. In the thirties *Marvel Tales* was one of the pulp magazines published by Martin Goodman. By 1939 the emergence of Superman had thrown the pulp magazine publishing industry into chaos. Publishers who had missed out on the lucrative newspaper funnies reprint sweepstakes in the early thirties were signing up anything that looked like a superhero and had color separations. Goodman commissioned an independent comic studio, Funnies Inc., to put together an original comic book in the fantastic science-fiction vein. The first issue was dated November 1939, and the title was *Marvel Comics* after Goodman's pulp magazine. (Subsequent issues were titled *Marvel Mystery Comics*.) The result was that two of the studio artists created masterpieces.

Carl Burgos dreamed up a character who was supposed to have been produced by the ever-present, well-intentioned scientist. In this case the scientist invented an android who would burst into flame and coincidentally come to life when exposed to oxygen. The good doctor kept him in an airtight case and occasionally would slip him some of the life-giving gas while newspaper reporters recoiled in horror and begged him to destroy his creation before it got out of hand. Of course it wasn't long before the Human Torch escaped, burning everything in his path. Next, a local arsonist conned the Torch into advancing his evil plans. Then, miraculously, the better side of human nature took hold of the Torch and he turned upon his Fagin, destroying the evil operation.

The Torch thus became a good guy, darting around the sky at will—since heat rises, it followed that the Human Torch could fly when lit—and becoming very adept at hurling fireballs that could melt solid concrete. Overnight the Torch became a national favorite. He appeared in *Marvel Mystery Comics* for ten years as well as in his own *Human Torch* comics.

His presence alone would have secured the success

of *Marvel Mystery Comics*, but in a bit of good fortune that befalls comic readers only once in a decade, a second character in that first issue of *Marvel Comics* achieved stardom in his own right.

The Sub-Mariner was the creation of Bill Everett, art director for Funnies Inc. Prince Namor, as the Sub-Mariner called himself, was the ruler of an underwater race dimly related at times to the lost continent of Atlantis. The group lived beneath the frozen waters of Antarctica. There they had no contact with the surface people until one day an American naval fleet showed up and started dynamiting icebergs. Thus threatened, the underwater kingdom sent its leader Princess Fen to seduce the Fleet Commander, while an army of underwater people was supposed to take the fleet by surprise and drive them from the area. Unfortunately, Princess Fen fell in love with Commander McKenzie and her army was routed. Betrayed by McKenzie and great with his child, Princess Fen gave birth to Namor and raised him to avenge her people. (This story is one of the few that contains the actual "birth" of a comic book hero. Most superheroes were normal humans transformed by a freak accident or created by a mad scientist.) Namor was possessed of extraordinary powers even for the underwater race. He could live on land as well as in water, he could fly and his strength was that of the traditional thousand men. He also had blue-green skin when underwater, thanks to a mistake in the original printing. This last quality has appeared and disappeared over the years depending on how the editors felt at the time.

Appearing together in *Marvel Mystery Comics*, the Torch and the Sub-Mariner were a compelling duo. Their respective premises complemented each other nicely. Personifying the opposing elements of fire and water, their personalities were quite different as well. The Torch was an outcast, a horror who was always trying to belong. His enthusiasm and flammable nature caused many to brand him a menace. The Sub-Mariner, on the other hand, was a sworn enemy of the human race. On several occasions he even gained the upper hand. However, he was a being of very rigid principles and would never accept a victory that was not totally his. In later years he would even fight on the side of the surface people against a greater foe, causing other superheroes to give him grudging admiration.

It did not take long for Burgos and Everett to hit upon the idea of staging battles between the Torch and the Sub-Mariner. Such a battle was a major event and today the original comics containing these battles are revered as collectors' items.

As the war clouds over Europe and Asia drifted toward the United States, Goodman's Timely line of comics produced another character that would ultimately reach beyond the confines of comic books and become a national institution. Captain America, originated by Jack Kirby and Joe Simon, started out as frail Steve Rogers. A certain Professor Reinstein was experimenting with a serum that would turn ordinary men into superb mental and physical specimens (for the war effort of course). As is so often the case in comic books, he got to try it only once, on Steve Rogers—and just in time, because an enemy agent got wind of the formula and tried to steal it. In the ensuing adventure Steve used his new abilities to thwart the spy but not before his uniqueness was insured by the murder of the professor and the destruction of the formula. Steve realized it was his duty to devote his life to destroying the evil forces that threatened the country. As Captain America, clad in a red, white and blue costume and brandishing a bullet proof shield, he struck terror into the hearts of spies, saboteurs and fifth columnists everywhere.

Like all good Americans of the time, Steve Rogers enlisted in the army. During the day he was just another G. I., but at night and on weekends he would don his Captain America outfit and battle the agents of the Axis. One day a small lad named Bucky Barnes inadvertently learned Steve's secret. Thereupon Bucky was provided with smaller red, white and blue suit and he served Captain America much as Robin served Batman. Soon Bucky became nearly as popular as Captain America himself and as a result he was featured in his own comic, *The Young Allies*.

In many ways this title was the predecessor of the whole genre of kid gang stories that would become a major force in comics. Bucky's cohorts, with the exception of Toro, a younger version of the Torch, were "Our Gang" types—Knuckles, Whitewash, Jeff, and Tubby. The effect was that no longer did a kid have to dream of becoming a superhero when he grew up. Thanks to the wartime emergency youthful applicants were being accepted. The Timely organization further played on the desire of young readers to participate in the action by forming Captain America's Sentinels of Liberty. In full-page ads Captain America practically ordered kids to send their dimes for Sentinel badges and membership cards. Young readers responded in the hundreds of thousands, and America won the war. This badge plays a pivotal role in the vintage Captain America story, "The Vampire Strikes," which first appeared in summer, 1942. This tale, reprinted here, is a typical production of the World War II era at Timely. The same comic book provided the prose piece "The Man in the Moon," a somewhat chauvinistic piece of science-fiction written by a Timely editor who would later become one of the country's most popular authors: Mickey Spillane.

The triumvirate of the Human Torch, the Sub-Mariner and Captain America were the backbone of the Timely empire. Besides appearing in their own magazines and *Marvel Mystery Comics*, they also showed up in *All-Winners Comics, All-Select Comics,* and *U. S. A. Comics.* The three *were* Timely comics, and except for a few heroines Timely introduced in the late forties, no one else mattered.

There were two main differences between the Timely books and those of their major competitor, Superman—D. C. First, the Timely heroes were not nearly as omnipotent as Superman. Captain America could not fly and was not immortal. Superman had superhuman powers while Captain America's powers were merely super. Sub-Mariner and the Torch had powers beyond those of mortal men but not in the great abundance of Superman. They had to set up a situation where their special abilities could be brought to bear. In Superman stories there is no doubt that Superman is going to win. His main task is figuring out who to punch. It was easier to keep coming up with interesting stories for the Timely heroes because they had more limited powers.

The second and more important unique quality of the Timely comics was their visual flash. Superman—D. C. comics contained simplistic and often understated artwork, while Timely comics were an explosion of color and forms in motion. The Timely books were lurid in a nonsexual way. Before he created Captain America, Jack Kirby worked at Fox Publications for Will Eisner. Eisner, who created the Spirit, is generally given credit for adapting cinematic techniques to the comics. Kirby brought this knowledge with him to Timely. The combination of their pulp heritage and their exciting layouts made Timely comics among the best during the forties.

But when the Second World War ended, the Timely formula faltered. By 1950 it was all over: *Captain America* folded in 1949, the Sub-Mariner and the Human Torch had slipped into oblivion a few months earlier, and Goodman folded his Timely banner.

Soon thereafter, Goodman started publishing under the Atlas logo. Some of the Timely people, notably Bill Everett and Stan Lee, continued to work for him. They revived the Torch, Sub-Mariner and Captain America for a while during the early fifties but with limited success. Bill Everett's short piece, "The Sub—Mariner Meets a New Enemy . . . Fire" is reproduced here from the June 1955 *Sub-Mariner* as an example of an artist's style which was considerably more sophisticated than it had been during its most popular period. Then, with the institution of the Comics Code, Goodman, like most publishers, turned away from the characters and titles of the past. He settled into publishing a formula of science-fiction and mystery stories which were free enough from sex and violence to win the Code's seal of approval. Although Goodman published these books through a number of publishing companies (Atlas, Vista, 20th Century Comic Corp.), they were a product of a common art staff.* This staff was the beginning of the group that would later produce what has been called the "Mighty Age of Marvel."

The Atlas comics of the fifties were not very inspiring, a fact that was reflected in their erratic publishing schedule. Except for the Sub-Mariner and the Torch in the pre-Code early fifties, Atlas comics had no continuing characters. The story lines compared unfavorably with similar comics published by E. C. No doubt the Code kept the writers from getting very far-out. The artwork, on the other hand, was sometimes exceptional. One example is a story in *Mystery Tales* (No. 46, October 1956) drawn by Al Williamson in his neo-Alex Raymond style. As the fifties dragged to a weary conclusion, work by Captain America's creator Jack Kirby appeared in Goodman's current titles, *Strange Tales, Tales of Suspense, Journey into Mystery,* and *Tales to Astonish.*

Stan Lee had become an editor for Atlas during the fifties. In 1961 he launched two new titles that featured Kirby's artwork. *Amazing Adventures* and *The Fantastic Four,* and the Mighty Age of Marvel was begun. The latter title is still appearing today and recently celebrated its 100th anniversary issue.

The Marvel superhero formula owes a lot to the Comics Code. One of the difficulties in creating superhero comics lies in developing villains worthy of the heroes. When an interesting villain is dreamed up, the tendency is to keep him around. However, the Comics Code requires that good triumph over evil and that the villains be punished for their crimes. In other words, the bad guy gets disposed of in the last scene. There is a literary device almost as old as serialized fiction itself whereby the antagonist is treated as no more than a threat to the established order and does no irreversible damage. That is to say, in his bid for power he destroys no vast amounts of property and he kills nobody. If the villain took over, we would all be in trouble, but when the hero blocks his attempt all is well and the universe is no worse for the struggle. This device was in common usage in comics well before the inception of the Code. Batman and Superman both faced a number of villains who would escape at the end of a story only to return again. This was the device that *Mad* satirized, and that E. C. undercut in its horror and science-fiction comics. The Code restored the device and Marvel perfected it.

Virtually every antagonist in Marvel superhero comics escapes with his life at the end of a story. In fact, were a reader not conditioned by other fictional stereotypes, he might have trouble telling the superheroes from the supervillains. In Marvel comics the same character may be a protagonist in one comic and the antagonist in another. Blurring the boundaries between good and evil enables Marvel to portray action and conflict for its own sake, but physical conflict is only part of the story. In order to keep the readers coming back for more, the character confrontations are subordinated to the personal situations of the characters. Each character has his own concerns that remain with him from story to story, and it is with these concerns and not the physical conflicts that the reader identifies. No matter what hero the reader follows, eventually he will experience a vicarious defeat or two, and thus get a taste of man's fallibility. Conversely, a reader who identifies with a villain will one day find he has backed a winner. Utilizing this new twist Marvel Comics rose from relative obscurity to a strong second place in the comic industry.

It all really started with the Fantastic Four. They were created when Reed Richards, his fiancee Sue Storm, her brother Johnny, and Reed's ex-college chum Ben Grimm were exposed to a healthy dose of cosmic rays. The accident affected each of them differently. Reed's body became completely elastic just like Plastic Man of an earlier era. Sue became able to make herself invisible and project force fields with her mind. Johnny became a slightly more introspective version of the Human Torch. Ben Grimm got the worst of it, changing into the Thing. As such he weighs half a ton, has orange scaly skin, packs the wallop of a pile driver, and is generally not very satisfied with his lot. Whenever things get slow Reed works on a formula to return the Thing to his former state, but the reversion is never permanent. The Fantastic Four are better set up than most superheroes. Their headquarters fill the entire Baxter Building which houses all of Reed's scientific paraphernalia and their living quarters. The style of this supergroup (along with a review of their origin) is exemplified by "A Visit with the Fantastic Four," reprinted here from *Fantastic Four* No. 11 (February 1963).

Amazing Adventures, which preceeded *The Fantastic Four* by six months and thus gained the distinction of being the first Marvel comic, was not immediately successful. The first six issues featured Dr. Doom, drawn by Jack Kirby. The series did not catch on, and when Kirby was switched over to *The Fantastic Four*, Dr. Doom left *Amazing Adventures* to become the Fantastic Four's primary adversary. Issues seven through fourteen of *Amazing Adventures* had no continuing characters, but in issue fifteen (the title had now become *Amazing Fantasy*), Stan Lee collaborated with Steve Ditko and the Amazing Spider-Man appeared. According to Stan Lee, the public reaction was fantastic. *Amazing Fantasy* was discontinued and the first issue of *The Amazing Spider-Man* (March 1963) was published, retelling the origin of Spider-Man.

Peter Parker was a typical teenage high school student who lived with his aunt and uncle. One day Peter was bitten by a radioactive spider, and he found that he suddenly possessed spider powers, which consisted of great strength and agility and a sixth sense which warned of approaching danger. Peter designed web shooting devices and a spiderish-looking costume with the idea of breaking into show business. Unfortunately during his first performance, a burglar killed his uncle. Enraged, Spider-Man swung around the city on his webs until he found and apprehended his uncle's murderer.

Unlike most characters who are blessed with super-powers, Peter was at a loss to know what he should do. For one thing, Peter was still very young. He still had to finish high school and he wanted to go to college. Even more pressing, his aunt was nearly destitute now that his uncle was dead. In a subsequent issue he toyed with the idea of putting his powers to evil use but decided instead to give show business one more try. He drew a large audience but nobody would cash the check he received from the promoter. As one bank teller put it, "Don't be silly! *Anyone* can wear a costume! Do you have a Social Security card, or a driver's license in the name of Spider-Man?"

The perennial problems of Peter Parker (Spider-Man).

Although Spider-Man slowly became one of society's leading lone crime fighters, Peter Parker continues to have an identity problem. He manages to eke out a living by selling action photos of Spider-Man to Jonah Jameson whose newspaper, *The Daily Bugle*, attacks Spider-Man as a menace. Being called away to battle crooks keeps Peter from having any kind of social life. He has fallen for several young ladies, but with the exception of a certain Mary Jane, they all have turned cool the first time more pressing engagements forced Peter to stand them up. Invariably each issue of *The Amazing Spider-Man* leaves Peter having narrowly avoided personal disaster and facing an uncertain future. Meanwhile, college kids everywhere were starting to pick up on him.

In their September 1965 issue *Esquire Magazine* noted that Spider-Man was as popular in the radical sector of American universities as Che Guevera. Many responded to the incredible paranoia that filled Peter's life. Political activists shared his feelings towards the straight press. Everyone understood his constant poverty. In issue six Spider-Man spends several pages trying to figure out how to raise the bus fare to get to where the bad guy is. Peter was learning that becoming more powerful raised more complications than solutions. Perhaps the college students were finding out the same thing. In a very real sense Spider-Man exploded the Superman myth for good.

Unquestionably, Stan Lee had come up with two important successes, but he was not content. Between the premier issues of *The Fantastic Four* and *The Amazing Spider-Man*, Stan Lee and his staff developed permanent characters for the other Atlas titles. Thor, a mythical Norse god-warrior with a magic hammer, started appearing as a monthly feature in *Journey into Mystery* (August 1962). Ant-Man made his first appearance in *Tales to Astonish* (January 1962). Johnny Storm, the new Human Torch from the Fantastic Four, was pressed into double service as he began his own feature in *Strange Tales* (October 1962). The drawing for these stories was divided between Atlas staff members Dick Ayers and Jack Kirby, whose giant machines and exploding buildings had become a Marvel trademark. He also drew a fourth new character called the Hulk, a green version of the Thing with a Jekyll/Hyde nature. Unlike the Thing he keeps changing back to his human form, nuclear scientist Dr. Banner, who is less than thrilled by the whole business. Lee felt that the Hulk was strong enough to carry his own magazine, and the first issue of *The Incredible Hulk* was published in May 1962. Lee made one more move during this period which was indicative of things to come. Issue four of *The Fantastic Four* featured the Sub-Mariner as the villain. In later years it became standard Marvel policy to have new (and revived) characters do guest shots in other characters' strips before they got their own feature or book.

In 1963, Lee put everything together. For the first time, all the comics he was editing bore the now familiar Marvel logo on their covers. He started publishing letters from the readers in each of the comics and instituted the forerunner of the Mighty Marvel Checklist. The Checklist gives a rundown on all the other Marvel comics out the same month. All guest heroes and villains are duly noted, and readers get enough of the plot to whet their appetites.

On the superhero front, Iron Man, drawn by Don Heck and the omnipresent Jack Kirby, became the resident hero of the remaining Atlas magazine, *Tales of Suspense* (March 1963). Besides *The Amazing Spider-Man*, three more completely new titles were started in 1963. *Sgt. Fury and His Howling Commandos* (May 1963)—"the war comic for people who don't like war comics"—featured artwork by the team of Kirby and Dick Ayers and became an immediate best seller. There were two new super-group comics, *The Avengers* and *The X-Men* (both September 1963). The former was like the *Justice Society of America* (D. C.) in that it featured characters from other Marvel comics who banded together to fight really big menaces. *The X-Men*, drawn at first by Kirby, starred a group of teenage mutants assembled by Professor Xavier, himself a mutant. Each member of the group has a super power. These powers are distributed quite differently among the X-Men; for example the brains of the outfit, Professor Xavier, is bound to a wheelchair. The Professor, Cyclops, Iceman, Angel and Marvel Girl combat threats to humanity from the Brotherhood of Evil Mutants and other mutant phenomena which the atomic age has brought upon us all.

There were a few setbacks in 1963 along with all the triumphs. *The Incredible Hulk* folded due to lack of support but Lee soon found a home for him with *The Avengers*. Ant-Man wasn't helping the sales of *Tales to Astonish*, so Lee changed the entire premise of the strip—with two letters! In November 1963 Ant-Man became Giant-Man. They didn't even have to change his costume. They just drew him bigger.

Meanwhile *The Fantastic Four* was selling fantastically well. Fans were haunting second-hand magazine stores for back issues, and soon dealers were asking extraordinary prices for the first issue, and getting them. A giant-sized *Fantastic Four Annual* was brought out for twenty-five cents, reprinting the origin of the group from the first issue. Today that annual will cost a collector ten dollars, and it is not likely that one could buy that first issue for any price.

If it sounds like Stan Lee was running the world of the Marvel heroes according to a "master plan," he was. Every new character, every new title, even every guest appearance ("crossover") was designed to draw the reader further into "Marvelmania." But for all the planning, not all the successes were anticipated. Somehow *Strange Tales* became the insiders' Marvel comic. Lee decided to add a second feature to supplement the Human Torch, and so Dr. Strange started his run in the tenth issue of *Strange Tales* (July 1963), from which his first adventure is reproduced here. Dr. Strange *was* strange; unlike the other Marvel heroes he never punched anyone. Instead he cast spells and entered weird dimensions drawn by Steve Ditko. There can be little doubt that much of the "psychedelic art" that was to emerge from the West Coast two years later owed something to the vistas explored in the Dr. Strange pages. Under the leadership of the Ancient One, a man of endless arcane knowledge, Dr. Strange battled obscure menaces from metaphysical planes unknown to uninitiated mortals. The fact that Dr. Strange bore the title of the comic book even though he was the second feature, somehow added to the mystique. Even some of the Torch stories were strange. *Strange Tales* No. 14 (November 1963) revived Captain America, but as a bad guy. As it turned out it was not really Captain America but the Torch's old enemy, the Acrobat. But in the meantime readers saw many pages of the Torch versus what looked like the World War Two hero; shades of the old Timely era with a new twist. At the end of the story, Lee could not quite contain himself and wrote: "You guessed it! This story was really a test! To see if you too would like Captain America to return! As usual your letters will give us the answer!"

As Lee had suspected, the fans did want the Captain back. He had not been forgotten; quite the opposite. One of the first orders of business for 1964, then, was to give him a job with the Avengers. Later that year he got his own feature in *Tales of Suspense* (November 1964). The Hulk, who by this time had quit the Avengers, got his own feature in *Tales to Astonish* (October 1964).

Essentially, Marvel Comics held its own during 1964. Only three new titles were published that year and two of them were once-a-year annuals. The success of the previous year's *Fantastic Four Annual* prompted a second number and *Spider-Man Annual* as well. (The origin of Spider-Man was not printed in that annual. Instead, it appeared in the twenty-five cent priced *Marvel Tales* along with the reprinted origin tales of the Hulk, Ant-Man, Giant-Man, Sgt. Fury and Iron Man, whose own comics were now bringing good prices on the back-date market.) The third new title of the year was a kind of multiple revival—*The Daredevil*. First of all, from 1941 to 1951 Daredevil had starred in a comic book published by Lev Gleason. But Lee's *Daredevil* gave readers a double-barrel of nostalgia. Not only did the new character have the same name as a legendary figure from comics history, but now he was drawn by a

couple of artists from the era of E. C. comics, Wallace Wood and Joe Orlando. Mostly what readers got in 1964 was every character doing lots of crossovers in an attempt to get the reader to buy both the character's magazine and the one he was appearing in. Guest characters were expected to refer to their most recent escapades, whereupon Lee would document the name and number of the comic where the previous adventure took place. Besides the possibility that they might sell a few more comics, these notations also served as a key for anyone tracing the exploits of a character through stacks of back issues. No doubt many of the writers and artists at Marvel itself have made use of this key many times when memory became hazy.

In 1965, when *Esquire* discovered the Spider-Man on campus and some of the beautiful people discovered Marvel comic books, Lee tightened his grip on his followers and channeled their enthusiasm by forming the Merry Marvel Marching Society. Unlike Captain America's Sentinels of Liberty, no good reason was given for joining the M. M. M. S. The ads practically admitted that the stuff which would be sent for a dollar was useless, but in 1965 the hot phrase was "put-on," and there was a rush to become Merry Marvel Marching Society members. Soon Marvel started promoting more useful items like T-shirts and stationery. In the past, comic book companies had licensed their characters out to toy and clothing manufacturers. Then, during the late fifties and early sixties, *Mad* developed mail-order sales of Alfred E. Neuman stuff into a profitable sideline. Lee applied the same process to his line of comics. The M. M. M. S. was promoted by devoting a page to its activities, which appeared simultaneously in all the Marvel publications. It worked out so well that in December a second "house page" was added.

The new page was called the Marvel Bullpen Bulletin (the Bullpen is where the artists, inkers and letterers work). This page is where Stan Lee takes hold of his readers. Or as he puts it: "Face front! Here's a whole kaboodle of news and gossip straight from the Bullpen to you!" The Mighty Marvel Checklist, which until then had appeared on the letters page, was moved to the Bullpen page and the rest of the space was devoted to items purportedly written by Lee about Marveldom in general. New artists are given full billing in each comic (Kirby had gotten tired of pencilling most of the strips and so other artists were being introduced), and Lee often announces in advance when changes are to be made. Readers are encouraged to write often and voice their opinions on artists and characters. The general results of these responses are announced along with any other considerations which help to determine the functioning of the Marvel empire. There is also a great deal of half-serious chest-thumping. Every favorable comment on Marvel comics from the remotest media branches is faithfully recorded.

The year 1965 set the pattern for things to come. No new protagonists were introduced as such, but the line continued to grow. Introducing a new comic book or even a new feature obviously entails a fair amount of risk. Starting in 1965, new titles had to contain a large quantity of familiar material, and new characters had to go through an initial grinding routine of guest appearances. Two features were changed that year. Sub-Mariner, who had made numerous guest villain and good-bad guy appearances, replaced Giant-Man in *Tales to Astonish* No. 70 (August 1965). Gene Colan was the first illustrator of the new series; eventually Bill Everett drew some of the stories, resuming a job he had created twenty-five years earlier. The second change involved the closest thing to a new hero that would come out of Marvel for two years, "Nick Fury, Agent of SHIELD," which replaced the Torch and the Thing in *Strange Tales* No. 135 (August 1965). Actually Nick was Sgt. Fury from *The Howling Commandos* comic, with the difference that the Commando stories were set in the past and Fury had graduated to the contemporary SHIELD. The SHIELD feature has an unmistakable James Bond flavor but with gimmicks and machines that are more incredible. Kirby (of course) did the first story and in early issues he alternated with John Severin from the old E. C. staff.

The appearance of Nick Fury in *Strange Tales* put him side-by-side with Dr. Strange. There was virtually no similarity between the two features; in fact the implied political premises of the two strips could not have been more different. Stoned hippies who grooved with Dr. Strange (he lived in Greenwich Village) might have been appalled by the violence of Nick Fury. Presumably the red-blooded kids who dug Nick Fury found Dr. Strange a trifle gay. At any rate the unstated rivalry of the two features carried over to the artists. Each new recruit from the Bullpen would pore over Kirby's Nick Fury originals and employ visual pyrotechnics of flying flesh and infernal weaponry in an attempt to match by contrast the superbly cool style of Ditko's Dr. Strange.

Ditko left Marvel in 1966. After some shifting around Bill Everett took over Dr. Strange for a while and drew it even better. An extremely important addition to Marvel was made by the introduction of a new illustrator, Jim Steranko, who began drawing Nick Fury. A former magician and escape artist, Steranko at first worked very closely with Jack Kirby, who did rough layouts of the story for Steranko to complete. By March 1966 the artwork was all being handled by Steranko, and even the dullest of readers could sense that something new was happening.

Marvel had always been willing to experiment artistically. More than once photographic backgrounds had been employed. Page layouts were not tied to any standard number of panels. A large number of small panels might be used to focus on a change taking place over a very short period of time. Or huge panels would be used to portray violent confrontations between battling groups. Steranko expanded these devices further. But what set his work apart was his use of color. Operating on the "less is more" premise, he would sometimes drop one or more colors from a panel or page for emphasis. With each passing issue Steranko's efforts became more and more innovative. Entire pages would be devoted to photo collages or drawings which ignored panel boundaries and instead worked together on planes of depth. The first pages—the so-called splash panels—of each story became incredible production numbers similar in design to the San Francisco rock posters of the period.

By 1968 *Strange Tales* was doing so well that Nick Fury was moved into his own comic book and Dr. Strange took over *Strange Tales*. Steranko did four issues and seven covers for the new *Nick Fury* and then moved over to *X-Men* for two and a half issues. In his later Nick Fury stories Steranko had begun to inject a bit of sex into his drawings. Females had been present in Marvel comics, but up to this point with a few exceptions their anatomy was represented rather than rendered. Nick Fury's girlfriend and co-agent Val was another story. Her inspired anatomy was reminiscent of the glorious past of characters like Sheena and Phantom Lady. Steranko's move from *Nick Fury* to *X-Men* signalled a further development. Switching from heroines to villainesses, his work began to take on bizarre overtones. In *X-Men* No. 50 the evil Mesmero transformed Lorna Dane, mutant groupie and his acknowledged daughter, into the Queen of the Mutants. As such she had all the characteristics associated with the dominant woman: amazon figure, hard-edged facial features and a confining but revealing costume, to which Steranko added green hues. The effect was to soften the image slightly while injecting a feeling of weirdness.

After his work on *X-Men*, Steranko did three issues of *Captain America*. Not surprisingly he came up with a new green villainess, Madame Hydra, a most imposing representation of the dominant female, complete with green lips. Steranko's three issues of *Captain America* are probably the finest examples of his work, and will no doubt have a great impression on the cartoonists of the future. More than any other artist he typified the renaissance in comics brought about by Marvel.

Steranko has done only two more pieces for Marvel since the *Captain America* issues, one love story and the piece reproduced here, "At the Stroke of Midnight," from the first issue of the mystery title

Love story comic books have been standard fare since the early days when the industry adapted pulp magazine formats. This stylish effort from Marvel's *Our Love Story* is the work of the innovative artist Jim Steranko, to date his last effort for the company.

Tower of Shadows (September 1969). The unique layout of this story won it the best short story of the year award from the Comic Art Fans and Collectors organization. Recently Steranko has been working on a history of comic books. Volume One of *History of Comics* appeared in 1970 and presented information on newspaper strips, pulp magazines, and the early work of the D. C. and Marvel companies.

Steranko's work had proved that comic books could portray females as sensuous, alluring figures and still stay on the good side of the Comics Code. Lee was quick to press the advantage, and a larger element of sexuality was added to the Marvel lineup. Love comics, although theoretically put out for female readership, have often been used as furtive pin-up magazines. Lee seized on this practice and released two new love comics in 1969. *Our Love Story* is a straight heart-throb comic book designed strictly for girls, but *My Love* is quite frankly aimed at a mixed audience. As Lee said on the Bulletin page, "You don't haveta be hung-up on heart-throbs, but if you like to look at gorgeous gals—this is the place to find 'em Charley"; *My Love* was for "everyone who loves to look at groovy chicks—and who doesn't?"

But the two most exciting girls in the Marvel line are not in love comics. They are Medusa and the Black Widow. Medusa is one of the Inhumans, and has magic red hair. She used to appear frequently in *The Fantastic Four* because her sister Crystal had become a part-time member of that group. Medusa and her royal family of Inhumans did a number of the usual guest appearances and then became the second feature in *The Mighty Thor* (formerly *Journey into Mystery*). Currently they are appearing in the newly resurrected *Amazing Adventures*. Clad in a maroon leotard with matching tights and boots, with her magic tresses flowing at her ankles, Medusa personifies the young, natural woman of the seventies. Her soft outline and majestic beauty are backed up by an iron will and a determination to find peace for her race of freaks.

Sharing *Amazing Adventures* with the Inhumans is the deadly Black Widow, female counterpart to Spider-Man. She got her start as a guest villainess in *Tales of Suspense* No. 52 (April 1964). At that time she was a Communist spy. Over the years she broke away from the party and became a force for good. For a while she roamed Marveldom in a costume reminiscent of Harvey Comics' Black Cat. Eventually her left-wing upbringing was put to better use, and she has lately taken to fighting realistic oppressor-of-the-people types. She helps young Puerto Ricans clean up police corruption and saves young hippies from organized crime. Her own costume is a one-piece black jumpsuit.

The increased sexual awareness in some of the comics is simply an indication that Marvel is aiming those comics at older readers. There is a limit, however, to what the Comics Code Authority will allow in any comic book. Rather than fight the Code on the issue of female nudity, Marvel recently expanded into the field of black and white comic magazines. Lee put it this way: "For those of you who've wondered when we'd break with tradition and enter the next phrase of comic book presentation—namely, publications for the more adult reader, in illustrated panel form—you need wonder no longer . . . *Savage Tales* No. 1 is destined to become the biggest and fastest best-seller since Hugh Hefner discovered girls!" The new step for Marvel presumably was inspired by the success of James Warren's publications: *Creepy, Eerie*, and most especially the sexy *Vampirella*.

Marvel's approach to the black and white field is based on the pulp and old comic nostalgia market. *Savage Tales* features "Conan the Barbarian," drawn by Barry Smith and adapted by Roy Thomas, one of Marvel's best writers, from the pulp magazine stories of Robert E. Howard. The artwork is reminiscent of pulp illustrations of the thirties and forties, with the near-nude female form greatly in evidence. Another *Savage Tales* feature is "Ka-Zar, Lord of the Last Jungle." A strip revived from the old Timely comics, "Ka-Zar" also has its share of undraped female characters. The magazine is self-rated as "M," which has

STUNG BY THE BLACK WIDOW'S REACTION, TONY STARK DEMONSTRATES...

JOKING? WATCH *THIS!* THAT STEEL SAFE WEIGHS A TON!

INCREDIBLE! IF I COULD STEAL THAT ANTI-GRAVITY RAY, I COULD WRITE MY OWN TICKET BEHIND THE IRON CURTAIN!

The evolution of a comic book heroine. Marvel's Black Widow began (above, left) as a villainous Communist spy in civilian garb. This panel, drawn by Don Heck, is from her encounter with Iron Man in *Tales of Suspense* No. 53. The Black Widow became a costumed menace (above, right) and battled her way through several publications before she reformed. A costume change in an *Amazing Spider-Man* episode drawn by John Romita (below, left) completed her transformation into a heroine, and she is currently headlining her own feature in *Amazing Adventures*. The title-page (below, right) drawn by Gene Colan reflects the recent trend toward involving fantastic characters in contemporary social problems, a move which has gained widespread publicity for Marvel and its competitor, D. C.

AND, IN ORDER TO *ERASE* EVERY LAST *VESTIGE* OF THAT PAST... I'LL BEGIN BY DESIGNING A NEW *COSTUME* FOR MYSELF!

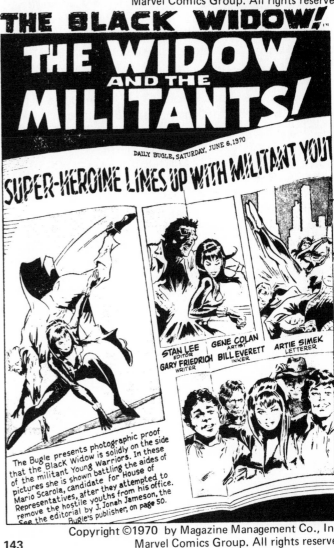

no real meaning other than that it was formerly one of the letters used to rate motion pictures. Conan and Ka-Zar also appear in their own four-color comic books accompanied by more fully clothed ladies.

Savage Tales is Lee's second attempt to break away from the Code-censored four-color comic book. In 1968 Spider-Man appeared in a black and white thiry-five cent comic magazine, *The Fantastic Spider-Man*, which was not Code-approved. Drawn by John Romita (who took over the strip when Steve Ditko left in 1966), the new publication was not successful. Perhaps the potential readers of a more adult comic magazine were not willing to accept the character who had been Code-approved for such a long time in his other appearances.

Lee, meanwhile, has not given up on treating controversial ideas in the Spider-Man stories. In *The Amazing Spider-Man* No. 96 (May 1971), there is a small incident involving a kid overcome by drugs. Spider-Man points out that hard drugs are extremely dangerous, but he wonders, "How do you warn the kids? How do you reach them?" Yes, how? The Comics Code did not allow any mention of drugs. A comic book could not even say drugs are a bad idea. And so *Spider-Man* became the first subscribing member of the Code to appear without its seal of approval. John Goldwater, president of the Comic Magazine Association, referred to the affair as "an error" when interviewed by *The New York Times*. "Everyone is entitled to one slip," he went on. More likely Goldwater did not wish to take on Marvel Comics, for were *Spider-Man* to sell well in the face of harassment from the Code, the Code would lose some of its authority. Distributors might not withhold *Spider-Man* from the stands if they were afraid of losing their Marvel contracts.

The result of this confrontation was a sudden change in Code policy. Marvel had made its point by challenging the Code, and now stories dealing with drugs are permitted, provided they depict drugs as a menace. This new ruling followed on the heels of several other changes in Code policy, which were announced in January 1971. These included the opportunities (previously denied) to show some sympathy for criminals and some suspicion of public officials. Furthermore, stringent dress codes were liberalized and the suggestion of seduction is now a

possibility.

But the new drug ruling, which came up so unexpectedly after the Code had just been altered, must be attributed to Lee and his publisher, Martin Goodman. The success of their stand against censorship must have been particularly satisfying to Marvel, especially in view of the problems the company had experienced three years earlier when organized outcries against televised violence cut short a series of animated cartoons based on their characters.

Marvel's new stand with regard to the Code seems to represent a change for a company which established its extraordinary popularity on the strength of its ability to concoct a formula which could work within the Code. The internalized and ambiguous conflicts of the Marvel heroes, combined with some outstanding artwork and a remarkable talent for promoting a public image, have made this company one of the most important in the history of comics.

Marvel's short-lived satire comic, *Not Brand Echh!*, juxtaposed parody versions of Archie and E. C.'s ghouls to recall the Comics Code Controversy of 1954.

Not Brand Echh! (whose title was presumably inspired by *Mad*'s label for its competitors) generally parodied Marvel's own heroes. Here writer Roy Thomas and artist Marie Severin mock the Mighty Thor, musical comedies and the restrictions of the Comics Code.

THE MAN IN THE MOON
BY SPILLANE

BRUCE HENDERSON looked at the calendar on the wall and grinned slowly. The date was December 31, 1941 ... New Year's Eve, but here in the wild jungles of Brazil one would never know it. Instead of snow, and the icy streets of New York, the moist wind rustled through green tree tops, and multicolored birds chirped madly. Sweat poured from his forehead as Bruce gathered up his rifle and boxes of ammunition and placed them on a small cart.

Minutes later he was trundling through the forest of ferns and shaggy trees with the load. He turned once, and looked at the house he had spent three years in, and then turned and went ahead. About fifty yards off was a clearing...one that represented tedious hours of back-breaking labor under a broiling sun. And there at one end was the greatest surprise of all ... a rocket ship! Sleekly streamlined, its shiny exterior glistening in the morning light, it thrust its pointed nose toward the horizon like a trained greyhound.

ADVENTURE! Space opened to man, to cultivate and develop! This was living. People could have their stuffy little offices, they could work in smelly research labs, but he, Bruce, would battle the dangers of space! Just one last look around, and he hopped in and bolted the door behind him. Quickly, he took his place at the controls, consulted the instrument panel in front of him, then he reached out and pulled back slowly on a lever.

Immediately a deafening roar blasted from the rear rocket tubes. Tropical plants disintegrated under the terrific power of the charges. Smoke and flame spat into the jungle, while the ship shivered slightly, eager to be off. Then the lever came back another notch. The ship lurched, slid forward, and under full gun tore down the clearing! For one awful instant Bruce thought he wouldn't clear the trees. He touched the controls slightly... and the space ship responded valiantly. It shot skywards, and a moment later was lost to sight of the naked eye!

Days went by swiftly. Whenever Bruce felt the urge to sleep, he set the robot controls and closed his eyes. Steadily, the moon grew larger, while behind him Earth diminished to a small, round sphere, with the continents clearly outlined. Outside, the sky was dotted with the brilliant globes of stars, and occasionally small pieces of space dirt rasped against the hull. Fortunately, the construction of the ship was strong enough to withstand the barrage, otherwise it would have been shredded into fragments!

Once a comet flashed across the ship's path, its long tail glowing brightly, and in an instant it was gone. Things never before seen by man were his to gaze upon in wonder. Asteroids...huge chunks of metal ...whirled by, their craggy outlines passing across the horizon of stars. Several times Bruce had to veer out of their way, or smash against them!

THE FIFTH DAY Bruce awoke from a sound sleep. He peered out ...then made a wild clutch at the controls. The Moon was upon him! Desperately, he shut off the rear tubes and threw on the forward ones, braking the ship to a stop. Short miles ahead the white surface loomed, like something long dead. Before he had time to think, the space ship hit, bounced, then settled neatly on the crust, sliding along for miles before coming to a stop!

Thrilled so that he could hardly move, Bruce donned a helmet, stepped into an air chamber, then jumped down to the ground. He made it! The first man to reach the Moon! He stepped forward, and then ... rose above the surface for ten feet! Gravity ... it was less than that on Earth ... he must remember that! Air hissed into his helmet. He dared not remove it, for there was none on Moon. Gravity was so light that it could not keep the air from drifting off into space!

Bruce had on his heavy space clothes, designed to keep him from freezing to death in the sub-arctic temperatures between Earth and Moon, but now it was uncomfortably hot. He struggled out of it and got a pair of tropical shorts from the ship. That was much better. Then, for the first time he took careful note of his surroundings. Gigantic pits were like ugly sores all over. Huge cracks yawned like the mouths of monsters. Meteors caused the pits... there was no air to burn them out before hitting, and the unbearable heat had opened up the cracks!

The whole place was a scene of desolate waste. The ground was a mass of white powder, and not a single speck of vegetation was visible. No life existed here for thousands of years. The small planet seemed to be an outcast from the Solar System, a true *desert of death!* Telescopes had often revealed this to the astronomers, but when seen so closely it was even more appalling!

Bruce had prepared for a long stay, but he wasted none of his time. First he got out a shovel, then began digging a ditch. Weeks later he was still at it. Finally the day came when his work there was done. Wait until *that* was seen from Earth! But the biggest task of all was still ahead... a visit to the dark side ... that which was never seen from Earth! Always, only one side pointed toward the mother sphere, now *he* would see what was on the *other* side!

A bicycle was dragged out of the ship and he was off! Fortunately, he was near the shadow line, and two days later he crossed into the dark country. Then...an amazing change came over the place ... the cold was unbearable... and only a few yards separated it from the hot side! Bruce donned his space suit, which he had taken with him, and went in! Here there was no light, only inky darkness ... and the cold. Not a sound broke the stillness except for a space humming. Further and further he went into the interior.

He tripped over jutting pieces of rock and fell, but there was no shock. When he went down the lessened gravity let him "float" down. It was a queer sensation, utterly different from anything he had ever experienced on Earth!

SUDDENLY...a shriek split the quiet. It grew louder, vibrating the ground! Just in time, Bruce looked up. A giant form was hurtling out of space toward Moon! It hit with a thunderous crash, knocking him off his feet. Bruce was showered with particles. The stuff rained down ... if it should penetrate his helmet, he was lost! But nothing happened. He had escaped unscathed! He flashed on his light, and in its rays saw the meteor ... or what he thought was a meteor ... split wide open ... and out of it came another space traveler!

And what an apparition it was! A horrible, eight-armed creature it was. Huge, devilish eyes gleamed dully as it crawled out of the wreckage of the ship. Then it saw him! The thing squirmed forward, its arms reaching out for him! Fully ten feet high it was! Bruce was petrified. He could not move. He tried desperately to bring up the rifle, but the thing's eyes held him motionless. And just as it was about to grab him it happened ... The thing collapsed!

Perhaps the shock of the crash did it, or maybe the intense cold, but it flopped to the ground like a sack of jelly... and started to shrink! A matter of minutes and it was a spot on the darkness of the crust. Quickly Bruce turned on his light and caught the thing in the beam. Smaller and smaller it got...and then it disappeared completely! What manner of creature was this that traveled through space ... and shrunk into nothingness when it died? This was too much!

Bruce turned and ran for the shadow line. He went in long bounding leaps, jumping crags and obstacles in a weird bouncing motion. He hit the line, ... slowly, so anxious was he to reach the security of the metal hull. But at last he made it. At once he took off his helmet, stowed his gear into the compartments, and leaped to the controls.

On went the motors! The ship sped along and lifted into the blue sky. The nose made a wide arc and he was homeward bound! Earth looked wonderful, even after so brief a leave. Days later North America spun into view, and grew steadily bigger. Bruce picked out a spot on the sandy desert of Arizona where he could do no damage in landing. The rockets in the nose blasted and the ship slowed. He leveled off and slid in beautifully. He was back!

LITTLE CLOUDS of dust on the horizon came closer. He had been seen ... and the curious were on their way. They showed up, all right ... armed to the teeth! They probably thought he was a visitor from another planet and were taking no chances! But when they saw that it was a man, questions poured out ... Bruce had to laugh them off. They wouldn't believe him anyway.

However, word reached the papers and he told them the whole story. The nation rocked with laughter. Prominent scientists said it was impossible ... he was crazy ... Bruce said nothing. Along about this time, the new telescope was erected in California, one that would bring the Moon to within twenty-five miles of Earth. Eager eyes peered into the huge barrel, gazing at the Moon .. and there, just as Bruce Henderson said it would be ... were the initials U. S. A., carved into the surface in letters each a mile long! It was the ditch he dug, deep enough to be seen from Earth—claiming the moon for the *United States!*

THE END

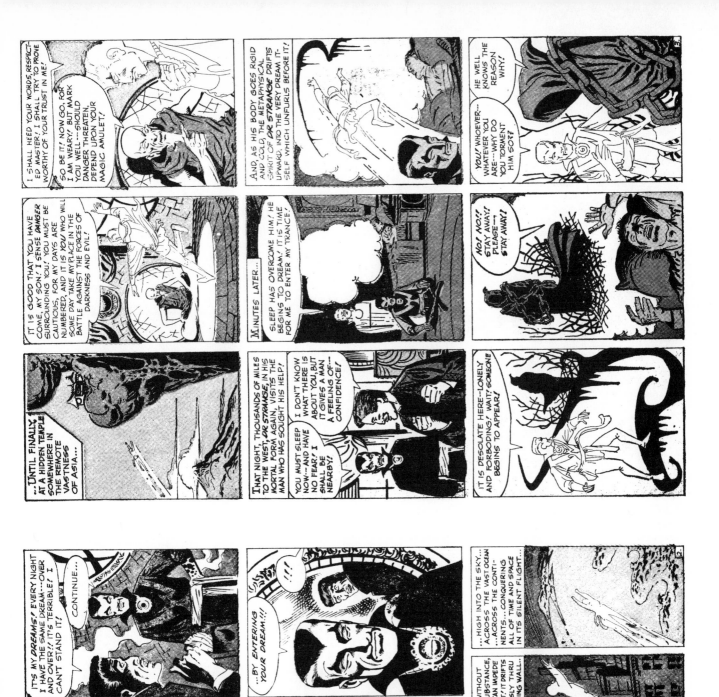

AND SUDDENLY, FROM THAT UNBLINKING ORB, A BLINDING HYPNOTIC RAY SHOOTS OUT, FREEZING THE AMAZED HUMAN TO THE SPOT, AS HIS LIMBS GROW STRANGELY RIGID!

AND, AS THE AWESOME AMULET LOSES ITS BLINDING RADIANCE, THE METAPHYSICAL SPIRIT OF DR. STRANGE ONCE AGAIN ENTERS HIS EARTHLY BODY!

NEXT ISSUE: EXPLORE THE MYSTIC WORLD OF BLACK MAGIC ONCE AGAIN WITH DOCTOR STRANGE AS YOUR GUIDE!

—THE END—

AN EYE SUCH AS NO MORTAL HAS EVER BEHELD ...SUCH AS NO MORTAL WOULD EVER WANT TO BEHOLD AGAIN!

I MADE IT! I'M SAFE IN MY OWN DIMENSION!

YOU'VE ELUDED ME THIS TIME, BUT I'LL GET YOU YET!

I WAS A FOOL TO COME TO YOU—I DIDN'T SUSPECT MY DREAMS WERE CAUSED BY THE MANY MEN I'D RUINED IN BUSINESS! CRANG WAS THE LAST OF THEM! I ROBBED HIM—BUT HE COULDN'T PROVE IT NOW—NOW I'LL CONFESS...

IT WILL BE THE ONLY WAY YOU CAN EVER SLEEP AGAIN!

...UNTIL IT SLOWLY OPENS, REVEALING A FANTASTIC METAL EYE WITHIN...

AND HALFWAY ACROSS THE WORLD, THE MYSTERIOUS GOLD AMULET ON DR. STRANGE'S CHEST BEGINS TO GLOW... BRIGHTER, EVER BRIGHTER...

AND, IN THAT SPLIT-SECOND, TAKING ADVANTAGE OF THE SUDDEN INTERRUPTION, DR. STRANGE DARTS PAST HIS ENEMY IN THE DREAM DIMENSION...

I SHALL RELIEVE YOU OF BOTH YOUR WEAPON AND YOUR HYPNOTIC SPELL! NOW SPEAK—AND SPEAK ONLY THE TRUTH, I COMMAND YOU!

IT'S OVER! YOU'RE STILL ALIVE! THAT MEANS I'VE LOST!

YOU KNOW THE RULES OF SORCERY, DR. STRANGE! THOSE WHO ENTER A HOSTILE DIMENSION MUST BE PREPARED TO PAY FOR IT—WITH THEIR LIVES!

BEHOLD, DR. STRANGE — YOU MAY WITNESS YOUR OWN DESTRUCTION! YOUR MORTAL BODY IS UNPROTECTED—ITS LIFE IS ABOUT TO BE SNUFFED OUT!

THERE IS ONLY ONE WAY TO HELP HIM—THRU THE ENCHANTED AMULET! I MUST CONCENTRATE—CONCENTRATE—

SUDDENLY, ANOTHER FORM APPEARS—FAR MORE MENACING THAN THE FIRST!

NIGHTMARE—MY ANCIENT FOE!

SO IT IS DR. STRANGE! YOU HAVE ENTERED THE DIMENSION OF DREAMS FOR THE LAST TIME! NEVER AGAIN SHALL YOU THWART ME!

HE IS IN A TRANCE—HELPLESS! IT'S JUST AS WELL! HE MUSTN'T BE ALLOWED TO LIVE WITH WHAT HE HAS LEARNED!

AND, ACROSS THE LIMITLESS VOID OF TIME AND SPACE, TWO ANCIENT EARS HEAR THE DESPERATE CRY OF DR. STRANGE!

HE CALLS!

I AM THE SYMBOL OF EVIL! THE EVIL ME HAS DONE! THAT IS WHY I AM CHAINED SO! IF YOU DO NOT BELIEVE—ASK MR. CRANG!

MEANWHILE, IN THE SEMI-DARK BEDROOM, THE SLEEPER AWAKES!

HE MENTIONED MR. CRANG! SO THAT'S WHAT IT'S ALL ABOUT! THERE'S DR. STRANGE! HE MUST HAVE HEARD IT ALL!

NOTHING CAN SAVE YOU NOW!

THERE IS YET ONE WHO CAN! MASTER! HEAR ME! I NEED THEE, MASTER!!

GOOD EVENING, TRAVELER...LOST YOUR WAY IN THE *DARK?* THAT'S NOT UNCOMMON IN THESE PARTS...*ME?* MY FRIENDS CALL ME *DIGGER*...FOR OBVIOUS REASONS/ YOU KNOW...YOU REMIND ME OF *SOMEONE ELSE* WHO PASSED BY HERE THE OTHER NIGHT...IN A *HURRY,* THEY WERE/ IT SEEMS THERE WAS SOMEWHERE THEY HAD TO GO...SOMETHING THEY HAD TO *DO*...AND OF COURSE, THEY HAD TO DO IT...

ᴏᴏ AT THE STROKE OF MIDNIGHT! ᴏᴏ

EDITED BY STAN LEE • WRITTEN AND ILLUSTRATED BY STERANKO • LETTERED BY SAM ROSEN

MARVEL BULLPEN BULLETINS • MARVEL BULLPEN BULLETINS • MARVEL BULLPEN BULLETINS

MORE BATTY BULLETINS TO BEWILDER, BEWITCH, AND BEDAZZLE THEE!

ITEM! We won't keep you in suspense a second longer! Here it is — our very next title of Marveldom for you to memorize and cherish fore'er! But first, let's once again summarize the first three we've stowed upon you. We started with RFO (Real Frantic One), to be used by those who buy three or more Marvel mags a month. Then, we added QNS (Quite 'Nuff Sayer), munificent moniker for those gifted ones who've had one or more letters published within these pages. Last ish we revealed to a breathless waiting world that TTB (Titanic True Believer), was the long-sought-after cognomen for anyone who has ever won a practically priceless No-Prize! And now — prepare thyself for the fabulous fourth rank of Marveldom Assembled — three letters which are destined to shake the literary world to its very core — three letters which shall soon be part and parcel of eternal Americana — three letters which, for sheer drama and stark simplicity have no possible peer — in short, the lustrous letters KOF (Keeper of the Flame), to be claimed with pride by any Marvel madman, anywhere in the free world, who successfully recruits a new disciple into the riotous ranks of Marveldom! Now, whilst you bow your head in silent reverie, we shall take this occasion to reveal next month's three letters — P.M.M. — the highest rank of all — whose deep, dramatic meaning shall be revealed to thee on this page next ish! And now, on to other matters, before we become too emotional —

ITEM! Here's another in our continuing series of newsworthy tidbits which you can very easily live without. Didja know that our mixed-up Marvel mags are actually reprinted in eight different languages thruout the globe? And as soon as we learn how to translate into cosmic Kree (in-joke for FF and Capt. Marvel buffs), we'll be making that NINE languages!

ITEM: Oh, speaking of our worldwide Marvel beachheads, we wanna explain something that's been bothering our brain-blasting British boosters. Those of you who've been following our yarns in the famous publications printed by England's Odham's Press have been worried that they'll be 'replacing our own tintinnabu-latin' titles. Well, perish the thought, Pre-cious One! The Odham's weeklies are simply REPRINTING our older classics (and doing a great job of it, too!) — but all the newest maniacal masterpieces we turn out will be on sale in Great Britain, same as ever, just as fast as we can ship 'em o'er! There now — is there anybody we haven't confused?

ITEM: We recently received a letter which we thought might interest you — so, here 'tis:

Dear Stan,
Operation Mailcall Viet Nam is a service by the American Government which gives people a chance to write to members of the American Armed Forces who are overseas. It's a chance to let them know that they're not alone — and that someone's thinking believe that many other Marvel Mad-men would be glad to correspond with someone overseas in my first letter I

just told a bit about myself as an introduction — my age, hobbies, etc. The letters should be in individual, stamped envelopes placed within another sealed, stamped envelope which is addressed to OPERATION MAILCALL VIET NAM, BOX 2602, WASHINGTON, D.C. 20013.

Yours truly,
Bill Reed, Craiglee Dr.
Scarborough, Ontario, Canada

Many thanks for the info, Billy — and we're passing it along as you suggested. We also want to mention one additional fact. Many of our politically aware readers have divergent opinions about the Viet Nam war — as do the Bullpeners themselves. This notice is not intended as an endorsement on our part of any specific policy regarding the war. We simply feel that many American boys have been sent into battle far from home — and anything we can do to make 'em feel that they're not forgotten is surely a worthwhile deed which transcends mere politics. 'Nuff said?

STAN'S SOAPBOX!

You've probably already noticed the way we've changed our cover mastheads on ASTONISH, SUSPENSE, and STRANGE TALES...featuring the name of each alternate character in turn, every other month. But that's only the beginning! 1968 will go down in comicdom history as the year of the big changes in the wonderful world of Marvel! We've got new titles that will soon be taking you by storm — and new features that'll make you realize the ol' House of Ideas is more daring than ever! In fact, we have one new mag now on the drawing board that's so dramatically different in concept, we confidently predict it will actually usher in the SECOND Marvel Age of Comics — an era even greater, even more glorious than ever before! So stay with us, fellow stalwarts — the best is just ahead! Remember — every wondrous winner has your name on it, and we kid thee not! Anyway, whatever you do—wherever you go—THINK MARVEL! It only hurts when you laugh!

THE MIGHTY MARVEL CHECKLIST
Marvel-ous Mags On Sale Right Now!

NOT BRAND ECHH #6: This is your last chance to latch onto the nuttiest issue of all! See what happens when LUV hits Spidey-Man, the Human Scorch, and Dr. Derangedl Chock full of goofy gags and way-out, wild guest stars, it's the funniest thing since Macbeth! Don't yecch — read it again!

FANTASTIC FOUR #72: Wouldja believe — another action-packed epic featuring the battle of the century? Wouldja believe — the Watcher? Well, you better believe it! This is the big one!

MARVEL TALES #13: Spidey, Thor, Giant-Man, and — latch onto your seat belts — from out of the glorious golden age...Marvel Boy, one of the most dramatically different super heroes ever! The House of Ideas has done it again!

AVENGERS #49: Magneto at the United Nations! War! And the mighty Avengers battling against their old comrades? The answer is yes on all counts — and adventuredom will never be the same again!

X-MEN #41: How do you fight a super-powered foe whose one overwhelming desire is to destroy the entire earth—and himself along with it? That's what our marvelous mutants must find out, and fast, when they battle the one and only... Grotesk!

DAREDEVIL #37: Sometimes a story's so great that there's no satisfactory way to describe it! All we can say about this one is — DD battles Dr. Doom like a man possessed—and you'll gape at the most frightening last page you've ever thrilled to! Howzat?

CAPTAIN MARVEL, starring in MARVEL SUPER-HEROES #13: A new weapon...a new life...and a mind-staggering menace that threatens to be not only Captain Marvel's first challenge — but also his last! For, at long last — the Sentry lives again!

THOR #149: Even a Thunder God can't win 'em all — especially when his frightful foe is the triumphant Wrecker! If you've ever wondered what happens when a super-hero is out-fought, this one's for you!

SUSPENSE #99: Whiplash! The Maggia! Jasper Sitwell! And...what's his name? Oh yeah, Iron Man, too! The biggest star-studded action-epic since "Gone With The Wind!" As for our star-spangled Avenger, together with the Black Panther, Cap finds himself pitted against Zemo, the fiend who cannot exist!

ASTONISH #101: Possibly the greatest Hulk tale you've ever read! See what happens when the giant rampager finds himself in Asgard, pitted against the might of the immortals themselves! Meanwhile, Subby battles for his life against a start-ling new super-villain near the site of the original Atlantis! This one's a blockbuster!

STRANGE TALES #166: Talk about cataclysmic climax issues — this one tops 'em all! Nick Fury and the Yellow Claw square off for a final, deadly fight to the 'finish — while Doc Strange goes into the last round of his epic encounter with Yandroth! You dare not miss it!

SGT. FURY #51: The Howlers crash land behind enemy lines — but that's not about to stop them from rescuing one of the most vitally important men in the free world! Oh, and guess who's with 'em? None other than Happy Sam Sawyer himself! Wah-Hooo!

CAPTAIN SAVAGE #1: The power-packed premiere of a pulse-pounding new battle-mag bombshell — in the great SGT. FURY tradition! It's destined to become a contemporary combat classic!

MARVEL COLLECTORS' ITEM CLASSICS #13: What would you do if you suddenly spotted a Marvel mag with the FF, Iron Man, the Hulk, Dr. Strange, and the Watcher, all in one ish? Snap it up, natch!

Let's meet 26 more M.M.M.S. members!

Ron Rererich	Dick Rader	Steve Robnett	Pete Ricciardi	Jean Reynolds	Vicky Roberts
Bergen, N.J.	Hillsdale, Mich.	Peoria, Ill.	Saddle River, N.J.	Palo Alto, Calif.	Ft. Knox, Ky.
Paul Torres	Tibor ulla	Keith Roy	Bill Rizzetti	Bill Rennert	Jim Riley
Los Angeles, Calif.	Victoria, Australia	Jenness, La.	Bridge, N.Y.	Boca Raton, Fla.	Annandale, Va.
	Robert Vanderheere	Joe Valasque	Bill Lark	Roy Rubinfeld	Glenn Harris	Wahkill, N.Y.
	Oneida, N.Y.	Newport, Ky.	Philadelphia, Pa.	E. Rockaway, N.Y.	New York, N.Y.	John Ray
	Dianne Rodman	Felicia Value	Mike Riley	Michael Tripp	Flory Tomasello	Sarasota, Fla.
	Sarasota, Fla.	Warren, R.I.	Seattle, Wash.	San Francisco, Calif.	Long Beach, Calif.	Joel Ramey
						Vancouver, Wash.

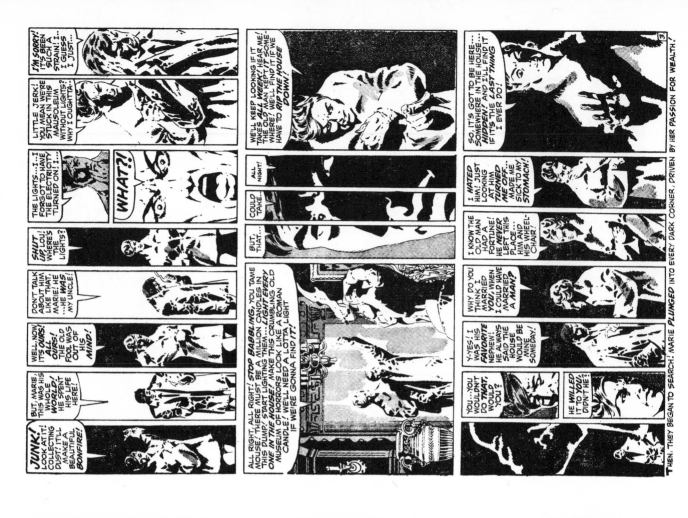

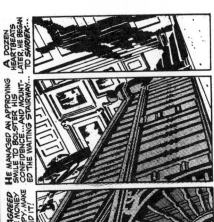

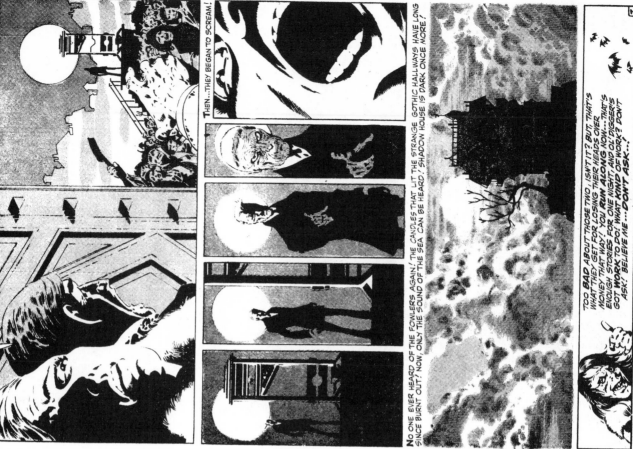

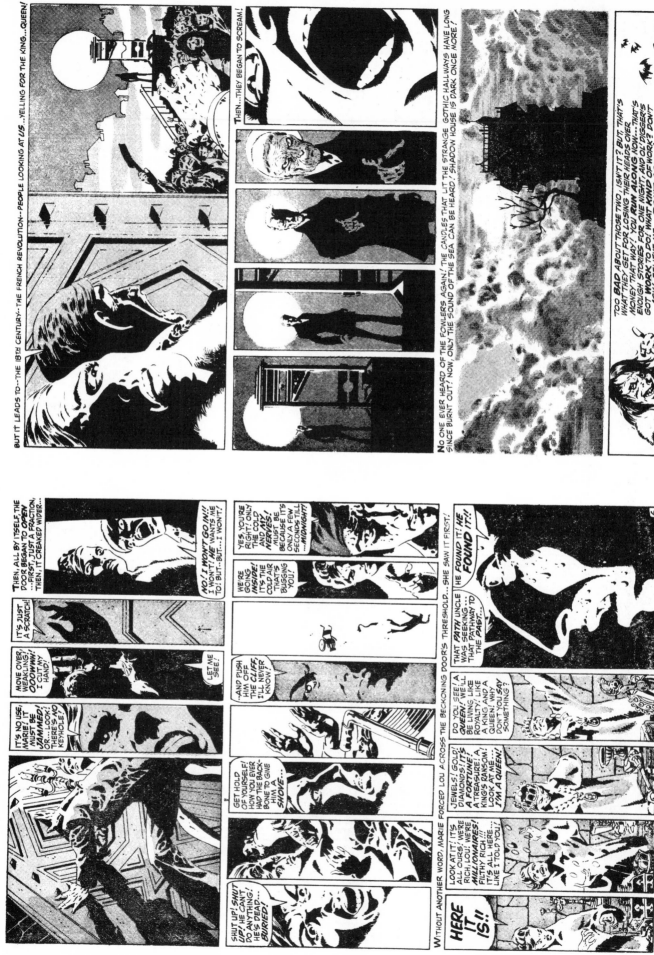

Chapter Eight: Underground Comics

So far, this history has concerned itself with the major manifestations of the comic book, those enjoying wide circulation and prominent public display. There is, however, another entire school of comic books that are not distributed through ordinary channels and are not bound by the economic considerations that make sales in the neighborhood of six figures a virtual necessity. These are the underground comics, which have existed in one form or another for as long as the medium itself, and have recently come into new prominence through the concentrated efforts of a handful of dedicated practitioners. The underground publications are indisputably the most controversial comics ever to be produced, and what makes them controversial is their totally uninhibited treatment of sex. The newest wave of such comics, which has made the "underground" designation particularly its own, is distinguished as well by a defiance of convention, a defiance which, embracing a variety of social issues as well as warm bodies, has distinctly political overtones.

Underground comics fall into three distinct groups, representing with some overlap three eras in American culture. The first is the small, pocket-sized pamphlet devoted steadfastly to the theme of sexual intercourse, and referred to by various designations including "eight-pagers" (the least colorful but most accurate of the names) and "Tiajuana bibles" (an attempt to identify a point of origin, which identification may actually be completely spurious). While no accurate documentation of this clandestine enterprise will ever be possible, internal evidence suggests that at least a few of these eight-pagers were in print during the twenties, thus giving them a claim to the title of the first comic books. They were definitely in vogue by the thirties, and continued to crop up for several decades before going into a decline which now has given them a current standing as antique items.

The second type which might be considered underground has never been described by a generic term, although they might be called "kinky comics." Again the prevalent topic is sex, but the emphasis has turned away from documentation of copulation. The feature of these comic books—printed without color, half-size, and sold for several dollars apiece—is the depiction of various forms of sadistic or masochistic behavior. Considering the possible range of these deviations, the variations employed are not very extensive, consisting generally of some mild flagellation and bondage, using every possible male and female combination. The material in most instances is presented with a distinct emphasis on comedy and cooperation to lighten the ostensibly grim nature of the subject matter. In contrast to the eight-pagers, bodily exposure in the kinky comics is kept within strictly defined limitations, without depictions of the legally questionable genital areas. Consequently, although the topics under consideration in the kinky comics may represent for some the ultimate in erotic appeal, the breasts and buttocks they traditionally bare are not specifically censorable, and so these comics are available over the counter at retail outlets in most major American cities. The date of their first appearance is fuzzy, but elements of their style and content seem to suggest that they came into their own during the forties, after the standard comic book form had been firmly established.

There is not much to be gained from a study of kinky comics. Distinguished by an extremely narrow range of subject matter, their settings and characters are as abstract and vaguely realized as any ever presented. A few artists who demonstrated a considerable technique emerged from this school; the most widely known are Stanton, Eneg, and Willie. But the monotony of the plotting, and the ludicrous ease with which characters fall into their perverted poses, make them the least impressive of underground comics, worthy of the term only because there is no other way to classify them, and included here primarily for the sake of the record.

The third and most significant group of underground comics are a far more public phenomenon. While the eight-pagers were without any legitimate circulation or recognition, and the kinky comics have remained generally unknown (due perhaps to the very specific and personal nature of their appeal), the new underground comics have had a sizable effect. They have alternately altered or reinforced the opinions of their readers, they have earned supporters and detractors through widespread publicity, and their dogmatic insistence on totally unrestricted self-expression has had a considerable impact not only on the "overground" comic book but on other arts with an ostensibly more serious purpose than comics. Also, they have come as far as they have in a very short time: this type of underground comic was unknown before 1965, and the first important title, *Zap*, did

not appear until 1968.

The new underground comics are part of a larger movement which is bent on inducing drastic changes in America's state of mind, not to speak of American society. As such, the artists producing them should be considered not only in terms of their individual achievement but as representatives of a philosophy of which they are both a cause and an effect. On the other hand, controversy over the general underground ethic often obscures the variations in viewpoint which exist among even the most prominent creators in the field. More to the point, it is important to note that a deliberate ambiguity exists in the concepts promoted in certain stories, and that any messages which might be gleaned from one piece may be apparently contradicted by the next, even if both are the work of the same hand. If some underground comics are pure propaganda, the best of them are distingiushed by an irony denoting skepticism at the notion of any simplistic solution. Such comics are equally likely to overstate their cases for the purpose of shock, a type of exaggeration that the undergrounders use as a major comedy device, gleefully secure in the belief that it will pass over the heads of the uninitiated.

The original shock value comic books, of course, were the eight-pagers, famed in mail-order advertisements (which were actually for fraudulent, censored imitations) as "the kind men like." The authentic items were created and circulated anonymously, and despite their rumored origin south of the border, they have a distinctly American flavor. Strangely enough, they are not entirely without what the courts refer to as "redeeming social content." Indeed, it is possible that these hot items have been thought to represent the depths of depravity not only because of their concentration on sex but because of their sociological and revolutionary implications. These implications, humanistic and anti-authoritarian, make some of the eight-pagers the obvious but unacknowledged predecessors of today's underground press. Simply by defying the ban on the explicit depiction of sexual activities, forbidden despite the fact that they are personally familiar to most readers and conceptually familiar to all but the youngest child, these comics were an avatar of the current growing insistence on the right to present all human activities in works of the imagination without restriction. Moreover, the concept of introducing the sexual element among familiar personages from the headlines and funnies pages often had a liberating effect exclusive of titillation by demonstrating the vacant and emasculated quality of "approved" entertainment.

There seems to be an important difference between the comics that draw on other comics characters and those that draw on public figures. The most widely known of the eight-pagers are those that used characters from the most familiar of comic strips

The original underground comics: the covers and the comparatively restrained first panels of two of the notorious "eight-pagers," which featured explicit sex and implicit social commentary.

and comic books as the protagonists of erotic adventure. As was noted in an earlier chapter, this use of established personalities in activities which their creators would never have sanctioned anticipated by a generation the *Mad* innovation of the fifties. Yet it would be inaccurate to imply that the eight-pagers examined the themes of the legitimate sources in any thoughtful manner. Operating in a twilight mode halfway between parody and plagiarism, the eight-pagers were clearly less concerned with exploration than with exploitation. The real commentary on the material which they treated was implicit in the contrast between the immaculate originals and the inflammatory imitations. Somewhere between the two extremes of purity and pornography lay the truth about human behavior, and the exaggeration of the eight-pagers, as a response to asexual entertainment, impressed many readers as eminently reasonable.

The other (and earlier) type of eight-pager, involving fantasies concerning actual public figures, had a more specific type of comment wrapped up inside it. One of the recent examples of this form presented Alger Hiss in a number of compromising situations, and the new undergrounders have made a lot of mileage out of the possibilities of presenting their prominent political opponents in scandalous situations. However, the original type of character to move from the headlines into these two-by-four inch comic books were notorious criminals. The Depression created a mystique around such infamous figures, based on their willingness to defy a power structure which seemed to be in a state of near

collapse, and on their apparent freedom and financial success during a period of crippling poverty. One example features "Pretty Boy" Floyd in a story called "The Fugitive," which brings the fleeing gunman to the exclusive "Madame Dora's School for Girls," an institution which the context endows with most of the qualities of a prison. He seduces an innocent inmate and lures her off into a life of passion and adventure. The hero's armed aggression is presented as a symbolic equivalent of sexual power, success with the former automatically giving way to success with the latter.

More directly anti-establishment is the attitude presented in a John Dillinger eight-pager, "A Hasty Exit," which elaborates the simpler plot of "The Fugitive" by expanding to include two girls and a police detective. Contrasting personal and official attitudes toward underworld behavior, "A Hasty Exit" is also tied in with certain aspects of the cultural changes wrought by industrial development, most specifically the mass-produced automobile. The auto changed the face of crime, and, even before the advent of the drive-in theatre, increased mobility made Henry Ford the father of the sexual revolution. His most impressive public statement was "history is bunk," and this story serves to undermine the official historical view of gangster morality.

Dillinger, like Floyd, is presented as attractive to women, but the two girls in this piece are far from naive, and they are in fact attracted by his infamy, rather than merely tolerant of it. Their rivalry for his affections begins when the outlaw encounters Evelyn and Nellie under their broken-down car, and casually donates his own stolen vehicle in exchange for their company—a small demonstration of the appeal of illegal affluence. A potential three-way love scene is degenerating into an argument when the law arrives in the form of Captain Tracy, who presumably got his name from the comic book detective, although there is no physical resemblance. The law's incompetence is demonstrated when Evelyn disarms its representative, and its corruption is shown in the last panel where Tracy and Dillinger have discarded their social roles as aggressive antagonists and formed a camaraderie born of similar desires. They share the girls, and Tracy gives the police chief a telephoned report that the criminal has escaped to Mexico. The "revolutionary" note here is that Tracy's devotion to duty is undermined not by force but by passion.

Such material indicates that there was often more to the eight-page comic booklets than has usually been considered. If their commentary was a peripheral issue, it was still discernible in numerous cases.

Finally, one can also say that the eight-pagers doubtless had an educational value in introducing some readers into the mysteries of sexual behavior, which was presented in their pages in a reasonably straightforward and comprehensible manner. At their first appearance, they were probably the only place in America where such information was available on a wide scale. Perhaps it was the recent surge of open discussion of sexual matters which cast the form into oblivion.

The new wave of underground comics, which are undoubtedly the most significant despite their comparatively brief lifespan, progressed through their speedy growth in a manner which reduplicated the progress of the standard comics. They began in newspapers, and gradually branched out into the comic book form. But since the new comics were to be totally free of censorship, they could evolve only in a new kind of newspaper.

The first newspaper to afford an opportunity for such uninhibited comics was New York's *East Village Other*, which began in 1965. By the spring of 1966, there were at least four other papers in the nation with similar policies: the Berkeley *Barb*, the Los Angeles *Free Press*, the Detroit *Fifth Estate*, and the Michigan *Paper*. These five became the nucleus of the Underground Press Syndicate, an organization devised to provide free exchange of features among member publications committed to the same radical point-of-view. To fully explore or explain the policies or the politics of the underground press would require a separate book, but certain positions were obvious: opposition to the draft and the war in Vietnam, opposition to drug prohibition, support for oppressed minority groups, demands for sexual freedom including women's liberation, and a general mistrust of

government and academic institutions. The newspapers mentioned above were gradually to be joined by dozens of others to become the most readily indentifiable voice of what has been described as the "new left."

The importance of comics to the success of the Underground Press Syndicate was made immediately clear when the announcement of its formation was printed with an illustration by Robert Crumb, who rapidly moved into the spotlight as the underground's most prominent cartoonist. He was probably not the first, however. The earliest continuous comics to appear in the underground press were the work of William Beckman, whose miniscule strip, "Captain High," was a pioneer effort in the pages of the *East Village Other*. Drawn in a style which suggested that the time taken to read the strip equalled the time taken to create it, "Captain High" was a slight effort which constantly abandoned its tentative grip on continuity to involve its characters in bouts of marijuana smoking. The casual attitude taken toward drugs was somehow more effective in defining the editorial position of the underground press than any number of reasoned or impassioned prose arguments, and the door had been opened for the freewheeling treatment of controversial social issues which was to distinguish underground comics.

©1966 by Bill Beckman and The East Village Other

The comics became the most continually impressive material available for syndication through the various outlets of the U. P. S. (the initials coincidentally duplicated those of the widespread United Press Syndicate)—and the comics succeeded because they were entertaining. Whatever one may think of the underground views of life and society, it is reasonably clear that they have had their best moments when expressed through the arts rather than rhetoric. What shines through the comics medium is the openmindedness about human and artistic experience that is the movement's spiritual core, a notion too often obscured by the debilitating dogmatism of narrowly focused debate.

To Robert Crumb must go the credit not only for contributing many of the best underground newspaper comics, but also for making the independent underground comic book a viable form. In addition to his early experience with *Help*, Crumb had solidified his technique through a job drawing for the American Greeting Card Company, where he specialized in the modern snide style of cheer for a line of cards labeled Hi-Brow. He also began developing his first major character, Fritz the Cat, a funky feline who with successive appearances took on more and more the attributes of the bohemian. Serialized adventures of this character appeared in *Cavalier* magazine after they had been drawn in a wallpaper sample book, and they were finally collected in a paperbound volume, *Fritz the Cat*.

What appears to be Fritz's earliest manifestation is a piece dated April 1964 but not published until 1969, in the small pamphlet, *R. Crumb's Comics and Stories*, clearly named in tribute to the famous *Walt Disney's Comics and Stories*. Actually, this pamphlet contained only one story, which saw a vagabond Fritz returning to his home with vague stories of wordly success, and ended with him seducing his younger sister after a midnight swim, an incestuous incident suggested rather than seen. The story ended in a blackout which, in Crumb's future work, would be replaced by unblinking illumination. The more fully realized Fritz pieces in *Fritz the Cat* include a negligible spy spoof, and two others which are keen depictions of the sources and substance of the developing "hippy" life style. At first a glib yet searching college student, the cat soon drops out to become "Fritz the No-Good," a disillusioned disaffiliate who loses his wife and home and becomes a revolutionary political activist more out of boredom than conviction. He runs into enough trouble to drop out of that, too, and eventually becomes the type of bewildered, downtrodden figure who is everywhere in his creator's work.

Fritz is in a sense the source of many of Crumb's characters; he actually traveled the route that brought the protagonists to the state we find them in at the beginning of their stories. As such, it was perhaps inevitable that he be abandoned to leave the way open for personalities who are at home at the point where he seemed to have reached the bottom (even if his optimism is essentially unimpared by the fall). Discarding Fritz also indicated a significant change for the artist, who has since concentrated primarily

©1967 by Robert Crumb

A Crumb drawing from Philadelphia's *Yarrowstalks*.

on human characters. Strangely enough, they rarely behave in as normal or naturalistic a manner as their animal forebear. It is indicative of Crumb's reversals that he should depict bestiality as an especial attribute of people rather than beasts.

Crumb wrote and drew the first important underground comic book, *Zap*, in 1967. Its appearance was delayed when a misguided acquaintance walked off with the original unprinted artwork, which is rumored to have ended up in England. As a result, it was a second volume that was finally released in 1968 as the first *Zap*. The previous collection of stories was rescued when the artist re-inked Xerox copies of his own missing drawings. The result was an issue numbered *Zap* zero so as to preserve the correct sequence. These two issues are the only *Zap* comic books to contain just Crumb's work, although he continued to appear in later issues and has also issued a number of other solo efforts under different titles, including *Despair, Motor City, Big Ass, Uneeda, Home Grown Funnies* and *Mr. Natural*. In addition, he has contributed to such titles as *Yellow Dog, Bijou, San Francisco Comic Book* and *Slow Death Funnies*.

The *Zap* comic books, printed in black and white with color covers by Don Donahue's Apex Novelty Company, contain the necessary ingredients for tracing many of the important developments in the underground comics field. To date there have been six irregular issues, the "original" zero plus one through five. The inside cover of zero featured what was to become a frequent occurrence in Crumb's comic books: pages offering the author's message in ludicrous self-portrait-style strips. "Mr. Sketchum is at it again!" proclaims the headline, beneath which a smiling figure with a pencil behind his ear stalks a ramshackle studio littered with old copies of both *Mad* (its last comic book issue) and *Humbug*. He cheerfully promises readers "the latest in humor! Audacious! Irreverent! Provocative! You Bet!" By *Zap* 1 the same chap had become "a raving lunatic" who threatened his audience with strange powers and warned that they were putty in his hands. The title was "Definitely a Case of Derangement!" Two years later, the *Despair* comic book saw the same figure cackling at the desperate plight of others, confessing that from childhood he had been afflicted with a "Morbid Sense of Humor." No longer content to be simply manipulating reactions, he had become a proponent of "psychological sadism . . . with you, the reader, as victim!!" These statements, tongue in cheek though in some respects they are, offer about as complete a sketch of the cartoonist as he is likely to provide; he remains an elusive subject for interviewers, reluctant to discuss his work or its implications.

The same elusiveness infuses his stories, which gain much of their humor from the manner in which they teeter on the brink of a distinct and possibly even profound significance, only to retreat into obscurity or nonsense at the moment when revelation seems at hand. A case in point is "Meatball," the lead story in *Zap* zero, which transformed round hunks of hamburger into a source of spiritual awareness. Dropping out of the sky onto the heads of a chosen few, the inexplicable meatball brings equally inexplicable relief to all it touches, becoming in the story a somehow convincing symbol of transcendence while still retaining the physical properties which make it such an unlikely choice for a source of the sublime. In the last panel the meatball comes alive, winking and waving a greeting to its converts and to those who wait in vain for its approach. (Part of the irony of the piece lies in the contrast between its use of "meatball" and the use that had been crystallized by the article in *Mad* No. 32 of radio personality Jean Shepherd, "Night People versus Creeping Meatballism." In this article, the term was used to describe the kind of materialistic mindlessness which the Crumb meatball cures.)

Crumb's range of targets is indicated by the last story in the same *Zap*. Having explored the possiblities of transforming humanity through miracles of the mind, he moved into "The City of the Future," where scientific development has alleviated all human suffering. Here the cartoonist mocks the pronouncements which assure the public that technology will make life perfect within a decade or two. Such absurd

devices as soft plastic buildings and vehicles (to avoid accidents) appear side by side with such dream creations as android slaves and machines that give the individual complete fantasy existences. Yet the pitfalls of the completely controlled society come to the fore at the end of the piece, when the clowns organized "just to keep us on our toes" take on a sinister cast as they deliver a pie in the face of an elderly golfer, the pie poisoned to bring about compulsory euthanasia used as a population-control measure.

The same issue presented some of Crumb's regularly featured characters, including the "snoids," grotesque, snickering little creatures who pop up at the perfect moment to increase embarrassment. Also featured was his most fascinating and enigmatic creation, Mr. Natural, an ancient wiseman who wavers between

©1967 by Robert Crumb

Mr. Natural confronts a nameless truth-seeker in one of his earliest appearances. Later Crumb comics show more care in lettering and borders. From *Yarrowstalks*.

inspiration and charlatanry. Some brief early appearances featured the sage with a black, shaggy beard, but it soon became the fluffy white one which gives "Natch" some of the physical qualities of Santa Claus, although he is less likely to give gifts than to receive them. His relationship with his followers suggests that he is some sort of confidence man, surviving on contributions for which he offers nothing in return except the opportunity to search fruitlessly for truth in his presence. There is no doubt, however, that he is happier and more competent than those who seek him out. His attitude toward life is based on a wide range of adventures recounted in a prose biography in the *Mr. Natural* comic book. Bootlegger, medicine man, magician, musician, migrant, and taxi driver in Afghanistan, the crusty old philosopher embodies much of the history of the bohemian movement in the United States and abroad. On a few occasions he has proved himself capable of performing something that could pass for a miracle. He does have strange powers, then, but they are "natural," the result of his own personality and experience, and thus impossible to transmit to followers through the sort of simplistic formula they demand. The result is that attempts to uncover his secret finally drive the wiseman to wisecracks and sometimes even to slapstick violence, as on the cover of *Mr. Natural*, where his hobnailed boots are delivering a swift kick in the pants to his disciple, Flakey Foont.

Flakey, Mr. Natural's most consistent foil, is a neurotic young man whose fervent desire for enlightenment leads him into confrontations with the guru which seem to teach him nothing. "Why do I keep thinking you can tell me anything?" he asks. Yet he will not quit, perhaps because his efforts to defy the sage end in complete futility. This was never more apparent than in *Zap 5*, where he determined to spend the rest of his life in a bathtub.

This bizarre bit of behavior might have been more readily accepted from another Crumb creation, Shuman the Human, a bald truth-seeker even more desperate than Flakey. Shuman has had his head reduced to minute proportions for his effrontery in demanding a confrontation with God; he has also suffered a nervous breakdown when Mr. Natural frustrated his attempt to became an eastern mystic. His ability for self-pity and self-deception point up the value of Mr. Natural's attitude.

Other important personalities developed in Crumb's early comic book period include "Whiteman," a business executive obsessed with the need to maintain his inhibitions while striving for success, and mocked by a group of relaxed blacks who then invited him to join in their celebration. The artist's treatment of blacks is based on the stereotype common to an out-dated tradition, but it seems certain that this is less a reflection of prejudice than it is a commentary on the prejudice he sees around him. The point was emphasized by the introduction, in *Zap 2*, of "Angelfood McSpade," a voluptuous native of Africa whose existence is an endless series of exploitations by white lechers.

The pages of *Zap 2* were opened to three other artists besides Crumb—Rick Griffin, Victor Moscoso, and S. Clay Wilson. Griffin and Moscoso have very similar styles and techniques, almost indistinguishable at first glance. They are the most careful draftsman of the underground cartoonists; the straight lines of their panel borders are one feature which sets them apart from their more casual cohorts. Their "stories" are comics only in a very limited sense. They generally abandon both plot and text to concentrate on conglomerations of abstract shapes and symbols which change from panel to panel in progressions based solely on the visual value of the material. Both have a fondness for Disney characters, mice and ducks who are reduced, especially in Moscoso's work, to their component parts and then rearranged with other objects like light bulbs and empty, shaded speech balloons. The effect of disintegration and reintegration provides the only subject matter, and apparently is intended to suggest the visual effect of psychedelic drugs. While Moscoso's objects seem to be chosen arbitrarily, Griffin's material reflects an interest in the occult, and some of his best pieces are full of arcane symbols like sphinxes, scarabs, and flaming hearts. Originally a poster artist, Griffin is most impressive in single pages which rely less on linear development than on direct relationships between component parts. His most coherent piece, "Bombs Away," reflects the doctrine of Karma in its tale of a duck and a mouse converting a pig into a sausage while a bomb drops from the sky onto their home.

The drawings of Griffin and Moscoso have been a relatively isolated phenomenon; the only other comics with similar concerns are the attractive but unintelligible productions of John Thompson. The debut of S. Clay Wilson, on the other hand, was to have immediate and powerful repercussions. He is, for better or worse, the cartoonist and writer who defies more taboos than any other in the history of comics. He has shocked and amazed every reader who encounters his work not only because of the subject matter but because of the repellent but fascinating drawing style in which it is presented. While Crumb's great popularity is doubtless increased because of a certain roundness and cuteness in even his most reprehensible characters, Wilson's figures are as hideous as his considerable skill can make them. Yet his work has had a direct and acknowledged influence on Crumb and all the other underground cartoonists, by making them aware of how much further they could go in challenging conventions of taste and judgment.

Wilson's fantasies of depraved sex and violence made everything that preceded him, even in the underground, seem tame indeed. He makes the eight-pagers look romantic, and the kinky comics look chummy.

Zap 2 featured three of his stories. One saw the contents of an unflushed toilet bowl flung into the faces of three characters, another featured a sailor whose oversized sex organ was amputated and eaten. Each of these pieces was only a page in length, with the ultimate outrage ending the story the way a punch line ends a humorous strip. The indignities which Wilson gleefully inflicts on his protagonists are so incredible that they actually do become jokes; it is because they are intolerable that they are absurd, and thus, in the last analysis, they are funny. The technique of exaggerating and exposing morbid fears is one which Wilson's comics have developed to the point where their crudity becomes cathartic.

Wilson has a number of thematic concerns. The third story in the same issue of *Zap*, "The Hog Ridin' Fools,"—a longer story than the others—explored one of the artist's favorite subjects: the world of contemporary motorcycle gangs. In this comparatively restrained effort, the "Fools" have the misfortune to tangle with the Checkered Demon, one of the rare Wilson characters who survives long enough to appear in more than one story. Various sorts of demons populate Wilson's tales, using their supernatural powers as a sort of moral force to restore order among survivors of his typically bloody battles. In addition to the bikers, Wilson has a fondness for depicting eighteenth century pirates. There are similarities between these groups, which have been emphasized in a series of "time warp" tales in which the two types are mysteriously juxtaposed, resulting in predictable mayhem. More staggering are pieces that depict the battle of the sexes in its most debased form, involving mortal combat between gangs of equally vicious men and women.

While the *Zap* comic books and Wilson's conflicts poured out of the West Coast, a New York cartoonist was creating a different sort of conflict in the pages of the *East Village Other*. This was Manuel Rodrigues, who works under the name "Spain." Wilson's violence has its sources in the domain of abnormal psychology, Spain's comes from the arena of political ideology. His major creation is Trashman, a radical revolutionary struggling against a repressive government in an indistinct period of the future. The Trashman series, which Spain produced and in which he kept a reasonably organized plot line in progress for over a year, constitutes the most sustained effort yet attempted in the field of underground comics. When the best strips were reprinted in a tabloid-size comic book by the Berkeley *Tribe*, the total effect suggested some of the qualities of an epic. In late 1970, years after the character's initial appearance, Spain pro-

duced an origin story for the *Subvert* comic book. The story made it clear that the civilization that produced Trashman was the result of an atomic war which had created a new ruling class, only partially in control of the population, and afflicted with a megalomania which found expression in mass slaughter, human sacrifice, and cannibalism. The hero, originally auto mechanic Harry Barnes, became a rebel after his wife was murdered by government agents. He received instruction from mysterious cloaked figures, gaining mastery of obscure skills described as "parasciences." Despite such hints of supernatural guidance, the bearded, black-clad Trashman is clearly a mortal, with magical powers apparently limited to the ability to interpret instructions from such unlikely sources as cracks in the sidewalk. Although the science-fiction elements make it possible to view the series as simply a work of imagination, there is little doubt that it is intended to reflect contemporary reality. Indeed, certain events over the past few years have shown the accuracy of Spain's implied predictions as the new radicals have moved away from a philosophy of peace and love toward the kind of militant confrontation embodied by Trashman and his band of urban guerrillas. Politics aside, Spain is closer to the traditional action comic book style than any of his colleagues. His backgrounds and battle scenes are often reminiscent of the work of Jack Kirby, and his theme is in the tradition of *Blackhawk*.

More recently, Spain has returned to the present with a new protagonist, Manning, a vicious plainclothes police detective who prefers force to reason. Crude, corrupt, and not very bright, Manning represents the radical's concept of the policeman as a "pig." His favorite investigative technique involves administering a brutal beating or a few bullet wounds to whoever happens to be on the scene when he arrives. Probably the rottenest cop ever to be imagined, Manning finally surpasses belief, although his presence in comics is an important indication of the extent to which certain groups, whose attitudes are exposed in the underground press, view "law and order" as a threat to their security. Spain frequently manages to include sordid sex scenes amidst the carnage his characters create (Trashman is one of very few comics heroes to catch a venereal disease), but his real importance is in his portrayal of the violence seething within contemporary society.

Another important contributor to the *East Village Other* is Kim Deitch, who dreamed up a number of weird personalities during a long stint as one of the paper's leading cartoonists. His most memorable creations are Sunshine Girl, whose round body is topped by a daisy-shaped head, and Uncle Ed, the India rubber man and acrobat of love. Deitch was eventually to become editor of the *Other*'s comic supplement, *Gothic Blimp Works*, which was inaugu-

©1968 by Spain Rodrigues and The East Village Other

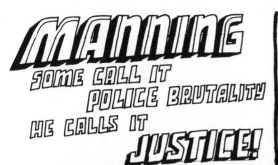

rated in 1969 under the editorship of Vaughn Bode, a cartoonist with a fondness for drawing reptiles.

This tabloid-sized publication, which lasted only a few issues, featured most of the top underground artists, and set itself apart from other productions in the field by including a few pages in color. The color separations were the work of Trina Robbins, who has gained a reputation as the foremost female creator of underground comics. She had some success in *Gothic Blimp Works* with Panthea, a creature half lady and half lion who was transported from Africa with painful results. The somewhat submerged concern for feminist principles which this series suggested was to emerge in 1970, when Trina became the principal contributor to *It Ain't Me Babe*, the first comic book devoted exclusively to Women's Liberation. The cover, which featured renderings of Sheena, Wonder Woman, and Mary Marvel, suggested how much comic book fantasies have done to provide images suitable to a new view of women and her place in the world.

Possibly the most widely syndicated of all underground cartoonists is Gilbert Shelton. After years of producing first the Wonder Warthog series for *Help!* and then *Drag Cartoons*, Shelton moved into high gear in 1968 with the *Feds 'n' Heads* comic book, which established his position as second only to Crumb in the ranks of the radical cartoonists. The Hog was to be gradually abandoned, perhaps because his predilection for crime-fighting made him too much of a "pig" for the new audience. He did exhibit some tolerance when, after accidently knocking a hole in the house of four shocked pot smokers, he remarked, "You folks go back to what you were doing, and I'll be back in a minute to fix your wall."

This sympathy for the drug culture was to take its most impressive form in the adventures of Shelton's new heroes, Those Fabulous Furry Freak Brothers, who have become a regular feature of the Los Angeles *Free Press*. Living by the motto "Grass will carry you through times of no money better than money will carry you through times of no grass," those three long-haired clowns have become the most consistently humorous characters in underground comics. Fat Freddy, Phineas and Freewheelin' Frank demonstrate the pleasures and pains of life on the outskirts of society in a manner reminiscent of the great silent film comedians. Most of these stories are a single page in length, and they appear regularly throughout the Underground Press Syndicate as well as in various comic books. Their longest adventure to date is "The Freak Brothers Pull a Heist," from the second Shelton comic book, *Radical America*, a special issue of a journal ordinarily devoted to revolutionary prose. The ingenuity employed to feed the ravenous pothead Fat Freddy provides an amusing commentary on the gullibility of a public conditioned by television giveaways and similar mass media nonsense.

FABULOUS FREAK FABLES

BY *Gilbert Shelton*

©1968 by Gilbert Shelton

Gilbert Shelton reports that this gag, reprinted from *Bijou Funnies*, had its original source in the *Reader's Digest*.

Shelton has also produced at least two classic pieces that do not involve the Freak Brothers. One is a poetic tale of a farmer who liberates his chickens in a psychedelic frenzy; the other is "Believe It or Leave It" from *Zap 5*. The latter presents radical complaints concerning policies of the American government, thinly disguised as descriptions of conditions in foreign lands, the argument being presented in vividly contrasting pictures and captions.

Just as the underground comics have their own newspapers, so they have their own presses and, as has been seen, their own comic book titles. An important feature of Shelton's career is his involvement with San Francisco's Rip-Off Press, a cartoonists' cooperative which prints many of the important underground comic books. Until recently, most of the rest came out of Berkeley's Print Mint, operated by Don Schenker. He has distributed the *Zap* comic books, the tabloid *Yellow Dog* (recently converted to standard comic book format) and even the Chicago-originating *Bijou Funnies*.

Next to *Zap*, *Bijou* is the most consistently impressive title currently being produced. Crumb and Shelton have been regular contributors, but the *Bijou* staff also includes two artists, Jay Lynch and Skip Williamson, with important individual achievements.

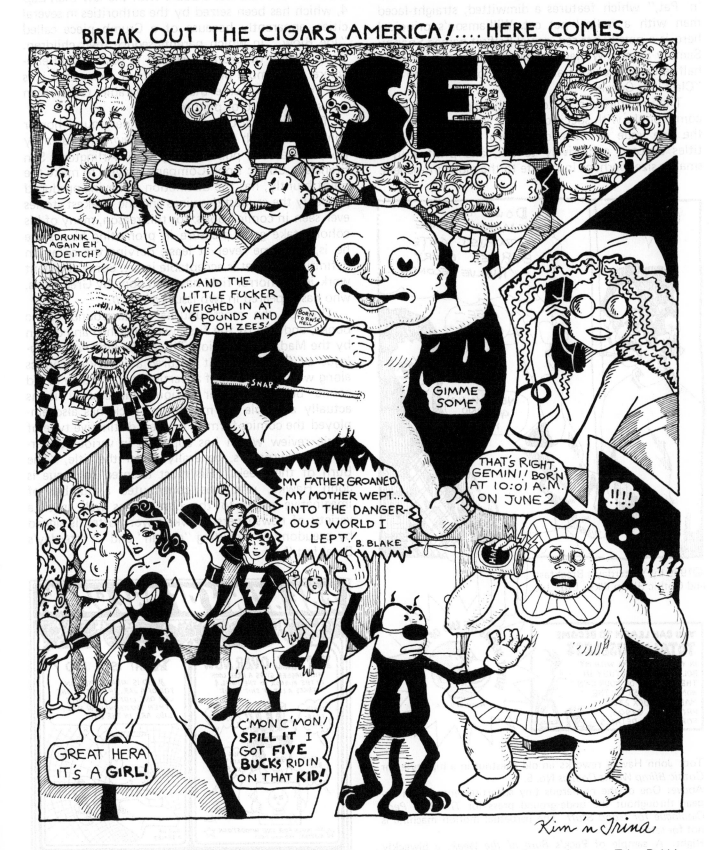

An undergrounder's underground comics page: the privately circulated birth announcement drawn by proud parents Trina Robbins and Kim Deitch.

Lynch, the editor, has a low-key, slightly archaic style which works to good advantage in his tales of "Nard 'n' Pat," which features a dimwitted, straight-laced man with a radical pet cat. Williamson's principal hero is a nattily attired, genial halfwit named Snappy Sammy Smoot. Williamson has also created a series of half-sarcastic views of armed rebellion under the title "Class War Comix."

The underground cartoonists have produced a few comic books with specific themes. Most notorious are the one issue of *Jiz* and the two issues of *Snatch*, titles devoted exclusively to sex, and printed in a smaller size, perhaps in tribute to the old eight-pagers.

©1969 by Yesterday's Breakfast and Gothic Blimp Wks., Ltd., Inc.

Top: John Hawke reworks an old chestnut in a hip style for *Gothic Blimp Works Comics* No. 5.
Above: One of the numerous tiny advertisements which appear throughout the underground press for *The Mad Peck Catalogue for Good Stuff*. The perpetual motion machine is not for sale.
Right: A sample of Peck's *Burn of the Week*, a biweekly feature which featured two thoughtful messages.

For some reason, these remarkably graphic entries seem to have had less trouble with the law than *Zap* 4, which has been seized by the authorities in several cities, apparently because of a Crumb piece called "Joe Blow," in which parents seduce their children. Since several of Crumb's stories in *Snatch* and elsewhere show more physical details, it seems that it is the incestuous theme that is intolerable, rather than any specific word or picture.

There have also been a few underground horror comics, of which the first was *Bogeyman*, drawn by Rory Hayes and published by Gary Arlington's San Francisco Comic Book Company. Hayes, to make the point bluntly, has the distinction of having produced probably the crudest drawings and the weakest stories ever seen in comic books; for this reason, many of his cohorts take great pleasure in promoting him, since he is, on some level at least, defying the common definition of what is acceptable in art. Some excellent work in the horror field has been done by Greg Irons, who has appeared in two issues of *Skull*.

One of the most unusual underground comic books, and one of the first, was published and drawn by the Mad Peck Studios. Titled *The Mad Peck Catalogue of Good Stuff*, it featured a variety of comics along with a number of advertisements—drawn in old comic book style—for various unnecessary items actually available by mail-order. Peck has also employed the comics form to create a distinctive type of music review which has appeared in various underground newspapers, generally under the title, "The Burn of the Week." His most talented colleague is John Hawke, who has contributed a number of imaginative pages to the *Catalog*, as well as to a variety of newspapers. Hawke's work often is signed by pseudonyms including "ekwah" and "Yesterday's Breakfast."

The general success of underground comics, especially the work of men like Crumb, Shelton, Spain, Wilson and Lynch, has drawn a remarkable number of people to the field. One of the most underrated is Justin Green, who has realistically documented the traumas of adolescence. His views of the past have an air of actuality which few of his contemporaries can duplicate. Dave Sheridan has created at least one great strip, "The Doings of Dealer McDope," in *Mother's Oats Comics*, which has received general acclaim as the most accurate treatment of the psychedelic drug experience. And Jim Osborne has demonstrated a consistent development which may soon bring him into prominence.

Important for reasons other than artistic competence is Denis Kitchen, who has done reasonably good work in three issues of *Mom's Homemade Comics*. Operating out of Milwaukee, Wisconsin, Kitchen is most important as a publisher. His Krupp Comic Works (formerly Kitchen Sink Enterprises) has produced a number of titles, including the first underground comic book in three-dimension, and has re-

cently acquired publication rights for *Bijou* and the latest Crumb opus, *Home Grown Funnies*. It appears possible that he will be the individual who will consolidate the various phases of underground comics into a cohesive unit—if these artists, even more unpredictable than most, are to be consolidated.

©1969 by Justin Green and EXTRA!

Justin Green records traumatic moments of truth in biology (above) and political science (below).

©1969 by Justin Green and EXTRA!

The significance of the underground movement was summed up in a letter to Kitchen from Stan Lee of Marvel Comics. "In a way I envy you," it read, "it must be a gas to just let yourself go and do whatever tickles your funny bone." The point is that the underground cartoonists are free. Needless to say, they are also united in their opposition to the Comics Code Authority, which perhaps created their movement in 1954 when it eliminated the material which they enjoyed as children. Crumb, Spain and Irons are among those who have specifically attacked the Code in their work, and all their colleagues have labored against it by the simple act of offering an alternative.

They have undoubtedly had an effect on the regular comic book industry. In combination with the liberal stand of the Warren publications, they have created a climate in which the Code-approved product has begun to appear dangerously dull. Among the results have been Marvel's tentative moves toward defiance, and a new approach at D. C., where a perceptive editor named Carmine Infantino has changed the viewpoint of several of the company's heroes to accomodate a new concern with social and political issues. Both he and Stan Lee have spoken out publicly against certain restrictions, and it was finally announced early in 1971 that the Code would be liberalized, if not drastically. Perhaps someday it can be eliminated altogether.

The untrammeled underground comics may represent the coming trend, or they may be only a temporary aberration. Regardless, there is a sense in which they can be considered part of a larger comic book tradition, a tradition in which realism gives way to exaggeration, and even exaggeration gives way to pure fantasy. The world of comic books is inhabited by supernatural monsters and pseudo-scientific heroes, by animals who act like human beings and human beings who act like animals. Such subjects, because they have a slight relationship to the mundane events of ordinary existence, have caused comic books to be treated condescendingly even by those who can overcome the traditionalist's suspicion of a mixed medium which combines the visual and the verbal.

In the last analysis, however, it must be recognized that the incredible subject matter is not a weakness, but rather the greatest strength of the medium. The surface irrelevance masks a deeper significance. The best comic books probe the subconscious, creating concepts and characters of mythic proportions. Free from the burden of respectability, comic books have provided, for creator and consumer alike, an opportunity to explore the wild dreams and desires which seem to have no place in our predominantly rationalistic and materialistic society. In so doing, comic books have won themselves a small but significant place as a key to the American character.

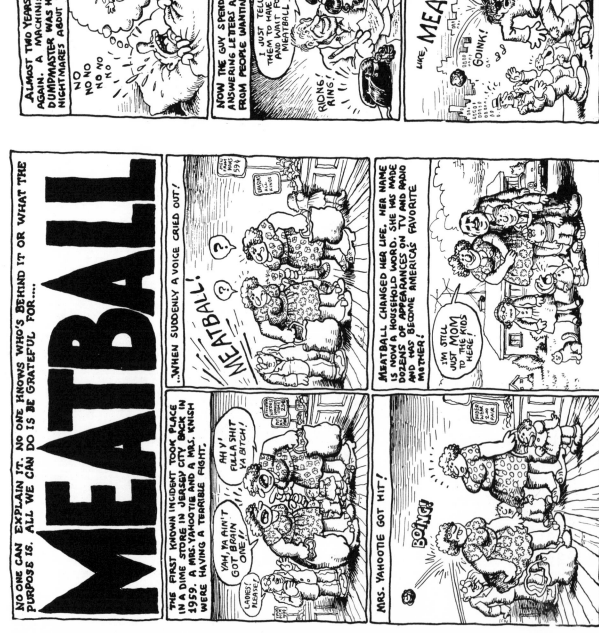

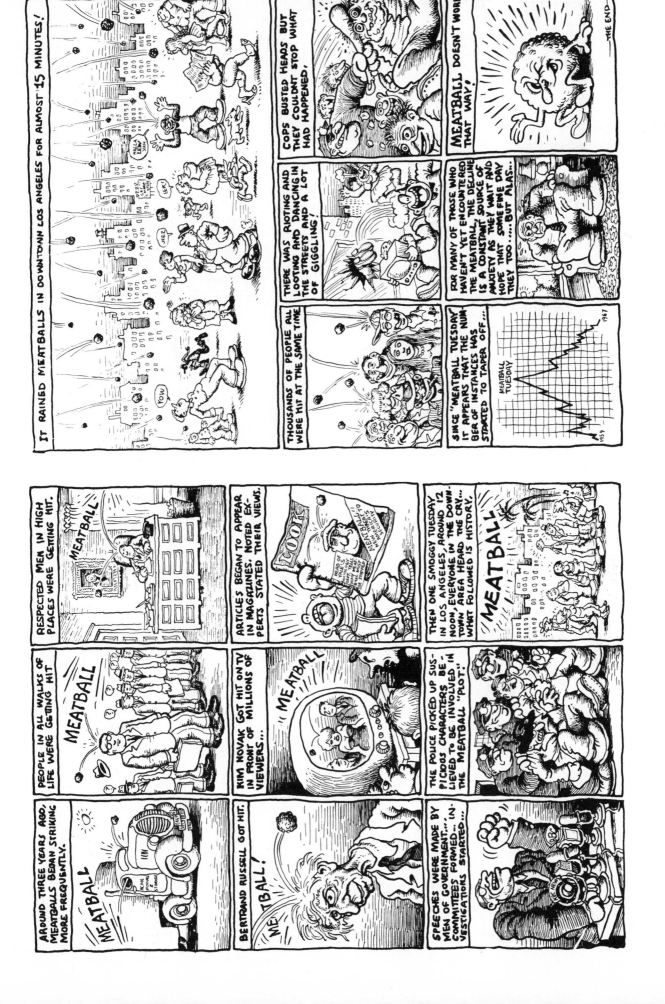

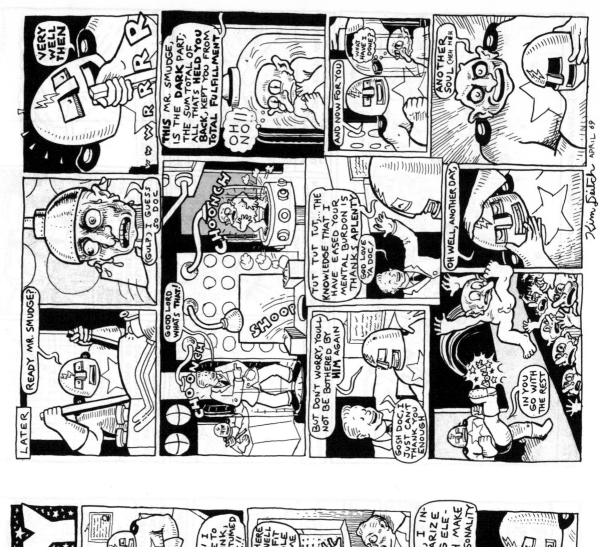

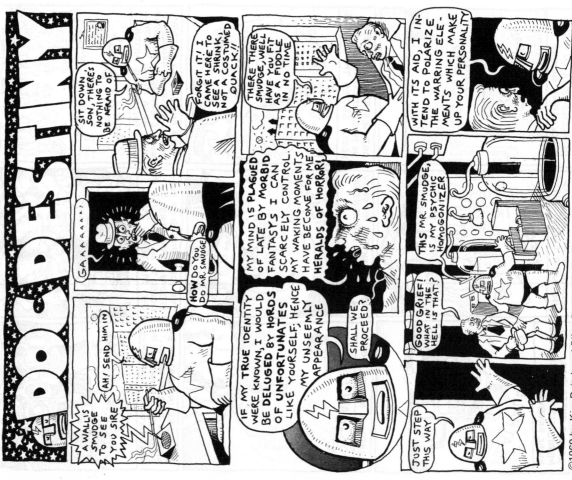

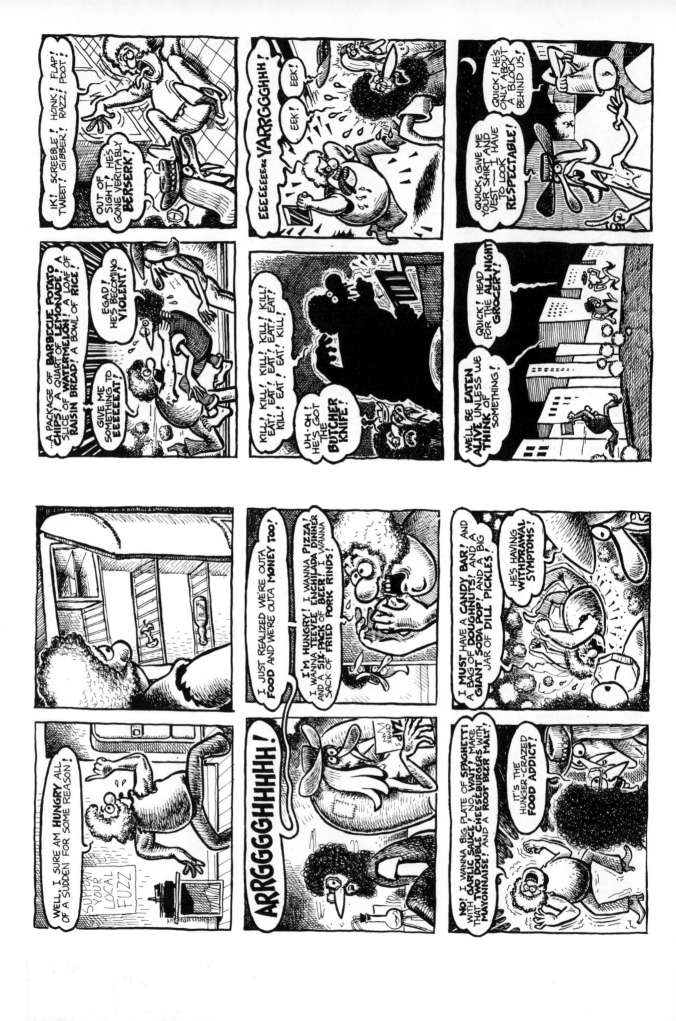

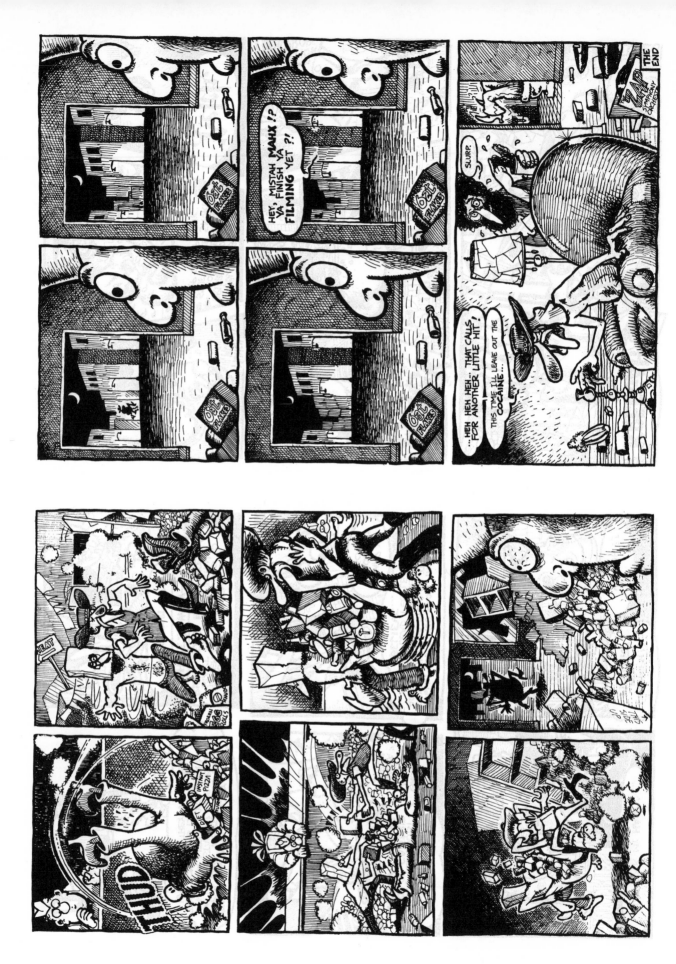

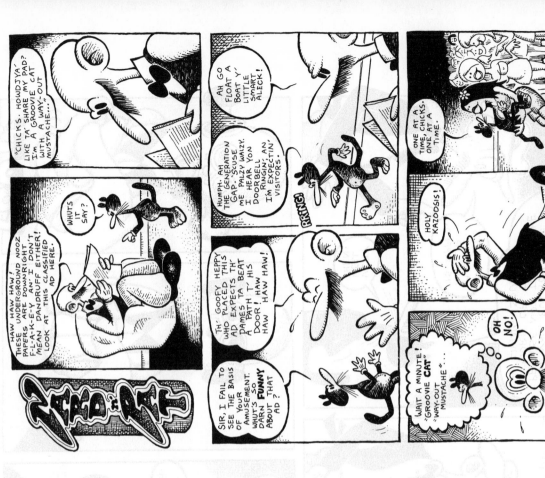

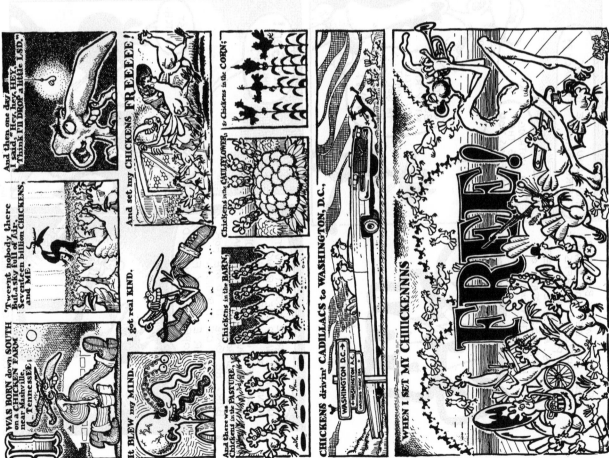

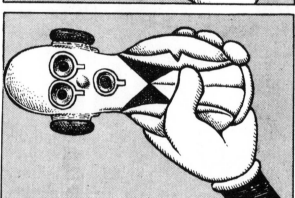

FEELIN' GLUM AN' BLOOZEY? WELL GET SET FOR SOME HIGH FREQUENCY LAFFS. THAT'LL PERK UP YER SPIRITS AN' UNZIP YER OL' LIBIDOS! READY OR NOT, HERE THEY COME! IT'S...

NARD n PAT

by JAYZEY LYNCH

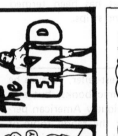

Notes

Bibliography

Chapter Three

*It should be noted that none of these characters was actually invented by Schlesinger, who was not an artist, but the head of business operations. Bob Clampett, a cartoonist and director for the studio, claimed credit for their creation in an interview conducted by Mike Barrier, the editor of *Funnyworld,* an amateur magazine devoted to the animal cartoon field. Barrier is also responsible for the definitive study of the Donald Duck comic books, "The Lord of Quackly Hall," which first appeared in his own magazine and was later revised for Don and Maggie Thompson's *Comic Art*, one of the most impressive and extensive nonprofit organs of what has been termed "panelology"—the study of comic book and strips.

Chapter Five

*Of course, Legman's book was not a best-seller, because he courageously cornered not only the comic books, but also cinematic and literary hotbeds of the uniquely American perversion which substituted bloodlust for the taboo topic of physical love. He even goaded such sacred cows as Hemingway and *Gone With the Wind*. Even today, serious thinkers are reluctant to consider Legman, although his academic interpreter, Leslie Fiedler, gained recognition and some noteriety with his *Love and Death in the American Novel*, which demonstrated that our principal literary themes are heterosexual necrophilia and homosexual bondage.

Chapter Seven

*During the early and middle fifties all the Goodman comics bore the Atlas logo on the upper-left-hand corner of the cover, irrespective of what the actual publishing company was. During the late fifties this trademark was dropped in favor of an indecipherable little symbol which had meaning only to the distributors. Presumably the change was made so that *Millie the Model*, another Goodman publication, would not suffer by association with the more adult fantasy books. Generally, comic collectors refer to all the pre-Marvel comics as Atlas publications, a convention which is followed here.

Couperie, Pierre, *A History of the Comic Strip*, New York, Crown Publishers, 1968.

Craven, Thomas, *Cartoon Cavalcade*, New York, Simon and Schuster, 1943.

Feiffer, Jules, *The Great Comic Book Heroes*, New York, Dial Press, 1965.

Lupoff, Dick, and Don Thompson, editors, *All in Color for a Dime*, New Rochelle, New York, Arlington House, 1970.

Overstreet, Robert M., *The Comic Book Price Guide*, Cleveland, Tennessee, 1970.

Perry, George and Alan Aldridge, *The Penguin Book of Comics*, Baltimore, Maryland, Penguin Books, 1967.

Steranko, James, *History of Comics*, Reading, Pennsylvania, Supergraphics, 1970.

Wertham, Frederic, *Seduction of the Innocent*, New York, Rinehart and Winston, 1954.

White, David Manning and Robert H. Abel, editors, *The Funnies: An American Idiom*, New York, The Free Press of Glencoe, 1963.

Index

What are YOU doing to protect yourself from

Misinformation

Half-truths

Mind Rot

MEDIA BURN

The Nation's leading mental crippler

Millions suffer from this dread malady without even knowing it. Even now you or one of your loved ones could be experiencing irreversable brain damage as a result of media poisoning. The electronic media is controlled by a few giant corporations who use it to sell you a bunch of stuff you could do without. No such monopoly exists in the field of comic book publishing. Some are printed by large concerns, others by rugged individualists in their basements. If you are a paranoid, right-wing fanatic or a worker's paradise zealot or anything in between there are comic books for you. The time to act is now, while you still can. Comic books have brought relief to millions of wretched souls who thought they were beyond help. You owe it to yourself to purchase this low cost protection right now before it's too late.

We don't ask you to believe us. Thousands of men, women and children - at first skeptical just as you are - have proved what we say. Many showed improvement after reading just one or two issues. So hot foot it down to your local drug store and pick up some comic books. In no time at all you will feel their deep penetrating powers throbbing through your cranial tissues giving you new strength to face the world without flinching.

If you are dissatisfied with the results, what have you lost? Comic books cost next to nothing to buy and they do not require expensive receiving equipment. So why wait. Get in on this cultural bonanza now. Join the satisfied multitudes who have found new meaning in their lives through comic books.

I must admit I didn't have much faith in it, But I hadn't been reading comix two weeks before I could see it helping me. I can now play electric bass, and the girls think I'm really groovy.
Eugene Feldspar
Columbus, Ohio

I'm tickled to death with the results. In just two week's time - no dandruff!!
R. C. W.
Cicero, Ill.

I amazed my friends and myself too. Comix have put me in a position to do things I'd thought impossible just a few weeks ago
M. Balicsky
Newark, N. J.

COMIX

contains complete stories featuring the great artists and characters of the past & present

YOU OWE IT TO YOURSELF!